Culture, Institutions and Economic Development

Culture, Institutions and Economic Development

A Study of Eight European Regions

Michael Keating
European University Institute, Italy
University of Aberdeen, UK

John Loughlin
Cardiff University, UK

Kris Deschouwer
University of Brussels, Belgium

Edward Elgar
Cheltenham, UK • Northampton, MA, USA

Published by
Edward Elgar Publishing Limited
Glensanda House
Montpellier Parade
Cheltenham
Glos GL50 1UA.
UK

Edward Elgar Publishing, Inc.
136 West Street
Suite 202
Northampton
Massachusetts 01060
USA

A catalogue record for this book
is available from the British Library

Library of Congress Cataloguing in Publication Data
Keating, Michael, 1956–
    Culture, institutions, and economic development : a study of eight European regions / Michael Keating, John Loughlin, Kris Deschouwer.
        p. cm.
    Includes bibliographical references and index.
        1. Europe—Economic conditions—1945——Case Studies. 2. Europe—Social conditions—Case studies. 3. Europe—Civilization—1945– 4. Regional economic disparities. I. Loughlin, John. II. Deschouwer, Kris. III. Title.

HC240 .K383 2003
306.3'094—dc21

2002037925

ISBN 1 84064 701 9 (cased)

Printed and bound in Great Britain by Biddles Ltd, *www.biddles.co.uk*

Contents

Preface and Acknowledgements

This book has its origins in a request from the Foundation Europe of the Cultures 2002 to Michael Keating, following a seminar in Leuven and memorable weekend in Dublin, to examine the relationship between culture and economic development in European regions. The research was funded by grants from the government of Flanders (in association with the Foundation Europe of the Cultures 2000) and the Administration for Foreign Affairs of Flanders. Michael Keating and John Loughlin also used material on Scotland and Wales from their project funded by the Leverhulme Foundation programme on Nation and Region in the United Kingdom and the ECRC programme on Devolution and Constitutional Change.

Assistance in various stages of the research was provided by Gunter Lauwers, Sabine Menu, Maite Puigdevll-Serralvo, Roberto Requejo and Ruth Van Dyck. William Genieys, Joseph Le Bihan, Ramón Máiz, Antonio-Carlos Pereira-Menaut, Emmanuel Négrier and Ferran Requejo helped with contacts. Zoe Bray copy-edited the text.

This is a three-authored book and we bear joint responsibility for its contents, but there was a clear division of labour. Michael Keating was project leader and wrote Chapters 1 and 2, the case studies on Catalonia, Galicia and Scotland, and the conclusion. John Loughlin wrote the case studies of Brittany, Languedoc-Roussillon and Wales. Kris Deschouwer wrote the case studies of Flanders and Wallonia.

1. Culture, Institutions and Development

MODERNISATION AND CULTURE

The origins of this book lie in a question about the relationship between culture and regional economic development. At one time, this might have seemed strange as these have long been regarded, at least in mainstream economics, as two distinct fields of endeavour, the one based on affective ties and tradition, the other on rational calculation and modernity. Recent work on economic sociology, however, especially at the local and regional level, has analysed the economy as a complex social system, intimately bound up with other aspects of collective human life. We did not seek to find a direct link between a culture expressed in popular values, and development as defined by economic growth, although other projects have addressed this. Rather we chose an institutionalist approach, looking at the way in which culture is shaped and used by elites in the construction of a development coalition. Development itself we define rather broadly to include a range of goals, which themselves may be subject to trade-offs and compromises. We do not seek a single formula for success, but illustrate the ways in which different regional growth coalitions seek to integrate their territories into the emerging global and European markets while retaining a degree of cultural and social cohesion.

For much of the nineteenth and twentieth centuries, the dominant modernisation paradigm postulated an increasing division of labour in society and a separation of the realms of the market, the state and civil society. As markets evolve, they approximate to the neo-classical idea-type, marked by strict individualism and instrumental rationality. The state adopts a more or less uniform bureaucratic-rational form and integrates its various territories and communities into a unitary national form. Political culture is unified and cultural distinctiveness, in so far as it remains, is relegated to the domain of civil society and depoliticised. Modernity is associated with the advance of the market and the state, while minority cultures are condemned as backward or doomed to extinction. Globalisation, in some versions, is a late twentieth century extension of modernisation theory, with integration at the planetary level. European integration is, in its neo-functionalist version, similarly based on the model of the modernising integrating state, extended to a continental scale. Prophets of globalisation have emphasised the decline of the nation-state, the mobility of capital and technology, trade flows, the rise of the transnational corporation and the emergence of international regimes. Some insist that there is only one model of the economy, one norm of political order and that, indeed, history has come to its culmination (Fukuyama, 1992).

Yet there is a powerful counterpoint to both statist and globalist accounts of modernisation from those who question its sharp distinctions among the realms of the market, the polity and civil society, or the analytical separation of market rationality from other cultural norms. Social scientists have rediscovered that the market is itself a social institution, with its own norms, which may vary from place to place. Institutions more generally are recognised as bundles of norms incorporating their own values and assumptions and powerfully conditioned by historical experience and, crucially, by interpretations of that experience. Boundaries between the state and the market are also unstable and change over time, as we have seen in recent years. Globalisation has given new relevance to these insights, as the role of states is reshaped. States seem to be losing power to the global market place and to transnational regimes, but at the same time they are undermined by new local and regional cultural, social and political movements. For some, these trends stand in stark contradiction, positing radically different modes of regulation and spatial scales.

Recently, however, there has been a growing appreciation that they may be complementary, with economic change, social mobilisation and politics restructuring simultaneously above and below the state, leaving the latter as something of a hollowed out shell. New systems of production, with distinct relationships among the market, the polity and culture, may be emerging not at the level of the nation-state, but in the regions, themselves tied ever more directly into European and global markets. The somewhat rebarbative term 'glocalisation' has been coined to capture this dual movement of restructuring (Robertson, 1992). Kenichi Ohmae (1995) has written of the 'borderless' world and presented a picture of 'regional states' based on local productive systems competing directly in world markets unencumbered by the institutional, social and political weight of the old nation-state. Others have talked of the rise of 'global city regions' based on large urban concentrations linked into international trading and financial networks (Scott, 2001; Sassen, 2001). Two aspects of these changes form the core of our concern here: functional restructuring, especially in economic development; and the rise of new or revived cultures and identities. By the late twentieth century, it was possible to formulate a hypothesis, contrary to the old modernisation wisdom, that in the new conditions of production, a distinct local culture might be an asset for development and a means of coping with globalisation. There might, contrary to the old modernists and to much neo-classical economics, be multiple paths to modernity and development.

Our interest is in the rise of such new spatially-specific forms of social regulation and collective action beyond the state. We focus on the regional level, identifying the region as an intermediate level between the state and the locality, with a certain sense of common identity and institutions. Rather than taking these for granted, we are interested in the way these territorial systems of actions are constituted under conditions of economic, cultural, political and institutional change, in the context of globalisation and European integration. This takes us into the realm of institutions, not in the formal sense of organs of government, but in the broader sense defined by new institutionalism, and covering both state and civil society. In pulling together the strands of political leadership, institutional development, culture and identity, we seek in particular to avoid two pitfalls. The first is a certain functionalist determinism in much writing about the new regionalism, the assumption that political and institutional form follows from the functional demands of the global economic system. The second is a tendency to cultural reductionism, the belief that change is driven by embedded cultural patterns and values largely immune from political or institutional influence; related to this is a tendency to reify 'identities', giving them a certain primordial essence and stretching the concept to cover too much. We focus on economic development policy as a main preoccupation of the new regionalist debate, but without restricting this to measures of economic growth in a narrow sense. Instead, we examine regional development as a complex project, with economic, social, cultural, environmental and political dimensions, the balance among which differs from one case to another.

Our approach is thus contextual, exploring the links among actors, institutions and processes at the territorial level, and this in turn means that we have chosen the case study method. Rather than tell a set of distinct stories, with the banal conclusion that places are different, we have placed our studies within a common framework and looked at the same issues in each of them. Regions can, of course, be defined in multiple ways; this is one of the issues which we explore. Yet we need a starting point and our concept of the region is institutional, the formal regions established by governments in four countries, with their own administrative and political structures. The question is how political, social and economic actors within these regions have been able to frame a development project permitting the insertion of the region into national, European and global markets on terms at least partly of their own making. More specifically we are interested in the uses of identity and shared culture in the forging of such systems of action. Since culture is essentially contextual, referring to differences, often rather subtle, among places, we have chosen a comparative case study approach, seeking to understand each case and then the differences among them.

THE CASES AND THE ISSUES

Since the goals of each regional development project are rather different, this precludes a systematic or quantitative assessment of the 'success' of each. Rather we are trying to explain why different regions are constituted differently, and why different types of development projects emerge in different parts of Europe and even of the same state. Our eight cases are chosen in pairs, with two each in Spain, France, Belgium and the United Kingdom, allowing us to hold the state framework constant and, at least in Spain and France, to examine regions with the same formal competences. We then have a cross-state comparison of all eight. This is achieved by looking at the same factors in each case, although recognising that not all are as important in each. All eight are deliberately chosen as historic and culturally specific regions, allowing us to incorporate the cultural dimension and explore the uses of historical referents and symbolism in the construction of a development coalition. We use the term region in a completely neutral way to cover all the cases, although we have all three grown up in environments in which the terms region, nation and community carry a heavy charge. Some of our cases, indeed, are stateless nations and this has affected their construction as institutions and systems of action, but all eight are recognized as regions on a European level. Finally, we have chosen in each case a region which is commonly regarded as successful in institution-building and has a higher level of economic development, and one that is regarded as less successful. This is only a starting point, since sometimes these characterisations are mere stereotypes and we can detect elements of dynamism and of weakness in all the cases. The 'strong' regions in our sample are Catalonia (Spain); Brittany (France); Flanders (Belgium) and Scotland (United Kingdom). The 'weak' regions that we selected are Galicia (Spain); Languedoc-Roussillon (France); Wallonia (Belgium) and Wales (United Kingdom).

We have sought in each case to trace the strategies and styles of development emerging from the dominant political and social coalitions in these regions. The emphasis is on economic development, but to assess the qualitative rather than the quantitative aspects we have looked at cultural and linguistic policy, at social inclusion and at environmental policy. Again, we are not interested in the whole field of cultural policy, but at the way in which it is linked to a development project or, conversely, the extent to which economic considerations and the demands of global markets constrain the region's ability to foster a distinct culture. Similarly, we cannot cover the whole of social policy but are interested in the way in which social considerations are included in the overall project, or alternatively consigned to national government. Environmental policy is a test of the ability of regions to mobilise for collective purposes, since it is concerned with largely non-divisible public goods. Like culture and social inclusion, it might be incorporated into an overall programme, seen as an integral part of development or even, as in the 'high road' scenario, contributing to development; or it might be seen as a costly luxury. We conclude that culture does play a role in region building around economic development, but in order to understand how and why this should be so, we need to take a rather lengthy detour through current theories of regional development to see just where culture and identity might fit.

2. The New Regionalism

THE CHANGING SCALE OF PUBLIC ACTION

Recent years have seen a debate in political geography and related disciplines about the 'new regionalism', the rise of new territorial frameworks for action below the state, often linked into transnational networks. The context for the new regionalism is fivefold. First, there is the crisis of the model of state territorial management and spatial economic policy elaborated in the years following the Second World War. Second, there is the constellation of effects captured by the term globalisation. Third is the rise of new forms of spatially-based production systems and forms of social regulation. Fourth is the resurgence of cultural regionalism, including minority nationalism and identity politics. Finally, there is the effect of institutional structuring as states have put in place intermediate or regional tiers of government.

TERRITORIAL MANAGEMENT AND REGIONAL POLICY

For over a hundred years, the context for regional politics and policies has been the nation-state, with regions being the object rather than the subject of policy. In the nineteenth century, tariff protection was an important instrument for territorial as well as sectoral accommodation in the developing industrial state and unified Germany and Italy have both been analysed as examples of territorial/sectoral compromise. In Germany, this was the alliance of grain and iron, while in Italy the industrial bourgeoisie of the north made common cause with the agrarian elites of the south behind an agreed policy of protection. The Catalan bourgeoisie's demands were focused simultaneously on a demand for local self-government and for a tariff regime that would deliver them the Spanish home market. The earlier phase of globalisation identified by Hirst and Thompson (1999) had some profound effects on territorial relations across Europe. Peripheries of the global trading hegemon the United Kingdom, including Glasgow, Cardiff, Belfast and Manchester, tied into world markets, became strongly free trading. Catalonia, competitive in Spain but not in global markets, reacted to the loss of its captive imperial markets with a retreat to protectionism. In protectionist France, Brittany, formerly linked to a maritime Atlantic economy, became a terrestrial periphery, while the development of Languedoc was subordinated to the needs of a centralised French state (Lafont, 1967). Galicia was similarly peripheralised. The collapse of the world trading system in the 1930s led to new coalitions of interest again, as territories sought protection within the state framework.

It was, however, in the post-Second World War era that western European states embarked on their most ambitious programmes of territorial economic management, linked to Keynesian macro-economic strategies and to the welfare state. The aim of policy was to incorporate territories with economic difficulties, whether of underdevelopment or of industrial decline, into national economic space. Under the principle of comparative advantage, regions were complementary, each having its role in a national division of labour. In a period of overall growth and full employment, regional economic problems were seen as marginal, arising from market imperfections rather than fundamental defects in the market economy or its spatial articulation. The disadvantages from which certain territories suffered were seen as stemming from peripheral location or inadequate infrastructure, which could be remedied by investment in infrastructure. Territory itself was not generally invested with any social or political context so that, given the right investment conditions, territories were almost interchangeable. Regional policies had economic objectives, which were to enhance national production by bringing into use idle resources in the periphery and modernise the national productive system. They had social objectives, to overcome unemployment and provide more equal opportunities for all citizens. Politically, they served to secure support for the state and for governing parties in regions that might otherwise be disaffected. They also had the advantage that they could be presented as a non-zero-sum game, in which everyone could win. Poor regions would gain from the additional development and employment; rich regions would gain from the relief of congestion; and the nation as a whole would gain from the ability to increase national production without generating inflationary pressures. These top-down, state-driven regional policy approaches were far removed from political regionalism, which was an ideology and political movement whereby regional populations, usually elites, sought control over the affairs of their regions. In the period immediately after the Second World War regionalism was widely thought to be backward and regressive. Regionalists who wished to develop a more progressive and modernising approach often had to disguise their antecedents by adopting positions such as Europeanism or neo-Marxist internal colonialism theories.

The main vehicle for modernisation and development was industrialisation, and policy focused on bringing new manufacturing plants into underdeveloped or declining regions. This was to be achieved through diversion of investment from booming regions, using grants and tax incentives, and by the provision of infrastructure in developing areas. There was an emphasis on hard services like roads, railways, airports, industrial estates and telecommunications to overcome inherited disadvantages. State owned industries were also used to divert investments, especially in basic industries like steel and the energy sector. Beyond the broad brush diversionary approach, based on large regions identified by unemployment rates, there developed a more refined spatial focus based on growth poles. This concept, which originated in non-spatial economics, was adapted to the needs of regional development in the form of strategically located investments which could attract complementary activity (Thomas, 1972). Basic industries in the energy or metals sector were often a key element; in other cases, the automobile industry, which creates a large demand for parts suppliers, was the basis for a growth pole. The general assumption was that, given the right cost structure and infrastructure, almost any region could be adapted to the needs of the manufacturing economy and find a place in the national division of labour. Place was thus culturally neutral.

Beyond this there was a variety of national experiences. Some states embarked on efforts at cohesive spatial planning, tying economic development policies to regional and local land use plans, including housing and social infrastructure. In France, the presence of a corps of modernising planners within the regional development agency, DATAR (*Délégation à l'Aménagement du Territoire et à l'Action Régionale*), together with a strong field bureaucracy, favoured synoptic planning. Smaller countries like the Netherlands and Sweden were able to achieve a quite high integration of the instruments of spatial intervention (Drevet, 1991). The United Kingdom was less successful, given the functional divisions within central government, although there were some ambitious efforts at spatial planning in west-central Scotland and ambitions, largely unrealised, for the Highlands (Wannop, 1995). Spanish regional policy under Franco was largely confined to massive public works projects, while urban development was chaotic and largely unregulated.

Policy, based as it was on the integration of regions into national markets, tended to be centralised, top-down and rather depoliticised. A favoured instrument was the regional development agency, specialising in economic development in the strict sense and largely insulated from local political and social pressures. Existing systems of local government, in particular, were seen as too tied into distributive politics and in some cases to clientelism, to be able to take the necessary tough decisions on investment priorities. There were reforms of local government in all countries, justified by the need to modernise structures and to engage in urban and regional planning on a larger scale, corresponding to functional patterns in economic development, travel to work and leisure activities. Another motive, more or less explicitly stated, was to reduce the influence of the old local elites, replacing them with more managerially minded people who could see the larger picture and collaborate with the state in the modernisation project. The most radical reforms were in the United Kingdom, where the system was overhauled in the mid-1970s with a drastic reduction in the number of municipalities. French governments proved less successful, given the entrenchment of the local elites in national politics, and the number of communes remained at over 36,000, more than in the rest of the European Union put together.

Attention was also focused on the larger, 'meso' level of government, or region, as a key level for economic transformation and planning and here too states sought partners on the ground for their modernisation strategies. Again, the aim was to co-opt the dynamic and modernising forces emerging in the regions (the *forces vives* as the French called them) while reducing the weight of traditionalists. The result was a set of planning mechanisms intended to strengthen the capacity of the state to plan and intervene at the regional level, while bringing in a regional input through consultative committees, all the while maintaining the national orientation of policy and resisting politicisation by oppositional forces. In France, this took the form of the CODER (*Commissions de Développement Economique Régionale*), established in 1963 and consisting of nominees from business, agriculture, labour and local government together with independent experts. Regional prefects were appointed to co-ordinate the field services of the state at regional level and, in collaboration with DATAR, this regional apparatus had the responsibility for translating the National Plan to the regional level. Shortly after, the United Kingdom followed suit, with regional Economic Planning Councils, to represent the dynamic forces within the region, complementing regional Economic Planning Boards composed of central government departments. In Scotland and Wales, where the Scottish and Welsh Offices already had the job of regional planning, there was no need for the Boards, but otherwise the machinery was similar. Belgium, too, established regional Economic Councils (Houthaeve, 1996), as did Italy. Such was the political sensitivity of anything to do with regions in Francoist Spain that, despite pressures from the rising technocratic elites, there was no question of adopting even top-down regional planning (Cuadrado Roura, 1981; García, 1979).

These efforts to channel and contain regionalism by defining it in restricted economic terms and seeking a consensual, technical response, largely came to grief in the face of political realities and the issue rapidly became politicised (Keating, 1988). In some regions, development coalitions of local modernisers had sprung up spontaneously, with their own ideas about regional development. Perhaps the best known was the Breton CELIB (*Comité d'Etudes et de Liaison des Intérêts Bretons*), formed in 1950 by business leaders, farmers, trade unionists and academics to press for a regional plan. The subordination of the CELIB to the CODER after 1963 led to the emasculation of CELIB and the resignation of one of its most prominent members, Michel Phlipponeau (Hayward, 1969; Phlipponeau, 1981). In the United Kingdom, it was never made clear whether the REPCs were there to provide a bottom-up element in regional planning or to apply the central policy in the regions, and they never recovered from the collapse of the first National Plan in 1967 (Lindley, 1982). Yet, while the new arrangements did not in general successfully integrate the new regionalists into the central development strategies, they did in many cases destabilise existing mechanisms of territorial representation and exchange, while raising the salience of the regional level. This coincided with a certain revival and revalorisation of minority cultures and the rise of new social movements, which also often mobilised at a regional level; the United Kingdom, Spain, Belgium and to a lesser extent France, experienced a revival or minority nationalism (Keating, 1988, 1998a). So the 1970s saw an explosion of regionalist movements and a politicisation of development issues, escaping the limits of state territorial management. The issue of regional autonomy began to take centre stage.

Failure to institutionalise the policy or to integrate the top-down and bottom-up perspectives was one reason for the decline of traditional regional policies from the 1980s. Another was a critique of the failure of policy itself. Some critics saw the focus on large-scale, capital-intensive projects as a means for the state to subsidise big capitalism and socialise investment risks (Dunford, 1988; Tarrow, 1978). The big development schemes, especially in southern Italy, too often failed to generate complementary industries or self-sustaining growth and were labelled 'cathedrals in the desert'. All the major investments brought to Scotland by regional policy in the 1960s were closed down in the 1980s or early 1990s. Measures intended to be short-term, while regions were integrated into national economic circuits, took on an air of permanence and some critics claimed that regions were being maintained in a state of dependency, from which they would never escape. The *Cassa per il Mezzogiorno*, set up in 1950 for ten years (Galasso, 1978) was finally abolished in 1985 and even then managed a few more years of shadowy existence. The oil crisis and recession of the 1970s struck a severe blow to traditional regional policy as governments faced straitened financial circumstances and unemployment hit formerly prosperous regions (Hansen et al., 1990). Diversionary policy was more difficult to sell as a zero-sum game and by 1983 the British Regional Studies Association (1983) could announce that regional policy could now be justified only on social and not on economic grounds. As neo-liberal ideology came into the ascendant, there was less support for planning, for grand schemes or for market-correcting diversion, although governments did maintain selective spatial interventions, often at the local and urban scale.

There is abundant evidence that traditional regional policy, while it did have serious problems, was not a complete failure (Artobolevskiy, 1997). Its demise owed something to changed circumstances, notably the difficulties for states in managing spatial economies in a globalising world. Firms denied permission to invest in one part of the national territory could now locate more easily out of the country altogether, while still having access to local markets. European competition policies also hampered many of the old measures used to stimulate investment in marginal regions, especially after the launching of the single market programme in 1985. Thereafter, the European Commission sought to regulate national regional policies through the competition directorate, while the regional policy directorate sought, with limited success, to Europeanise the policy field. We would also argue that a vital element in the demise of traditional regional policy is the change in the intellectual political climate, which has led to the old idea of regions as complementary pieces in a national division of labour giving way to the idea of competitive regionalism, in which regions seek their own place in the European and international division of labour. There is a dual intellectual basis for this, in the debate on globalisation, and in what amounts to a paradigm shift in thinking about regional development matters.

THE GLOBALISATION DEBATE

Globalisation is one of those very general concepts which have been so widely diffused and invoked as to cover almost every aspect of modern society and thus lose their explanatory power. It is, in fact, a set of distinct processes, which might be linked and whose relationship to each other is not always obvious. Perhaps the most important aspect of globalisation is the economic one. Increasing trade flows have made nation-states more inter-dependent thus increasing the costs of protectionist policies. Easy and rapid mobility of capital has undermined the ability of governments to manage their currencies, and thus their monetary policies, and rendered them prey to speculators. The rise of the transnational corporation, itself eased by the liberalisation of capital flows, has forced governments to compete for investment and technology, reducing their ability to regulate business and perhaps obliging them to accept terms dictated by international capital. In the more extreme versions of this theory, governments are powerless within global markets, a prospect celebrated by some and deplored by others.

The second most prominent aspect of globalisation is the communications revolution, especially the Internet, which provides instant links among people across the globe. For some, this defines a whole new stage in social evolution, the 'information society' (Castells, 1997) as the constraints of time and space that have defined the limits to human endeavour are shattered. By its very nature, the new technology is resistant to regulation by states, thus empowering individuals and oppositional groups. It also permits the emergence of virtual communities, of social and political movements divided by space but united by interest, taste or preference. This might potentially sustain cultural pluralism as the ease and cost of communication within distinct cultural groups is reduced, but the main effect of globalisation in the dominant accounts is cultural uniformity, together with atomisation and individualism. A global culture and lifestyle, especially among the young, may be emerging with the dissolving of old territorial communities and the ease of diffusion of fashions in dress, music and thought.

There is also a political dimension to globalisation in the rise of global social movements, dedicated to causes including environmentalism, the rights of autochthonous peoples or feminism. Some of these are opposed to globalisation itself, at least in so far as it fosters the dominance of market forces and corporate interests. Institutionally, globalisation takes the form of international regimes and organisations concerned either with promoting free trade and capital mobility, or dealing with its social and environmental consequences. Within Europe, this has taken the specific form, not replicated elsewhere in the world, of a dense network of organisations and regimes spanning economics, defence, human rights and aspects of environmental and social regulation. At the centre is the European Union, itself subject to a variety of interpretations. For some, the EU is merely a form of globalisation, an effort at the continental level to create a free space for market forces, further undermining the state and tilting the playing field against social and other interests. Most observers, however, recognise that the EU is also a political project, creating a new political space with its own characteristics, neither a state in the making nor a mere intergovernmental regime. This is indeed one of the issues at stake in the construction of Europe, pitching neo-liberals who favour a market-driven vision against those who see Europe as a way of preserving the historic social compromises and the welfare state in the face of global market pressures.

Globalisation is thus a complex set of processes and it is not surprising that it has spawned a number of critiques. There are those who think that the whole thing has been exaggerated and that the nation-state remains the fundamental basis for political authority. They point to the resilience of the European welfare state, the fact that governments consume as large a share of the national product as ever and the dominance of the new international regimes by states themselves. Some critics see the whole idea of globalisation as an ideological construction to justify cutting back welfare spending and building neo-liberalism into political structures. What is lacking in this view is not the ability of the state to regulate markets but the willingness (Boyer and Drache, 1996). Others question the extent of globalisation and argue that, to the extent that it is a reality, it is nothing new, since very similar statistics about capital flows and trade emerge from a study of the global economy at the end of the nineteenth century (Hirst and Thompson, 1999).

There is some merit in most of these arguments. The problem is that the issue of globalisation has too often been approached at a rather abstract and general level and its affects deduced rather than investigated. We would argue that the state remains a key element in social regulation, in economic life and in politics, but that it has been undergoing a process of transformation. This has had important effects on its ability to define territory and to manage its spatial economy. In turn, this has created a context in which new forms of sub-state regionalism can mobilise but this mobilisation takes a variety of forms and is in no way pre-determined. To simplify, we can see the nation-state, as it has existed since the nineteenth century, as a territorial framework within which coincide a number of social, economic and political systems. We can talk of a national economy, not because the state is a 'natural' economic unit, but because states have moulded their economies, and because the national territory is a unit of economic management. National cultures are in part the product of shared social and linguistic patterns, but owe a great deal to the ability of states to shape and reproduce culture and language. National identity, in so far as it corresponds to state identity, has also been moulded by state policies in education, media regulation and a variety of socialisation instruments. This in turn has underpinned a political community, or *demos*, and served as the foundation of democracy as well as for social solidarity. The state has furnished the basis for systems of representation and the mechanisms of policy making and authoritative decision making. These are not discreet items, but come together to create a functioning national community, within which politics can take place and social compromises can be worked out. Recent changes have not so much destroyed the state or public authority; rather they have led to a certain disaggregation of these functions. So economic restructuring is following a global and, to some extent, local logic rather than being encompassed by state boundaries. National culture is challenged by global and sub-state cultures as the state loses its monopoly of the instruments of socialisation. Policy making is increasingly moving out to networks, spanning the public and private sector and crossing state boundaries. The old social compromises are more difficult as capital, being mobile, finds it easier to escape social obligations, while labour is largely confined to state boundaries. Representative institutions are challenged because of their apparent impotence in the face of global and market forces, while new social and political movements search for new forms of democracy below and beyond the state.

THE NEW REGIONAL DEVELOPMENT PARADIGM

Globalisation and the transformation of the state have in some accounts broken the link between territory on the one hand, and function and identity on the other, heralding the 'end of territory' (Badie, 1995) or a borderless world. Yet it is increasingly recognised that they have also encouraged a reterritorialisation of function, identity and social life, and the emergence of new systems of territorial regulation and collective action. In particular, they have formed the backdrop to a new vision of territorial economic development, which has to a large extent displaced the old vision of integrated national spatial management. In this vision, the region is more the subject than the object of policy and the context is provided not just by the state but also by the international market place and the demands of inter-regional competition. The new literature on regional development is large and complex and it would be mistaken to take it as a single school, but there are common elements. Drawing on economic sociology and institutional economics, they tend to see the market and systems of production as socially constructed rather than the product of perfect competition and in permanent equilibrium (Swedberg, 1993). The behaviour of economic actors is moulded by institutional incentives, learned behaviours and routines and, in some versions, cultural values and norms. Consequently, markets work differently in different contexts, not just because some groups have yet to experience 'modernisation' but as an inherent feature of the market itself. The perfectly competitive market in which transactions take place on the basis of value-free exchange is only one possible form, and is at best an ideal-type.

All versions also seek to reincorporate territory back into explanations of economic and social change, rather than merely seeing it as a stage on which any play can be performed. To some extent, this represents a return to Marshall's concept of industrial regions, observed in nineteenth century Britain but building on one particular aspect of this. Generally, for Marshall, industrial districts were sites of specialised production in which complementary firms congregated because of their mutual dependence as suppliers and consumers. Marshall did, however, also identify a less tangible attribute of locality, 'something in the air' and it is this insight that forms the basis for much of the new regional paradigm. Regions and localities, as the site of dense networks of institutions, understanding and knowledge, construct the market in very specific ways. As a consequence, territories are not interchangeable as locations of production, even if the cost structures are altered by state policies of subsidy, diversion and infrastructure investment. There is a scepticism about Ricardian theories of comparative advantage and equilibrium economics, according to which the market will distribute production optimally, with each region finding its place in the national or global division of labour (Begg et al., 1995). An equal scepticism is expressed about the 'spatial Keynesianism' of traditional regional policy in which state intervention can overcome market imperfections, re-integrate territories into national markets and remedy temporary disequilibria. Rather, regional development is a matter for regions themselves, in a context in which they are pitched into competition in global markets, without the protective umbrella of the nation-state, so linking the arguments about regional development to the globalisation debate.

Beyond these common features, there are many variations of the new paradigm and a number of distinct schools. Transaction costs versions, based on institutional economics, see collective action as a way of overcoming problems associated with purely individualistic accounts of the markets. Such accounts cannot handle the need for non-simultaneous reciprocity, the production of public goods, or the problem of externalities. Capitalism requires a delicate combination of market competition and co-operation, and these can be provided by local production systems. The California school, influenced by the experience of the Los Angeles area as well as other parts of the United States and of Europe rely to a large degree on the idea of a transition of production, from large-scale, mass production to flexible specialisation (or from Fordism to post-Fordism) (Storper, 1995, 1997; Scott, 1996, 1998; Scott and Storper, 1992; Scott et al., 2001). They stress the conditions of production, transaction costs and the advantages of distinct regions under different modes of production. Modern flexible specialisation generates specific and new forms of agglomeration economy, such that firms tend to cluster together rather than dispersing (Storper, 1995). These economies are rooted in the conditions of flexible specialisation itself, notably the need for firms to know rapidly about each other and about changes in technology and fashion, and for workers and employers to adjust to changing demands for products and skills. Modern conditions of production, the need to adjust rapidly and the importance of access to technology are such that the old concept of comparative advantage, in which each region has its place in the national and global division of labour, has given way to absolute or competitive advantage, in which regions are competing against each other constantly (Storper, 1995; Scott, 1998). Unlike neo-classical economists, they hold that there is not one unique combination of production factors capable of achieving absolute efficiency, but a whole range of possibilities, depending on local circumstances and resources. So multiple worlds of production are capable of co-existing in equilibrium, without any one driving out the rest.

Other versions go beyond this purely transactional reasoning to locate regional systems of production in deeper historical and social patterns. The Italian school (Bagnasco and Trigilia, 1993; Garfoli, 1991) initially based its work on the experience of the dynamic regions of central Italy which seemed to have made a successful transition from standardised mass production into specialised production of high quality goods in competitive global markets, after the industrial conflicts of the late 1960s and the oil crisis of the 1970s. Here there appeared to be dynamic networks of small firms, using their small size to achieve flexibility, and the wider networks to attain the economies of scale normally associated with larger units of production. At the same time, they were able to combine the competition necessary for a dynamic market economy, with co-operation in the production of the public goods necessary for capitalism to survive and thrive. For some, this pattern of flexible specialisation was a response to the crisis of 'Fordist' mass production; for others it was an abiding feature of these regions, which had enabled them to adapt to successive changes in production technologies and markets over the centuries. From Italy, the idea spread to southern Germany, where scholars also found industrial districts, and to Scandinavia before becoming something of a model for industrial policy more generally. More recently, Crouch et al. (2001) have emphasised the diversity of local production systems that can exist in different places at any one time, distinguishing broadly among old industrial districts (based on reciprocity and mutual learning), networked firms (with more highly structured links of based on the dominance of one large firm) and empirical clusters (with a lower presence of reciprocity and community norms). They also introduce an element of dynamism, and change on Schumpeterian lines. Local production systems are constantly poised between conflicting tendencies and forces and, while enjoying periods of stable equilibrium, are also prone to crises, change and reconstitution in new forms.

British scholars have approached the question from the point of view of institutions, emphasising associations and networks. Amin and Thrift (1994) write of institutional thickness as a key element in regional performance. Cooke and Morgan (1998) write of the 'associational economy' characterised by associations, networks and linkages among firms, social groups and government. They go beyond the Italian or California schools in seeing this as a new economic system, an alternative both to market capitalism and to centralised state planning. They also go beyond the narrow issue of economic production by claiming that this new model is not only more efficient but also potentially more socially integrative, recalling the 1980s debate about models of capitalism. The basic idea is that the new forms of production put an emphasis on social co-operation and common understandings as well as sustaining human capital and that this may facilitate social solidarity. Putnam's (1993) work on Italy also goes beyond the question of economic production to make large claims about the territorial conditions underlying rival models of society, presented as stark contrasts in civic virtue. Central Italy sustains not only a more vibrant and adaptive economy, but also a higher degree of civic participation and better democratic performance generally.

There are enough points in common to these accounts to allow us to talk of a new paradigm, but there are clearly differences in the scope of the claims made by the various schools. All see the market as socially embedded within territorial spaces. Territory is conceived as more than mere location but refers to the whole pattern of social and economic relationships, conventions and culture, which together make up the distinct *milieu* of each place. Traded dependencies, as the basis for economic transactions, are complemented by untraded dependencies that arise from spontaneous interaction among firms and individuals, promoting patterns of collaboration and competition in different ways. The locality or region is seen not merely as the location of productive activities but as a productive system itself, able not only to exploit new conditions but to innovate and learn, so continually adapting and improving its productive apparatus; this is the learning region (Morgan, 1997). In conditions of globalisation, these regional productive systems are in competition with each other for advantage, seeking technology and markets. Beyond this, there are differences in the various approaches. Some scholars see flexible specialisation as a system of economic production rooted in the social practices of particular regions, and thus not applicable everywhere, while others see it as a condition of modern industrial technology and thus generalisable. Among the former, some extend the idea beyond productive relationships to make a whole theory of social regulation, encompassing social integration and political life.

The new thinking has had an immense impact on regional development policies across Europe and within the European Commission itself (Bachtler, 1993; Yuill et al., 1993). Policy has been decentralised to local and regional levels and at the same time Europeanised. There are strong functional and efficiency reasons for this (Cappellin, 1995a), but it also follows political and institutional trends in the nation-state itself, as does the emphasis on partnership, flexibility and adaptation (Loughlin, 2000). There is a strong emphasis on institutions, particularly on partnership between public and private actors and on networks of knowledge-sharing and co-operation. Less stress is put on investment in hard services and infrastructure, partly because most development regions acquired these in early phases of regional policy, but also because soft services are considered the key to the modern performing, learning region. There is heavy investment in human capital, including education, training and skills upgrading; most states have devolved manpower training to the regional level, where it complements the other instruments of intervention. Research and development, along with technology transfer, are seen as key elements in growth and adaptation. While inward investment is still promoted, there is a new emphasis on endogenous development and the promotion of entrepreneurship (Cappellin, 1995b). There is less synoptic planning or large-scale intervention and policy takes a lighter touch, attempting to 'steer' development or intervene selectively. Spatial redistribution has given way to the idea that regions need to help themselves (Stöhr, 1989). Regions, once seen as complementary elements in integrated national economies, are now seen as competitors within European and global markets. These ideas have gradually diffused from the academic world into government and the European Commission, and among regions through networks of co-operation and partnership. By the 1990s these ideas had become the common currency of regional political and administrative elites (Kohler-Koch, 1998).

Yet there have been many criticisms of the new regional development paradigm. Some of the earliest complained that it relied on a tendentious and starry-eyed generalisation from a few cases, themselves often poorly understood (Lovering, 1999). Scholars revisiting these regions themselves have discovered the other side of flexible specialisation, including exploitation and low wages (Hadjmichalis and Papamios, 1991). Some, while not dismissing the new model, warn of its uses as an excuse for states to disengage from responsibilities to troubled regions (Amin, 1999). Others have asked whether, since the new model is based upon the unique qualities of individual regions, it counts as a model at all (Storper, 1995), especially as most regions are still rooted in traditional forms of mass production or in services. There is a danger of reifying the region or of attributing collective interests to it without considering internal divisions. More fundamental questions can be raised about some of the concepts on which the model rests, which are often poorly specified and over-stretched. Above all, we still know too little about just how and why particular regions develop the social preconditions for successful development. Hence our focus on the comparative case study method.

THE RISE OF CULTURAL REGIONS

One effect of the demystification of the nation-state has been to provoke a new interest in alternative identities, including those based on the smaller cultures, languages and regions. This is not merely a matter of rediscovery, since while historic stateless nations have indeed been revived or transformed, new ones have been invented. Minority languages have been revalorised and revived and traditional cultures rediscovered. It is increasingly recognised that individuals and communities can have multiple identities depending on the context and the issue at stake. In Belgium, the language issue has divided the society and linked with territorial and political considerations to generate powerful disintegrative pressures on both the Flemish and Walloon sides. Basque, Catalan and, to a lesser extent, Galician nationalism, have become defining features of Spanish politics. Scottish, Welsh and Irish nationalism have revived strongly in the United Kingdom since the 1990s. There has been less such mobilisation in France, although there is a strong movement in Corsica and continuing movements in Brittany and Languedoc. In all these cases, political movements have combined elements of culture, identity and territory to demand a drastic decentralisation of the state or even the right to secede.

Under the old modernisation paradigm such local particularities were often seen as an obstacle to economic and social progress, evidence of social retardation. Some observers now see them as evidence of a new historical era, postmodernity, in which universal values and grand narratives give way to particularism. Without getting into this debate, we can certainly see the revival of local identities and cultures as part of a broader process of social change and not just evidence of atavism. They take multiple forms and not all are territorially based. Yet they do coincide in time with the rediscovery of local and regional production systems, and an institutional restructuring of the state and there is a strong tendency for such movements to develop on a territorial basis. Territory thus provides a prism through which to examine the interaction of cultural reinvention and functional economic restructuring, and the relationships between the two. National and cultural revivals, and the new political economy of regions, however, have tended to be the subject of distinct literatures, from different disciplinary backgrounds and employing different methods. To put it differently, we do not have a political economy of the new regional cultural movements. Yet there are reasons to think that the forms of identity and collective action fostered by the new cultural regionalism may be linked to the social mobilisation required in the new regional development paradigm, and we do find political leaders in cultural regions seeking to advance on both fronts together.

THE REGIONAL STATE

Another widespread trend has been for states to institutionalise an intermediate, regional or 'meso' level of government. The impetus came partly from the functional logic of regional development policy and the need to institutionalise and strengthen the horizontal level of planning and intervention. It also came from pressures to democratisation and decentralisation and from demands for recognition from cultural and historical nationalities and minorities. Yet there was an implicit tension between state regionalisation from above, and political regionalism from below. While these pressures and conflicts can be detected widely across Europe, the outcome was specific to each state and its domestic political balance. Regionalism in France was largely contained by adapting the old system of territorial management and representation. After the failure of De Gaulle's referendum on regional reform in 1969, itself aimed at undermining the old Fourth Republic notables in the localities, Pompidou established indirectly elected regional councils controlled by the notables themselves, so co-opting them into the regional planning mechanism. In government from 1981, the Socialists launched an ambitious programme of decentralisation but, unable to choose among the three levels of local government, gave something to each of them. The result was a rather weak tier of elected regional governments, with more power going to mayors of big cities and also to the *départements*. The main role of regions was still to engage in planning, in partnership with the state, and to programme public investment, but some regions were able to make more of these powers than others.

In the United Kingdom, the functional regionalism of the 1960s was overtaken by the debate devolution provoked by the rise of Scottish nationalism. Proposals for devolution to Scotland and Wales failed because of parliamentary obstruction, lack of will on the part of the Labour Party which was sponsoring them and, in the case of Wales, heavy defeat in a referendum. Schemes for regional government in England were abandoned and the Thatcher government even abolished the Regional Economic

Development Councils, as attention shifted to selective intervention in urban areas. Regionalism went out of fashion although in Scotland opposition to Conservative policy fed into a revived home rule movement from the late 1980s. After the change of government in 1997, elected assemblies were set up for Scotland, Wales and Northern Ireland, and unelected regional development machinery revived in England.

In Italy, the earlier regional development machinery, notably the *Cassa per il Mezzogiorno*, technocratic in inspiration, had by the 1960s fallen into the hands of the party system ('partitocrazia') and been subordinated to a clientelistic logic. The centre-left coalition from the early 1960s was committed to implement the clauses in the post-war constitution providing for regional government, but these were not set up until 1970 and only in the late 1970s did they receive their powers. Even then, they were under the control of the national parties and had little policy discretion, although from the 1990s they began to acquire more powers and a higher political profile.

In Belgium, on the other hand, a combination of functional arguments and the demands of the language groups produced a double system of devolution, to territorial regions and language communities, which was eventually to transform the state into a federation. In Spain, no serious moves were made on regional structures until the transition of the late 1970s, when the need to accommodate Basque and Catalan nationalism started a process of decentralisation which rapidly affected the whole country. As a result, by the end of the 1990s all the countries in our sample had elected meso-governments, albeit of very different powers and status.

Regional governments thus came to reflect tensions in the way they were set up. They are used by the state for the purposes of national economic and spatial planning (notably in France) but also represent a impulse for self-government on the part of the regions themselves. They have an important role in facilitating development according to the new models of self-sustaining, endogenous growth, but are also concerned with safeguarding and promoting regional culture and identity. Regions vary greatly in their powers but nowhere do they have the panoply of competences that the nation-state in its heyday possessed to pull together the domains of culture and identity, economic development and politics. Rather they must operate in complex and rather pluralistic environments, in which policy making is a matter of networks and relationships, integrating different territorial and functional actors. Their work is less about the authoritative allocation of values in Easton's famous expression, and more about social mobilisation around shared objectives, notably in economic development and growth. They also have interests in their own strengthening, especially in those regions controlled by parties engaged in nation or region building.

There have been various efforts to capture this new dynamic, from both right and left of the political spectrum. Ohmae (1995) writes of 'regional states', although what he refers to are rather local competing regional systems of production locked in battle for competitive advantage. His analysis and prescription are a curious mixture of neo-liberalism, in which government is seen as an obstacle to market-driven growth, and neo-mercantilism, in which regional states seem to have moral imperative to do everything they can to promote competitive advantage. A more sophisticated version is presented by Courchene (1999, 2001) who draws on the literature on the new regional development paradigm and on trends in the international economy to argue that regions must adapt to their external environment. Since this entails keeping their cost structures in line with those of their immediate competitors, there are large implications for politics and public policies. The 'state' in this formulation does not carry the implications of sovereign authority which are its defining characteristics in political science and law, but refers rather to a system of regulation and public policy making within a looser federal type arrangement. A social democratic version of the regional state or 'new regionalism' paradigm is presented by the California school. Scott (1998) sees the region as the locus of new production systems in conditions of globalism and 'post-fordism' but broadens the agenda of regionalism to include issues of worker rights, gender, the environment and political representation. Avoiding the term 'regional state' he sees a need for new forms of regional regulation in the form of 'regional directorates' in order to integrate these diverse concerns in the face of weakened nation states. Alain-G. Gagnon (2001) applies the idea to the stateless nation of Quebec, a 'state' without all the attributes of sovereignty but at the centre of a development coalition seeking to secure its place in North American and global markets.

INSTITUTIONS AND CULTURE

We have, then, the transformation of the state; a process of functional restructuring; the rise of cultural regions; and a restructuring of government, all components of the new regionalism (Keating, 1998a). These we postulate as common effects across our cases. Our aim is to explore the divergent responses in different places, the scope for regions to shape the terms of their insertion into the new order. This is not merely about economic development, subordinating all other considerations as in Ohmae's vision, but about development in a broader sense, encompassing questions of social integration and of cultural expression.

Our framework for analysing this is provided largely by the 'new institutionalism' (March and Olsen, 1984; Peters, 1999; Steinmo et al.,

1992; Hall and Taylor, 1996). A reaction to the universalising assumptions of much of behavioural social science in the 1960s and 1970s and of public choice in the 1980s, it focuses on differences among social systems and the explanations for them, while trying to avoid essentialist or purely cultural arguments. Institutions are conceptualised broadly as patterns of routinised behaviour and expectation, as well as the formal apparatus of government. There are three forms of new institutionalism, which tend to complement rather than contradict each other. Rational choice institutionalism is a corrective to rational choice models themselves, and holds that actors' choices are constrained by the institutional opportunities open to them. Normative institutionalism emphasises the role of institutions in shaping people's values and norms, again correcting some of the more extreme rational choice assumptions. Historical institutionalism traces the role of institutions in transmitting patterns of behaviour over time, explaining the remarkable historical continuities that we find in some territorial societies. These ideas are valuable and we will be adopting a broadly institutionalist approach in the case studies in later chapters. Yet the application of the theory to territorial societies and issues of regional development is a difficult one. If institutions are defined very broadly, then they come to constitute all forms of social practice, extending the concept so far as to undermine its explanatory usefulness. Normative institutionalism can similarly be stretched to cover all social norms and practices and become no more than a politically correct term for what we used to call culture, until the reaction to the rather ethnocentric 'civic culture' studies of the 1960s, with their findings that the Anglo-Saxon democracies represented a higher form of civic life to which less enlightened nations could only aspire. So we cannot escape altogether from culture, into a value-free world of rational choice. Historical institutionalism is predicated on the concept of path dependency, the idea that decisions are constrained by previous ones, implying that change will be gradual and that different societies can remain on different trajectories even when faced with the same external pressures. Yet we do not always know what the 'real' history of a society is. We do know that history is constantly made and remade in successive waves of revisionism; so that what may really matter is whose version of history prevails.

There are also problems in the application of the new institutionalism to the new regionalism, that is the emergence of territorial spaces as dynamic centres for economic and social change. Amin and Thrift (1994) talk about 'institutional thickness' as a key factor in regional success, while Cooke and Morgan (1998) write of the 'associational economy'. Putnam (1993) sees participation in associations as a key explanation of regional performance in Italy, an idea subsequently extended to the United States (Putnam, 2000).

Yet there is a counter-argument, associated with Mancur Olson (1982) that the existence of multiple institutions, far from enhancing flexibility, impedes it by introducing additional veto points and increasing the transaction costs of co-operation. Networks can help common action but they represent sunk costs and may therefore be resistant to change (Bergman et al., 1991). It all depends, as Amin and Thrift (1994) note, on what type of institutions we are talking about and what their effects are on human behaviour. They write that institutions must not only be present, but interact, foster coalition-building, and sustain a common enterprise. Putnam writes of the rich network of private associations in central Italy, but there are equally dense institutions in the south, run by organised crime. He considers the decline of bowling clubs in the United States as a good proxy for the decline of civil society, without explaining the precise social function of particular types of associations as opposed to others. At one point, he argues that it does not matter what the avowed aim of the associations is, that choral societies or bird-watching clubs will do, although in more recent writing he has accepted that there may be both benign and perverse forms of associationalism. This is a question which it is surely impossible to answer in the abstract. Guilds, for example, might in one context be sources of dynamism as repositories of knowledge and skills; in another they may be monopolistic rent-seekers, stifling innovation and social mobility. They may represent an expansion of the public domain and of social reciprocity, or its closure. Similarly, some patterns of associational life and solidarity might be more functional than others. It may be that in the United States the Tocquevillian associationalism of enlightened self-interest has been replaced by a privately oriented form of associationalism in which community is seen less as public space than a mechanism for the defence of private space (Keating, 1993). Clientelism is usually thought to be inimical to development, since it promotes vertical dependency rather than horizontal collaboration, and the patron has an interest in stifling self-sustaining growth which would enable the clients to dispense with his services. Yet there are circumstances in which clientelism can allow an individual to mobilise the resources and have the incentives to engage in positive development (Piattoni, 1997). Familism can similarly be interpreted as sustaining healthy associationalism or as fostering resistance to change and individualism (Mutti, 1996). The confusion surrounding all this is well illustrated by the debate on social capital, a concept frequently invoked to explain the differences among regions.

Social capital was originally taken to refer to relationships among actors that facilitate social co-operation (Coleman, 1988). The term has over time been extended and vulgarised so as to become something of a catch-all for civic virtue. There is general agreement that it represents a further stage in the specification of factor endowments, beyond the familiar physical and technical capital and the more recently noted human capital. While human capital refers to the endowments and capacities of individuals, social capital is about relationships. This is of obvious relevance to the construction of territorial production systems as discerned in the new regionalist literature. Beyond that, however, there is great conceptual confusion and stretching, and a lot of attempts to capture the concept ideologically (Schuller et al., 2000). There is a fundamental problem about its very definition or specification as an independent factor, since many exponents define it in a circular or tautological way (Portes, 2001). Putnam (1993) does this as does Woolcock (2001: 6) who writes that 'social capital is generally defined as the relationships, networks and norms that facilitate collective action', but then contradicts himself by saying that it must be defined by what it is, not what it does. There is a fundamental ambivalence about whether it refers to institutions or to cultural norms, the most important of which is trust. Woolcock (2001) sees trust as the *result* of social capital. Putnam (2001: 45) agrees that trust is not part of the definition but a consequence, but then continues that since 'it is certainly a close consequence' it 'could easily be thought of as a proxy' and proceeds to use it as such. So, in a manner all too common in these studies, he uses the dependent variable of the analysis as a proxy for the independent variable. Like others, he seems to use it sometimes to refer to institutions and at others to refer to cultural norms. Other scholars trying to operationalise the concept have reduced it to little more than associationalism, often counting the number of associations as a measure. This takes us back to the problem identified earlier, that there are functional and dysfunctional forms of associationalism (Portes, 2001). If social capital means anything, then it refers to a set of relationships and norms embedded in society, which may take any number of institutional forms; indeed one might expect that dynamic regions with the right *milieu* could have rather few formal associations, relying more on informal networks.

Some approaches focus more directly on the concept of trust, although at the risk of expanding this concept excessively, for example in Fukuyama (1995) where it seems to cover all social relationships that work. The problem lies in specifying, operationalising and measuring what is essentially a contextual relationship. Surveys asking people in a general way whether they trust other people do not tap this interactive dimension and, like the measures of associationalism, do not distinguish between benign forms of trust and those underpinned, for example, by the Mafia. The origins of the practices underlying social capital are also obscure, largely because of the way in which it has been conceptualised both as cause and effect (Portes, 2001).

Much of the problem here arises from the disrepute into which the concept of culture came after the civic culture studies of the 1960s with their ethnocentric bias and assumption that there was just one route to modernisation. If we are to bring culture back in, we need to cast it in a more sensitive way and show how it is formed and changed over time. The word culture has been used to cover a multitude of social phenomena and too often invoked as a *deus ex machina*, to explain whatever cannot be explained by other, more concrete social and economic variables. There are three distinct but related elements. One refers to the performing and visual arts, whether in the form of 'highbrow' or popular entertainment and creation. A second meaning denotes the values and practices of a society which help condition behaviour and set expectations. A third refers to identity, another concept that has also been too poorly specified and stretched to try and cover and explain too much. There are three distinct elements in regional identity and its relationship to collective action (Frankenber and Schuhbauer, 1994). First there is the cognitive dimension, whether people are aware of the region, its geographical limits and characteristics. The salient characteristics in turn may vary, from the landscape, to the folklore, to the history, the language or the economic structure. Second is the affective dimension, how people feel about the region and the degree to which it provides a framework for common identity and solidarity, possibly in competition with other identities such as class or nation. Third is the instrumental one, whether the region is used as a basis for mobilisation and collective action. These may be successive stages in regional mobilisation, since the third is not possible without the first and second, but not all regions have reached this third stage. Nor can we say in advance what form mobilisation will take, whether of defensive resistance to change, or a programme for development and modernisation.

We see culture and identity as important elements in regional mobilisation around a development project, but we do not want to treat it as an unanalysed residual, something that itself cannot be explained. We do not share the assumption, often made, that culture, values and social norms are primordial elements or, as in Putnam's (1993) account, something derived from a historical period so remote that it can safely be misunderstood. Culture and identity, rather, are constantly being made and remade. Nor can we accept the perennialist view, that culture and identity are the underlying substructure of society, amenable to change only in the very long term. Values, identities and self-understandings can in fact change very rapidly at key historical junctures, and then remain fixed for long periods as the lessons of history are relearned and simplified to sustain the dominant self-image. J.H. Plumb's (1967) remarks about political stability are to the point here:

There is a general folk-belief, derived largely from Burke and the nineteenth century historians, that political stability is of slow coral-like growth: the result of time, circumstances, prudence, experience, wisdom, slowly building up over the centuries. Nothing, I think, is further from the truth. True, there are, of course, deep social causes of which contemporaries are usually unaware making for the *possibility* of political stability. But stability becomes actual through the actions and decisions of men, as does revolution. Political stability, when it comes, often happens to a society quite quickly, as suddenly as water becomes ice.

Culture and identity are, then, both the conditions under which political leadership operates and the product of that leadership. Region-builders, to take our case, may have considerable scope for social mobilisation by invoking cultural images and identities, using available raw materials but moulding them and valorising some over others. Yet serious problems remain over how to investigate culture and integrate it with other approaches to regional development.

STUDYING CULTURE

There have been two methodological approaches to the measurement of regional culture and its relevance to development. The first consists of studies of individual regions and the construction of a narrative about the region and its success. Most of these stories are about successful regions and the stories bear a remarkable similarity. As when witnesses in court tell exactly the same story, this may be less a testament to their accuracy, than to their common source. The story is essentially that, in this region, we have a common history and identity and a commitment to social co-operation. Decision-making circles are small, everyone knows each other and there is a lot of face-to-face contact. The strong look after the weak, and we present a common face to the world. Often there is a historical story to accompany this, based on a shared past and adversity, so while the story is the same, the detail is different, tailored to the individual place. This story is seductive but, having heard it repeatedly, one becomes a little suspicious. Could this not be a myth the people are creating about themselves, complete with invented tradition (Hobsbawm and Ranger, 1983) and selectively interpreted past? Sabel (1993) argues that the story may be precisely a strategy to promote co-operation. There is another story which, like the success story, is almost always the same. In this account, the region suffers from an inherent lack of self-confidence and an excessive individualism in which the concerns of the self and the immediate family preclude wider social co-operation. This is the story picked up by Banfield, who labelled it 'amoral familism' and retailed by Putnam a generation later. Yet the repetition of the story and the gap between the individual and the collective self-representation suggests that this, too, is a tale that has been learnt.

The other approach to analysing culture and development is based on survey data. Here culture is conceptualised as a set of attitudes and norms which can be measured by standardised questionnaires and systematically compared. Much use has been made here of the European and World Values Surveys. The Foundation Europe of the Cultures 2002, for example, has sponsored a series of studies measuring values at the regional level and regressing them against measures of economic growth. There are serious problems with these surveys, given their level of generality and the lack of systematic controls for the effect of variables. A more fundamental problem is their tendency to measure culture as a static concept, which is then given a determinate role in social outcomes (Jackman and Miller, 1996). Surveys are, further, vulnerable to the 'individualist fallacy' in seeking to make inferences about a unit of analysis, a national or regional culture, bigger than the unit of measurement, the individual. If culture does have an effect of social behaviour, it will not be because individuals simultaneously think the same way and act accordingly, but because in the dynamics of social interaction, people pick up cues and place signals in particular social contexts. Culture is what helps people interpret social and economic events and moulds their collective responses. It is about attitudes, but also about symbols, rituals and myths (Fach, 2001). It is therefore inter-subjective rather than subjective, fundamentally a social rather than an individual phenomenon. It is this which surely explains the paradox that, while survey research shows considerable convergence of attitudes in Europe under the influence of modernisation and globalisation, regional and local politics has taken on a new and greater significance. It is the local society that forms the prism through which global experiences are refracted. It is not a purely independent set of historically given attitudes laid down by events in the inscrutable past.

Cultural approaches are highly vulnerable to the charge that they are merely reproducing stereotypes, often learned and repeated. This is the case with the 'stories' of regional development success and failure that we have heard repeatedly in our work. It is also a feature of many of the surveys; indeed there are Spanish surveys that attempt precisely to probe regional stereotypes and their components (Sangrador García, 1996). The stereotypes themselves, moreover, may be open to multiple interpretations depending on the needs of the moment (Mella, 1992). So collective attitudes, strong private networks and associationalism may be interpreted as evidence of a blocked society, or as the basis of the new regional dynamism. Individualism is interpreted as the cause of lack of co-operation in the unsuccessful regions, and as the embodiment of capitalist virtue in the successful ones. Tradition may be an obstacle to progress or the basis for social capital. Catholicism is often seen as discouraging innovation and as militating against the free association and horizontal reciprocity essential to the performing region. Yet Berthet and Palard (1997) show that, of all places, in the Vendée, heartland of the counter-revolution and of traditional Catholicism, there is a performing industrial district. Here, Catholicism promoted the sort of values Weber attributes to Protestantism, while favouring social integration and cohesion. The Church, seeing the need for industrialisation to maintain its demographic and social base, took the opportunity here to encourage a specific model of industrialisation, rooted in traditional Catholic values. So we can accept that cultural norms are important without assuming that they are immune to political intervention. On the contrary, they can be used, reassessed and re-used in multiple ways.

This implies that the meaning and social power of particular cultural forms and legacies will differ from one context to another. Generalisations about the rise of Protestantism or secularisation assume that these have a uniform impact everywhere, when in fact it is their reception into specific local societies that shapes events. This opens up a potentially much richer field of research than any mere attempt to correlate a single measure of development against a single set of cultural variables, let alone a single variable like 'trust' or 'civicness'. This also means, as many scholars have pointed out, that attempting to distinguish the roles of culture and institutions is largely futile, since these are dynamically related. Nor, since culture is a formative value which shapes others, can we measure it by controlling for everything else and seeing what is left. 'Everything else' is shaped inescapably by culture, so there is no neutral, cultureless control case available. Nor should we see culture as necessarily implying shared positive values at all if this implies the existence of a monolithic or hegemonic mind-set. Rather culture may simply be a way in which society can look at itself, with all its internal conflicts and contradictions but regard itself nevertheless as a functioning society.

SPECIFYING THE PROBLEM

We are sceptical of purely functionalist accounts of the emergence of regions, which see them as the automatic outcome of economic restructuring. We are equally sceptical of primordialist and perennialist accounts and of essentialist visions, which attribute inherent vices or virtues to regions or their populations, or present them as trapped into historical trajectories from which they cannot escape. Against the common historical reductionism, there is plenty of evidence that regions like the Italian Mezzogiorno are capable of change (Trigilia, 1996). Instead, we adopt a more constructivist approach, treating regions as systems of social regulation and of collective action, built by political and social actors in given contexts, reflecting the balance of social and economic forces, and open to change. Such systems are emerging at various spatial levels, but our level of analysis is the administrative-political region within states that have given autonomy to governments at the intermediate or 'meso' level. We have chosen regions with distinctive cultures and histories, since our interest goes beyond inter-organisational relations to encompass broader historical, cultural and political issues and we are interested in finding out how historical themes and cultures are used in the construction and reconstruction of modern territorial systems. Our concept of the region as a system of regulation and collective action bears some resemblance to the concept of a development coalition or urban regime which is a staple in the study of American cities (Kantor, 1995; Stone, 1989; Harding, 1999). It is about purposive action in pursuit of development, and about the constellation of public and private actors, themselves socially embedded, that are involved. As we have noted, some approaches to the construction of regions around development are rooted in transaction costs theories in economics; others are grounded in sociological analysis, exploring norms, routines and networks. Our approach focuses on politics and political action, not because we think that this is more valid than the other approaches, but because this dimension has been less fully explored. While our point of departure is political leadership and institutions, however, we are well aware of the social and economic contexts in which these operate and the limits to political action; indeed these are a central part of our analysis.

The new regional paradigm has created a new context for regional politics. It has not, however, removed political conflict and choice and we are critical of a certain wishful thinking that sees in it the emergence of a whole new social order. Neo-liberals celebrate the weakness of the state. Ohmae (1995, 2001), as we have already mentioned, sees the imposition of competitive neo-liberalism as a unqualified good. Porter (2001) manages to suggest that all regions can win in the new dispensation by adapting to their comparative advantages; but the essence of competition is surely that there are losers.

Other authors embrace a different form of optimism, seeing in the new regional development models a way of escaping the old dilemmas and conflicts and getting onto a virtuous growth path. There is a general assumption that it provides a more socially benign approach to the economy, apparently on the basis that the new paradigm requires that the market be tempered by co-operation, so contributing to social cohesion. Putnam's (1993) concept of 'civicness', indeed, is an amalgam of all the good things about territorial societies, which he constructs as a compound variable and then regresses against measures of economic and institutional performance, finding a positive relationship. Apart from the conceptual difficulties of constructing such a compound, there are serious methodological problems since Jackman and Miller's (1996) secondary analysis finds that none of the individual components seems to fit the regression. Social capital has similarly been extended to cover both economic efficiency and social cohesion, since it answers the needs of policy makers seeking a painless way out of current policy dilemmas.

Cooke and Morgan (1998) claim that, at its best, the new paradigm can provide a model of development that is both economically more efficient and socially more benign. Amin (1999: 373), following Putnam, claims that many prosperous regions also show 'public sector efficiency in the provision of services; civic autonomy and initiative in all areas of social and economic life; a culture of reciprocity and trust which facilitates the economics of association; containment of the high costs of social breakdown and conflict; and potential for economic innovation and creativity based on social confidence and capability'. Writing tends to be celebratory and to mix scientific analysis with moral prescription, based on the return to an idealised past of solidaristic communities. This explains its adoption by bodies like the World Bank and the OECD, often accused of applying a savage form of neo-liberalism to countries in both the developing and the developed world, and its appeal to prophets of 'third way' politics (Giddens, 1998) in which circles are squared and conflicts wished away. In the process, however, it risks obscuring the real policy dilemmas and social conflicts within societies.

Others recognise the dilemma highlighted above, that inter-regional competition may provoke a race to the bottom, even though this may prove self-defeating by destroying the human and physical capital on which competitiveness depends, but postulate different responses. They then distinguish a low road and high road to development (Cooke et al., 1999). On the low road, regions compete on costs with low wages, deregulation of business and lax environmental standards, seeking to attract inward investment at all costs. On the high road, they will invest heavily in infrastructure, training, education and technology, seeking to promote and attract high value activities paying high wages, and firms that put a premium on attractive environmental conditions, a skilled and educated workforce and social stability. The high road in turn is interpreted, as above, as the basis for a development trajectory that is both more economically efficient and socially inclusive.

This is an alluring scenario, but again there are problems. If it is true that we are in a world of absolute advantage then, whatever the successful regions do, there will be others who lose out. Scott and others (Scott, 1998; Scott et al., 2001) recognise that global competition among regions may lead to increasing inequalities among regions, some of which will adapt better than others, and within regions, between those tied into the new global trading networks and those who are not. Others have traced patterns of winners and losers in the European single market. Indeed, the very concepts of the competitive region and of absolute advantage implies that there will be winners and losers in the new regional game (Dunford, 1994; Amin and Tomaney, 1995). Even among winners there may be costs as they are forced into a 'race to the bottom', cutting their social programmes and focusing on the needs of business in order to stay in the game. We need, in any case, to be a little critical of the notion of competition, a highly ideological concept that has come to dominate modern politics well beyond the world of production in which it originated. It may be that regions are, in some ways, competing for investment, markets and technology, yet to say so involves a certain reification of the region, its constitution as an actor with a unitary interest. This is not, as we have noted, a necessary consequence of changing systems of production but involves a political process in which the interest of the region is postulated as distinct from the competing interests within it. An insistence that the region is facing competitors from outside may thus be a device used by region-builders to consolidate their position and to close off internal political debate just as the theme of competitiveness is used in other realms (including modern universities) in an effort to predetermine policy choices. Regions are thus credited with unitary 'interests' and development policy is thus constructed ideologically as a form of neo-mercantilism in which territories are pitched into a zero-sum competition.

The high road to development may be more socially integrative, since it requires heavy investment in public services and education. Indeed, extreme neo-liberals like Ohmae apart, exponents of the new paradigm generally have tended to regard it as more socially benign because of its dependence on social co-operation and integration. Yet again we need to be cautious. It may be possible to gain agreement among neo-liberals and social democrats on increasing investment in education, since this can be presented as at once economically efficient and socially integrative, and this may explain the fashion for 'human capital', but this does not exhaust the question of social inclusion. There are still large questions about the distributional impact of any regional development strategy and the imposition of a shared territorial framework does not dissolve underlying conflicts along traditional class lines, or those of age, gender or ethnicity (Hudson, 1999).

We might say the same about culture and the maintenance of minority languages and traditions. It might be that there is no longer a conflict between sustaining small cultures and languages since these, far from being an obstacle to modernisation and insertion in the global economy, are sources of common understandings, co-operation and 'social capital'. Yet again it all depends on the circumstances and the way cultures and languages are promoted and deployed, whether as symbols of modernity or as vestiges of the past, and on the social meanings which they embody.

We understand development in a broad sense, going beyond the narrow issue of economic growth. While increases in GDP per capita are obviously considered desirable and are a policy goal everywhere, this does not exhaust the agenda. We are dealing here with cultural regions, in which there are projects for region or nation building and for the pursuit of political autonomy. In a globalising world and an integrating Europe, it has become received wisdom that maintaining a distinct culture requires economic prosperity, but how well the two goals support each other is, as mentioned above, an open question. A similar question arises with regard to autonomy. In modern conditions, regional autonomy means something more than having formal powers and competences devolved from the central state. It requires the ability to mount a distinct development project and to insert the region into the new networks of policy making spanning the public-private boundaries and crossing state borders. Yet this does not mean that economic development and autonomy are the same thing. It may be that wealthy regions can enhance their development by reducing their dependence on the central state and gaining more powers for themselves, but even the most prosperous regions in Europe are still tied to their states for important resources and forms of protection. For poorer regions, autonomy from the state might be at the expense of transfer payments and protection. There is also the issue of social solidarity and redistribution. It may be that inter-regional competition is forcing a 'race to the bottom' in which regions need to cut back on social expenditures and favour their most dynamic sectors and locations in the manner described by Peterson (1981) for American cities. It may, on the other hand, be that regions with strong cultural identities foster greater social solidarity and a more inclusive development model. It is possible, indeed, that a stress on social integration can be an asset to regions, allowing them to take the high road, avoiding the social costs of poverty and urban decay. Yet there will always be political decisions to be taken and trade-offs to be made.

While the distinction between the high road and the low road of development is a useful starting point, we think that it needs to be refined to allow for the existence of various models of growth. We could, as a starting point, posit four ideal types. The first would be a low-cost model of growth, corresponding to the low road, in which a region seeks to compete on the basis of low wages, a lack of trade union organisation, weak environmental regulation and an open attitude to the demands of inward investors. A second one, which might be described as 'bourgeois regionalism' (Harvie, 1994; Keating, 1998a) is a high-cost model in which there is an effort to move up the production scale to high-quality, high value-added production. This may require substantial public investment in infrastructure, training, research and technology transfer as well as an environmental regime attractive to clean industries and the people who work in them. This does not, however, automatically entail a policy of social inclusion or progressive redistribution through social policy. Public spending could be focused on improving the infrastructure of production, including human capital, without tackling issues of poverty, housing and social exclusion. A third model, the social democratic model, is more explicitly re-distributive and inclusive, placing an emphasis on social inclusion in its own right, even at the cost of certain types of growth. Public goods here are seen not merely as factors in production but also as valuable in themselves. While there may well be agreement between proponents of the bourgeois regionalist and social democratic models on the need for certain public goods like education and vibrant city centres, there is still a large scope for conflict over broader social priorities. Our fourth ideal-type is not strictly a competitor to the other three, since it may be combined with any of them, but most especially the second and third. This is the nation-building model in which the main aim of the political leadership is to construct a stateless nation, with or without ambitions to eventual statehood. Here there is an emphasis on enhancing regional autonomy, on the insertion of the region into international circuits and on culture and language as elements in their own right. There are some reasons for thinking that the nation-building model may be more socially inclusive, since nationalism usually has a cross-class appeal and seeks to promote the unity of the nation against competitors outside. On the other hand, it may be in tension with the social democratic approach, which is predicated on a class solidarity transcending cultural boundaries.

These broad orientations of policy can be linked to the composition of the development coalition and the patterns of political and social leadership within a given context. It is these that provide the explanatory element of our analysis. The first element of the context is the economic and geo-political state and location of the region. We do not subscribe to Porter's (2001) idea that any region can make it in the new economic dispensation merely by good organisation of its assets and productive potential. While raw materials may be a less important factor than in the past, some regions are better endowed than others with a good trading location, climate and accumulated investment assets. In other words, industrial traditional location theory still has some explanatory power. Beyond this, however, we are interested in the social and political construction of the region and its mobilisation around a development project. Here we consider the matter of culture to be critical, not in the primordialist or essentialist sense, but as a symbolic realm in which a territorial level can be endowed with meaning, and a set of values to which actors can subscribe. Culture in this form is open to change and development, affecting behaviour but in turn affected by it. Culture as a factor in the construction of social systems can take several forms. There may be a hegemonic culture in which language, social practices and norms enforce a specific way of thinking. Quebec before the Quiet Revolution provides an example, with an ultramontane Catholicism and the local political class sustaining traditional values of piety and resisting modernisation. Another form is social escapism, in which the symbolic representations of the society are divorced from reality, or culture is confined to the literary realm. Certain visions of Scotland from the late nineteenth century illustrate this, with their images of the 'kailyard' and 'tartanry', a nostalgic vision of an older society stripped of its social and political meaning. A third form of culture is more interesting from our point of view. This is culture as a set of images of society, a way in which a society can examine itself critically and sustain a debate on its common past, present and future. Culture in its broadest sense refers to a common frame of reference, an understanding of the membership of a society which might underpin a common project. Another way of presenting this is the idea of the *référentiel* underpinning systems of policy making (Muller, 1989). There are affinities, too, to Anderson's (1991) notion of a nation as an 'imagined community' of individuals who are bound together although they will never all meet each other personally.

This form of culture is neither determined rigidly by the past or by rooted social values, nor entirely open for invention and manipulation in the present. It is rather a dynamic element of social structuring that may resist change for a long time and then change rather quickly. It is also a set of images and values open to different interpretations, as we have noted above in the discussion of stereotypes. We therefore treat it both as a conditioning factor for development policy, and as a resource used by political and social leaders in the construction of a territorial frame of reference and to invest this frame with meaning. Culture might thus be an obstacle to change or the vehicle for change and fulfil different social functions. A common territorial identity and set of understandings might facilitate cross-class development coalitions, and the search for positive-sum outcomes of policy conflicts, reconciling competitiveness with social solidarity and encouraging the production of public goods. Yet localist cultures and minority languages might also cut a region off from the wider world and foster a social and economic conservatism and resistance to change.

Economic success might provide the resources to sustain local cultures, but also attract incomers unsympathetic to indigenous traditions. There is a constant balance to be struck between the localist theme and the cosmopolitan or global one. Localism sustains common action but threatens parochialism and exclusion. Cosmopolitanism offers an opening to the world but threatens social solidarity, attachment and local culture. The secret is perhaps to cultivate what Granovetter (1973) describes as 'weak ties', linkages that allow collective action and information exchange, but which do not trap communities into dysfunctional patterns or inhibit change. Another way of putting it is the search for a 'rooted cosmopolitanism' (Friedman, 1991) allowing the local and the global to interact.

A key element of the *référentiel* is the territorial level at which the aggregation of interests, the debate about choices and the construction of a collective interest takes place. Regions are not givens but can be defined in a variety of ways, as economic spaces characterised either by a single dominant form of production or complementary sectors; as landscape, tradition, music or cuisine; as cultural or historic spaces; as political spaces in which there is a public debate and reciprocity; as political and administrative units. These meanings may coincide in space, or they may differ radically. Where they do coincide it is rarely by chance or the invisible hand of social evolution, but as a result of social and political action and institution building within state and civil society. In this process, history matters a great deal as does culture but not always in the most obvious and direct ways. There are many potential regions and territorial systems of action but not all have become salient in the new conditions of globalisation and European integration, while in some instances there are rival projects to build imagined communities at different spatial levels. Some approaches to the new territorialism take as their unit of analysis the emerging systems of production, tracing the patterns of social relationships and their underlying logic (e.g. Crouch et al., 2001). The focus here is on the local level or industrial district. Our starting point is a little different, since we commence from the political system and examine its impact on the construction of a territorial community, and our level of analysis is the larger level of region. The region is thus defined largely institutionally and by political considerations, but this level has also often been identified as a key level of economic transformation, spatial planning and policy integration. This is not a matter of choosing the 'right' level as opposed to the wrong one, merely a different choice of perspective guided by our interest in the question of meso or regional government and the political movements that have emerged at this level.

Our case study regions all have their own distinct cultures and histories but, rather than seeing these as determining the future, we treat them as resources that can be mobilised for various purposes. In a global world of competitive regions, leaders in Catalonia or Flanders can pick up historical referents to their history as trading regions back to the middle ages and valorise this aspect over others. Galicia suffers from a negative stereotype but there are elements here too that can be presented as potentially valuable in the new dispensation. Wales and Brittany can evoke traditions of co-operation and solidarity, emphasising these more than those of class conflict or marginalisation. In a remarkable transformation, Irish culture has been revalorised and associated with modernity and fashion, in tandem with Ireland's rapid economic growth. Treating culture as something that is created and recreated, rather than a fundamental cause, also allows us to evaluate the 'stories' we pick up in our field research, the sustaining myths that people tell themselves to explain success or failure. These are neither dependent nor independent variables but part of the process by which public action is mediated and legitimated. We can similarly distinguish between the collective stereotypes of a region revealed in survey research and the attributes which individuals attribute to themselves, and which are sometimes in stark contrast. The one is a social phenomenon, the product of discussion and transmission, while the other is an individual level evaluation.

Our focus is thus less on culture itself than on the use of culture. We are also interested in the actors at whom it is addressed and the transmission of the territorial *référentiel* across the society. In each case, we look at patterns of political and social mobilisation, the extent to which representation is organised on a territorial basis, and the interactions among organised actors. Some general patterns have been recognised in the literature (Keating, 1998a). Big business has tended over the years first to nationalise, then to Europeanise and globalise, becoming less dependent on local networks and seeking to preserve its freedom of manoeuvre and location. Certainly even large firms require public goods and services and care a great deal about locational factors, but to a large degree can do this by shopping around rather than engaging in the regional political game. Small and medium sized businesses, on the other hand, are more dependent on the public goods provided by regional governments, especially in the form of business services and the 'enterprise support system' as a whole, and are less locationally mobile and often locally owned. They are thus likely to be more fully integrated into regional development coalitions and more regional in orientation. Trade unions have historically developed at national level during the twentieth century, and have succeeded to varying degrees in becoming interlocutors of national governments on labour and even broader economic issues, and sometimes partners in the delivery of welfare state services. Yet since the 1970s they have been involved in local struggles over plant closures and restructuring, which have drawn them into broader coalitions of territorial defence. There has also been some decentralisation of their activities and structures, although without a full return to their local roots. They have tended increasingly to look to regional solutions to issues of economic restructuring, while seeking to preserve national welfare state regimes. So in many cases, we have both business and union involvement in regional development coalitions, with shared goals of economic growth, but often with different social priorities. Business and unions also tend to disagree on the institutional structures for regional development, with the former seeking special purpose, depoliticised agencies in pursuit of a 'bourgeois regionalist' strategy, while the unions have increasingly looked to stronger elected regional governments, open to broader social interests, in the pursuit of a more social democratic model.

We place a strong emphasis on institution-building, both in state and civil society. All our cases have elected governments and, although their powers vary, economic development is a key element in all. Formal powers and competences are of vital interest here, but also important is the way in which institutions work, their legitimacy in the eyes of the population and organised groups, their success in establishing the regional frame of reference as salient, and their ability to position themselves at the centre of the emerging networks of economic development. Comparative examination of regions with identical formal powers within the same state shows that institutionalisation can be more or less effective and performance better or worse.

Regions have emerged as a level of government in many parts of Europe but, compared with state and local or municipal governments they have particular characteristics. They lack both the macro-economic powers and the panoply of coercive instruments at the disposal of states, although their legislative and administrative competences vary greatly. Unlike municipal governments, they do not usually have a large role in service delivery. So their powers depend to a larger extent on steering and concertation of other actors. This is particularly true in relation to economic and social development, a policy field requiring flexibility and innovation rather than bureaucratic routine, and involving close relationships with private and other public partners. It is for these reasons that the looser terms 'governance' or 'policy networks' have frequently been applied to the regional level. These have now spawned a literature of their own, have undergone the usual conceptual stretching and duly given rise to a series of rather scholastic debates on the meaning of the terms. We will try and avoid these debates, but recognise that institution-building is taking place within civil society and seek to trace the emergence of territorial policy communities sharing the same spatial frame of reference. This involves looking at the extent to which interest groups, social movements and non-governmental institutions are organised on a regional basis, the importance of the spatial frame of reference for their attitudes and activities, and the patterns of relationships among them. We are not looking for a form of 'regional corporatism' or tripartitism in which governments, employers and unions come together to bargain authoritatively over policy and priorities. Regions are too open as systems and both governments and social partners too weak, to allow this. We do, however, detect patterns of concertation and partnership over general orientations and over specific issues and can assess the participation of the various partners within this. We can also assess the extent to which cultural and social groups are incorporated into the regional coalition.

Since regions are not closed systems but embedded in wider state and European networks, the external dimension of region building is critical. We therefore examine the extent to which regions have not only been constituted as systems of action and policy making around development, but have become actors within broader systems. This is not an attempt to reify the region or to attribute objective interests to territories, but rather an exploration of the extent to which common understandings of a territorial interest have emerged, who is able to define these and how broadly they are shared. The old dyadic territorial exchange between state and region that characterised the heyday of the nation-state is giving way to a more complex order in which regions seek competitive advantage in global and European markets. Yet states are still very much present and we examine patterns of intergovernmental relations to see how these interests are projected into state politics on development issues and how the region is able to operate within the emerging European order.

The effects of European integration on regions are in some respects similar to that of globalisation. There are changes to the geography of production, new functional spaces are created and regions and localities are pitched into competition in European markets without the old protective mantle of the state. Yet European integration is more than this, since Europe is also a political system with its own decision-making structures and a range of policies in environmental, cultural and other matters going beyond the strict limits of market integration. We do not propose to enter into the old argument about whether Europe is fundamentally an intergovernmental organisation or a political system in its own right, but we do see it as an open and complex system, with multiple points of access, including national political channels, lobbying in Brussels, and the array of consultative mechanisms such as the Committee of the Regions and regional associations. There is a large literature on the role of the Structural

Funds in providing links between the EU and the regions and in stimulating regional mobilisation (Hooghe, 1996). Regional interest in EU policies, however, extends well beyond this, into competition policy, and sectoral policies, notably in agriculture, fisheries and industry, environmental regulation and culture. At one time, there was suspicion of European integration among some regionalists, who feared that Brussels would be even more remote and unsympathetic than their national capitals. During the 1980s and 1990s, this was replaced by a general belief, encouraged by the expanding Structural Funds, that Europe was an ally of the regions, eroding the state from above as they eroded it from below and providing new resources and opportunities for regional autonomy. Europe has also been used symbolically as an arena in which regions can project themselves, thus helping to consolidate their identity and sense of shared interest at home. The broad acceptability of the project of European integration has helped enhance the legitimacy of regional leaders, who can demonstrate that they are contributing to the cause.

Since the late 1990s, however, there has been more caution, as regions have become more aware of the homogenising tendencies in the single market programme and the threat this poses to minority cultures, and of the way in which the EU has increasingly encroached upon matters of regional competence. Europe thus remains a central element of the political debate within the regions and an important part of region building. More broadly, external activity, paradiplomacy and inter-regional networking are means by which regional leaders assert their regional personality, while seeking resources and allies in the outside. There is a wide variety of styles and strategies here with some regions concerned with enhancing political autonomy, others seeking cultural goals and all concerned to a great extent with economic development opportunities including inward investment, markets and technology. We therefore devoted attention in all the cases to the outward projection of the region.

3.   Spain: Catalonia and Galicia

THE SPANISH AUTONOMOUS COMMUNITIES

Spain is a regionalised state with seventeen autonomous communities, established under the provisions of the 1978 constitution. With the exception of the Basque Country and Navarre, which have extensive fiscal powers under historic provisions, all have in principle the same competences. In practice, there are differences in the speed at which autonomous communities have acquired full competences and there are important political differences between the three 'historic nationalities', the Basque Country, Catalonia and Galicia, and the rest. The division of powers between the state and the autonomous communities (ACs) is quite confusing, with a list of exclusive state powers, a list of powers to be devolved in the individual statutes of autonomy and a list of state powers which might also be devolved, often by bilateral agreement. As a result, the allocation of responsibility is not always clear and, because powers have been devolved to some ACs and not others, central ministries in Madrid have retained extensive administrative structures. In recent years, there has been a decentralisation of training and active labour market policies, which has permitted the development of distinctive strategies across the regions. Much policy is in practice made between the central government and the regions, but without the formalised provisions found in Germany. There are sectoral conferences covering the main policy fields but, in practice, intergovernmental relations are structured by party channels. Where the same party is in power at both levels, they can manage relationships internally; where territorial parties are in office at the regional level, they can use their position in the national parliament to negotiate concessions. Neither channel, however, is secure. A regional branch party giving unconditional loyalty to the centre may simply be taken for granted, while the distinct regional parties only come into their own where there is no overall majority in the national parliament. Regions have limited taxation powers, with the exception of the Basque Country and Navarre, which have historic rights to collect almost all taxes and pass on a share to Madrid. The others have, following gradual changes in the 1990s, the right to collect 30 per cent of the income tax, which they can vary within certain limits.

Wealthier regions have increasingly demanded more fiscal autonomy, citing the needs to compete in European markets and arguing that the poorer regions do not benefit from the assistentalist model of financing that has prevailed to date. Unsurprisingly, the poorer regions disagree. European Structural Funds are important, with large parts of Spain, including Galicia, eligible under Objective 1. Catalonia mainly benefited under the former Objective 2. Management of the Structural Funds in Spain has been rather centralised, with much of the funding going to central agencies and rather tight central control over programmes and priorities. Regions have, to varying degrees, been active in Europe but, despite strong pressures, the central government has refused to allow them to represent Spain in the Council of Ministers.

Under the Franco regime, there was a strong suspicion of anything to do with regionalism and regional development programmes were confined to large infrastructure projects including hydro-electric barrages, directed from the centre. Under the technocrats of Opus Dei from the 1960s, the regime sought to liberalise the economy without liberalising politics, with an opening to trade and foreign investment. This produced a sharp rise in economic growth, but planning remained weak, with a resulting imbalance in infrastructure provision, urban sprawl and seriously underdeveloped social services. Catalonia, which had faced discrimination in the early years of the dictatorship because of its role in the Civil War, resumed its role as one of Spain's leading industrial regions, although the region of Madrid also expanded rapidly. Galicia remained underdeveloped and peripheral. There was in fact a reduction in regional disparities measures as GDP per capita, but this was more the product of migration and a fall in the population of poorer regions than of convergence in productive capacities (Castells and Parellada, 1998). In the course of the twentieth century, Spain's population doubled, Catalonia's tripled, and Galicia's increased by about a third. Since the 1980s regional disparities have in general stabilised, although with variations in individual cases.

Francoism inhibited the growth of an autonomous civil society, but provided a high degree of social organisation through the corporatist structures and vertical unions of employers and employees, at national, sectoral and local levels. Wages and work conditions were imposed through these structures, adding to the rigidities of the society. These structures have only gradually been dismantled, with the result that Spain appears to be densely organised, although many of the structures involve minimal active participation. Spain's democratic transition was accompanied by a process of economic restructuring in which formerly protected heavy industries were run down and the productive tissue modernised to cope with European competition. This led to high levels of unemployment and social discontent.

Autonomous communities in Spain have had varying experiences of institutionalisation and of developing policy capacity. All have been engaged to varying degrees in region building and, in the case of Catalonia and the Basque Country, of nation building, through institutional development, cultural and language policy, and development, but the outcomes have varied. Our two cases are chosen among the historic nationalities, with their own cultures, languages and histories, but with very different economic bases and images. Catalonia is widely regarded as a success story, a wealthy region with a vibrant culture that has managed to combine localism and outwardness, tradition and modernity, under the leadership of its own elites. Galicia by contrast, is a poor and peripheral region, and suffers from an image of economic and social backwardness and a dysfunctional pattern of social relations akin to Banfield's amoral familism. Both regions face the challenge of region building within the Spanish autonomous system, in Europe, and in global markets, but under different governing parties and social coalitions. Catalonia has been dominated since the early 1980s by a moderate nationalism of the centre right, while Galicia has been under the rule of the national conservative party the *Partido Popular*, a generally centralist party but which has incorporated a certain conservative regionalism into its strategy.

CATALONIA

Catalonia in Spain

Catalonia has long been one of the most advanced regions of Spain. A Mediterranean trading power in the middle ages, it experienced a second economic take-off from the eighteenth century when it was the first part of Spain to industrialise. Its location as a region of passage, from the Carolingian age, when it was known as the Spanish Mark, through its status as a frontier region between France and Spain, to the European Single Market, has not only shaped Catalonia's trading relationships, but has moulded its culture. In the mediaeval era it was a central place in a Mediterranean-focused world, but was later marginalised with the rise of the Spanish empire and the shift of trade to the Atlantic. Within the European Union, it is resuming a more central position as a gateway from Europe to the Iberian peninsula and as part of the EU's southern flank and opening to Mediterranean region as a whole. This location has enabled Catalans to present themselves as quintessential Europeans and the theme of 'a return to Europe' has been even stronger here than in other parts of Spain. Another key factor is the position of Barcelona as a metropolis, the political and economic capital of Catalonia and also a major city in Spain and the Mediterranean.

In the early part of the Franco dictatorship, Catalonia suffered for its support for the defeated Republic, but from the 1950s was the location of many of the regime's development initiatives, with the consequent influx of waves of immigrants from southern Spain, bringing its population up from under three million in 1940 to just under six million in 1980. At the time of the transition, some 40 per cent of the population had been born outside the region. While growing, however, it lost its status as Spain's wealthiest region and converged towards the rest. In 1955, Catalonia's GDP per capita was 159 per cent of the Spanish average, but by 1975 this was down to 128 per cent. After further a dip in the 1990s, its relative position recovered so that it is now at 125 per cent, behind Madrid and the Balearic Islands. This is almost exactly the average for the EU as a whole. In the 1980s there was a painful process of restructuring in the older industrial regions of Spain as the traditional, industries were run down and reorganised. In Catalonia this was less painful than elsewhere but there were some serious repercussions in the large textile sector. Now that this process is largely complete, policy attention has moved to the growing sectors and the smaller and medium sized firms, but there are some remaining structural problems in the old industries, a lack of dynamism in many firms, and a heavy reliance on inward investment for technology, innovation and growth. The activity rate of the population has always been somewhat above the Spanish average and there is a larger proportion of the population employed in industry and a very small agricultural sector.

Catalonia since the transition has been marked by a process of nation or region building, with the imperative, as Jordi Pujol, long-serving president and leader of the moderate nationalist coalition *Convergència i Unió*, has put it, to *fer país*. There is a strong ideological dimension to this, as the dominant forces have sought to impose their own vision and make Catalonia the frame of reference for political and social change. It builds on elements of the social structure already present, and encompasses institutions, culture and economic development in a broad project for change. Some elements of this project are broadly shared within the society, while others are contested.

Culture and Self-Image

Catalonia has a very strong sense of identity as a minority nation within Spain, but separatism is relatively weak, compared for example with the Basque Country. Catalan identity is strongly correlated with the language, understood by 94 per cent of the population and spoken by 68 per cent

(Generalitat, 1997). Despite neglect or persecution under successive regimes since 1714, Catalan has survived and, like other European vernaculars, experienced a revival in the late nineteenth century in the context of the emerging nationalist movement. Under Franco, the language was banned in public and, for a while, in private use, and a section of the upper classes abandoned it, while mass immigration further limited its use. Yet it retained a high social status among the middle and professional classes as well as being the main medium of communication in the countryside and smaller towns. Proficiency in Catalan is much lower among the immigrant population, but the strong social incentives to learn it make it a vehicle for the assimilation of immigrant children. As a Latin-based language it is sufficiently close to Castilian to be accessible to anyone who wants to learn it and virtually all native Catalans are bilingual, switching easily between the languages. It thus serves as an important factor in group identity and social cohesion without raising insurmountable barriers between groups of the population within Catalonia. Its positive image and connections with the story of Catalonia as an outward-looking trading nation also favour its use as a vehicle of modernisation.

Catalan national identity is generally sufficiently open to accommodate incomers and to provide a force for integration without closing the society off from the outside. Surveys show most Catalans happily adopting dual identities (Keating, 2001a, 2001b). There is certainly a stronger sense of Catalanism among native-born Catalans, Catalan speakers and those of Catalan parentage, yet there is considerable assimilation, especially in the second generation. Data from the late 1980s showed that of those born outside Catalonia only twenty per cent described themselves as only Spanish and ten per cent even described themselves as only Catalan (Virós et al., 1991). Catalan voters have taken a little time to pick up the link between national self-assertion and European integration made by political elites. According to the European Values Study of 1990, Catalans, while broadly in favour of Europe, were somewhat less enthusiastic than people in other parts of Spain (Andrés and Sánchez, 1991) apparently viewing Europe more as a neutral political space less hostile to their aspirations than positively as a new form of identity. On the other hand, evidence from the mid 1990s shows Catalans becoming more European. Catalans in the majority continue to feel both Spanish and Catalan but the European identity is ever more salient and, among native Catalans, is now equal to Spanish identity (Sangrador García, 1996). In a 1994 survey, the mean score for Spanish identification was 8.26 in Catalonia against 5.71 in the Basque Country and 8.8 in Spain as a whole. The score for identification with Europe was 7.48 in Catalonia against 6.8 for Spain as a whole and just 5.2 per cent in the Basque Country, whose moderate nationalist leadership is also strongly pro-European. The picture is similar for the stereotypes that the various national groups sustain. Catalans come immediately after Basques and Navarrese in their negative views of Spaniards, with a mean score of 7.64. On the other hand, they have the second most favourable view of Europeans (after Valencians) at 7.36, against a Spanish average of 6.94 (Sangrador García, 1996). It appears, then, that dual identity may be giving way slowly to triple or multiple identities as Europe impinges more on daily life and politics.

Culture and values have been an important part of the nation-building project in Catalonia, and respondents almost always come up with two auto-stereotypes. The first is of Catalans' business acumen and entrepreneurial spirit. The other is the tendency to pactism and compromise and the tradition of *seny* (Giner et al., 1996), the latter being roughly analogous to the mythical Anglo-Saxon virtues of common sense, practical wisdom and moderation. There is evidence that Catalans are slightly more inclined to business values than people elsewhere in Spain and they are more secularised (Orizo and Sánchez Fernández, 1991). They certainly believe this about themselves. Surveys in 1976 and 1992 showed Catalans attributing their economic success not to natural advantages, to investment or to the state, but to the character of the people (García Ferrando et al., 1994). Catalans see themselves are more entrepreneurial and hard working than other Spanish peoples, an attitude reflected, albeit more weakly in the attitude of the latter toward Catalans (Sangrador García, 1996). Yet Catalans are much less likely to characterise themselves individually according to the austere, work-oriented and business-inspired stereotype than they are to apply this to their fellow Catalans as a whole. This suggests strongly that this is a created or imagined collective image, used instrumentally. Outsiders tend to give Catalan attributes a more negative interpretation, seeing them as closed, mean and egotistical (Sangrador García, 1996).

The pactist interpretation of Catalonia points to the tradition of limited sovereignty in the middle ages and the complex arrangements for accommodating social and political interests and the tendency since the transition to pactism and negotiated order. Critics point to the polarisation and violence of Catalan society in the first four decades of the twentieth century, and note that pactism has been a feature of Spanish political practice generally since the transition. There is even a counter-stereotype, again almost untranslatable, that of *rauxa*, denoting emotion and rebelliousness (Lobo, 1997). Once again, we are faced with the question of a usable past. Catalonia does have pactist traditions but it also has a history of extremism and the choice to revalorise the pactist tradition as a legitimation of present practice and a means for confronting the conflicts inherent in Catalonia's condition, is a political one, made by political and social leaders and made acceptable to their followers. It is not an automatic product of some path-dependent history. As it happens, this practice of pactism and accommodation and the search for consensus are effective mechanisms, not only for managing nationality conflict, but also for managing regional change and modernisation in the conditions we have noted above. Once again, this is not an automatic connection (which in this case would be teleological) but a social and political choice, made effective under favourable conditions.

Political Leadership

The dominant political orientations are a moderate nationalism represented by the governing *Convergència i Unió* (CiU) which is an alliance of liberalism (Convergència) and Christian democracy (Unió); and a moderate socialism represented by the *Partit dels Socialistes de Catalunya* (PSC), party of the Spanish socialist party, PSOE. PSC favours a federal Spain. CiU is heir to a tradition of Catalan nationalism going back to the late nineteenth century, which sees Catalonia as a nation within a plurinational Spanish state and aspires to play a role in Spanish politics as a whole. For the early Catalan movement, the dream was to 'Catalanise' Spain, converting it to Catalonia's modernising and industrial values. There was an echo of this in the mid 1980s when Miquel Roca was charged with putting together a coalition of liberal and regionalist forces for the national elections. After the failure of this operation, CiU has acted independently but sustained successive socialist and conservative governments in Madrid in exchange for concessions to Catalonia and on economic and social issues. The *Esquerra Republicana de Catalunya* is officially in favour of independence, but only in the long term and within an integrated 'Europe of the Peoples'. In the Catalan elections of 1999, the moderate nationalist Jordi Pujol was challenged by the Socialist Pasquall Maragall, who put together a coalition which was non-nationalist while still being recognisably Catalanist. The parties are also agreed that anyone who lives in Catalonia and wishes to be considered Catalan is so. This means that, while there are constant arguments over constitutional matters, there is still a broad consensus on their limits and a diffuse nationalism sufficiently moderate to incorporate large sections even of the immigrant population, especially in the second generation.

Catalan nationalism has a usable history in the memory of Catalan autonomy before 1714, and in the mediaeval legacy as a trading nation. This was reinforced and refurbished by the nationalist awakening of the late nineteenth and early twentieth century which, originally led by the commercial and industrial bourgeoisie, defined Catalonia by the combination of business dynamism and traditionalism. Catalan nationalism in this phase was highly protectionist, since Catalan goods were not competitive elsewhere in Europe and this combination of demands for self-government with the need for the protected Spanish market gave a profound ambivalence to the movement. Before the Civil War, this was challenged by a more left wing and radical nationalism incarnated in the *Esquerra Republicana de Catalunya*, which dominated under the Second Republic. The revived nationalist movement since the Civil War includes both these left wing and right wing traditions, although it has largely lost the support of the upper bourgeoisie and big business, remaining stronger among the middle classes. The dedication to economic success remains a defining feature of middle class nationalism. Catalan nationalism is also now strongly pro-European and has been at the forefront of the Europe of the regions movement, seeking a new political order in which stateless nations will have a defined place alongside, but not entirely replacing, the old state system. Moderate nationalism is thus almost a hegemonic ideology, while containing enough variants to encompass most of the active population.

CiU wishes to transform Spain into a plurinational federation, with specific recognition for the historic nationalities but has been wary about trying to change the constitution since this is a complex process and would encourage the proliferation of other demands. In the meantime, it has pressed for the fulfilment of the statute of autonomy by the transfer of powers in social policy, culture and development, and for stronger links into Europe. Progress has largely depended on the relationships with the ruling party in Madrid and was more rapid in the late 1990s when successive socialist and conservative governments had to make pacts with CiU to sustain their majorities.

Institutions

Catalonia's autonomous government, the Generalitat, is strongly entrenched by southern European standards and is a prime point of reference for citizens. It must coexist with field services of the Spanish state and there is considerable competition here. The Generalitat has sought to separate itself as much as possible from the state administrative network, notably by setting up its own system of intermediate administration, the *comarcas*, in order to by-pass the four provinces recognised by the state. Indeed, it was prevented from abolishing the provinces only by the constitution. There is also political and administrative competition with the city of Barcelona, a fief of the Socialists, although the Generalitat was able to abolish the corporation of Metropolitan Barcelona, a bastion of the old regime and its officials. In this way, the Generalitat has been able to enhance its own decision-making and strategic capacity and promote an all-Catalonia vision. Political and generational change have transformed the bureaucracy from Francoist and pre-Franco times and performance levels are generally quite high. A 1996 survey showed that the proportion of people experiencing no difficulty in getting a response from the administration was, at 38 per cent, the average for Spain (Fundación Encuentro, 1997). This is not to say that clientelism is absent; opponents constantly complain that the Generalitat uses its cultural and social programmes to favour those who share its vision. The main infrastructure and economic development initiatives are not, however, subject to purely clientelist logic. The Generalitat has established a strong image locally, and Catalans see it as more efficient and less corrupt than the central government, and favour the expansion of its powers (García Ferrando et al., 1994). This is particularly so amongst those most fluent in Catalan and among the younger sections of the population.

As a wealthy region, Catalonia has constantly demanded more fiscal autonomy and was responsible for the successive concessions of 15 per cent and then 30 per cent of the income tax, wrested from minority socialist and conservative Spanish governments. CiU's strategy is to make the Generalitat the principal government of Catalonia, with wide powers in social and economic matters (see below).

Catalonia does have its own civil society, with a dense network of associations and groups, which have steadily grown in number since the transition. This matches the general perception of Catalans as a highly associational people. Paradoxically, however, the European Values Study suggests that Catalans are not great joiners, with lower levels of organisational membership than the rest of Spain (Orizo and Sánchez Fernández, 1991). This might suggest a typical dissonance between the stereotype and the reality, but matters are probably more complex. At the time of the transition, there were vibrant social movements, especially in the large urban areas, since this was one space where it was possible to mobilise under late Francoism. In the succeeding years, however, this energy has been absorbed and canalised by the political parties, which have grown to dominate civil society and organisational life. Many of the new associations have been fostered by the autonomous government as part of the extension and reform of the welfare state and are not part of a spontaneous grass-roots mobilisation (Sarasa, 1998). Associationalism is thus part of the strategy of the Generalitat in building the nation according to its vision and the prevailing self-image. It is also probable that, despite the low levels of overall associational activity, Catalonia has more groups in the urban areas and the modern sectors of social and economic life (Sarasa, 1998).

Its economy is quite diversified, and dominated by a dense network of very small firms on the one hand and large multinationals on the other, without a sort of middle-sized firms that are so important in Germany. After Madrid, Catalonia has been the most successful Spanish region in attracting inward investment, although from the 1990s direct investment gave way to acquisition. By 1994 more than half the large firms in Catalonia had majority foreign ownership, while the proportion of Spain's 1000 biggest firms that were headquartered in Catalonia fell to the benefit of Madrid (Sánchez, 1998). The small firms do appear to be more dynamic and flexible than their counterparts elsewhere in Spain, giving some substance to the Catalan stereotype of entrepreneurialism (Parellada and Garcia, 1997). Yet there are problems of collective action and co-operation. A notable feature of Catalonia is the absence of large locally owned banks, in contrast with the Basque Country, and the presence of a dense network of mutual savings banks. Catalonia is the seat of a third of the savings banks in Spain, and these account for two thirds of all bank deposits in the region (Cabana, 1998).

Catalonia stands out for the number of business associations it has historically supported, although these are under pressure from the concentration of business itself and the quest on the part of Catalan employers to expand their area of action. There is a Catalan employers' organisation the *Foment de Treball Nacional* but, despite its title and its origins in the eighteenth century, it is highly integrated into the Spanish employers' organisation CEOE, in whose founding it played a key role. Employers' organisations were very suspicious of the movement to political autonomy in the early years but have now learned to live with it and, as the Generalitat has become their main interlocutor, have even pressed for more autonomy (Bru, 1997). The Foment has in the process taken on board many of the ideas of the new regionalism, accepting the importance of projecting Catalonia as an economic unit within Europe and the world. Yet they remain very cautious about the broader political implications of this and especially of Catalan nationalism, preferring to see Catalonia as a dynamic region of Spain with an outward vocation. Small firms are represented by the *Patronat de le Petit i Mitjana Empresa* (PIMEC) and the *Agrupació Empresarial Independent*, which are more rooted in the Catalan world, operate in the Catalan language and tend take more nationalistic positions. Both the Foment and PIMEC are federations, including sectoral and local bodies, with some larger firms affiliating directly. There has been some tension between them and especially with another body, SEFEC, expelled from the Foment in 1987 (Casademunt and Molins, 1998). There are also the local chambers of commerce, especially the long-established Barcelona Chamber.

On the trade union side, the *Comisió Obrera Nacional de Catalunya* (CONC) is the equivalent of the traditionally Communist Spanish *Comisiones Obreras* (CCOO), although it does have a certain autonomy and campaigns on Catalan themes. The traditionally Socialist *Unión General de Trabajadores* is more tightly integrated into its Spanish parent body. While this does weaken an independent Catalan trade unionism, it nevertheless helps integrate immigrant workers, who might avoid an overtly nationalist union, into the Catalan community (Jordana and Nagel, 1998). Separate Catalan trade unionism is confined to a few Christian Democratic unions organising the staff of the autonomous government and favoured by CiU. Trade unions, here as in the rest of Spain, are highly integrated into the administrative system, with extensive rights of consultation and a network of sectoral and local collective agreements, but their membership is very low. Catalonia's rate of unionisation, calculated at 9.4 per cent of the workforce in 1995, is the third lowest among autonomous communities (Escobar and van der Meer, 1995). While their administrative role is thus quite important, they are not significant actors or partners with regional government in working out regional development policies.

Class relations in Catalonia also present paradoxes. On the one hand, given the predominance of small and family firms, there is less social distance between workers and employers, a feature also noted in Italian studies of diffuse industrialisation (Bagnasco and Trigilia, 1993) and a disposition to negotiation and compromise. On the other hand, Catalonia in the early twentieth century possessed one of the most revolutionary working classes in Europe, and violence was endemic, as witness the *Setmana Tragica* of 1909 or the confrontations of the Second Republic and Civil War. Once again, this shows the danger of generalisations and stereotypes. There are in Catalan history both traditions of conflict and traditions of compromise. Since the transition of the 1970s, the compromising elements have been promoted and predominated. Another marked feature of the Catalan class structure has been the predominance of a regional bourgeoisie and the relative lack of social importance of elites linked to the military or state service who have been so crucial in other parts of Spain. The regional bourgeoisie was vital in the industrialisation of Catalonia in the nineteenth century and in the reinvention of Catalonia as a nation. Many of the upper bourgeoisie, including leaders of the old *Lliga regionalista*, went over to Francoism during or after the Civil War (Riera, 1998) and later the rise of state-controlled firms and the Madrid conglomerates weakened the native industrial class further. Since the 1980s, large industry has increasingly come under the sway of multinationals. There does, however, remain, a distinctly Catalan bourgeoisie, rooted in the small business sector and this provides an important base for the parties of CiU. A final element of the class structure is the immigrant population, numbering around 40 per cent of the population at the time of the transition in the 1970s. This is largely working class, producing some overlap of national and class identity. On the other hand, there is also a substantial Catalan working class and, while there is some residential segregation, there is very little workplace friction or social confrontation between immigrants and natives, and a high degree of assimilation of immigrants in the second generation (Keating, 2001a).

External Relations

The dominating vision for Catalonia is that of a self-governing nation within a weak Spanish state encompassed in Europe, a vision rooted in its experience before the forcible incorporation of 1714, acting in several political and economic arenas, without raising the issue of independence or getting into confrontations with the Spanish state. Yet while early twentieth century Catalan nationalism raised protectionism to a fundamental principle, modern Catalanism is strongly committed to European integration and, free trade (Clavera, 1990). For CiU and to a lesser extent the Catalan socialists, Europe secures free trade but, beyond this, provides a whole symbolic realm for the projection of Catalanism as well as a series of opportunities to act either on its own or with Spain. Again Catalan leaders are careful to distinguish their activities from ambitions to independence or aspirations to rival the state itself. Pujol has emphasised that Catalonia does not have a foreign policy, but an 'international presence' (El País, 15 December 1993).

Consistently with the general style of government, the Generalitat has not sought to run all its international activities itself. A directorate for external affairs, attached to the presidency, co-ordinates matters and sets priorities, but implementation is the responsibility of functional departments, special agencies, chambers of commerce and public-private partnerships. There are some thirty delegations abroad, mainly in Europe but including offices in New York, San Francisco, Tokyo and the countries of the Mahgreb. These do not represent the Generalitat but are formally private bodies run by the professional and business associations, with public participation. They include the *Consorci de Promoció Comercial*, the *Consorci de Projecció Exterior de la Cultura Catalana* (COPEC), and the *Patronat Català pro Europa* responsible for European matters (Petschen, 1992) and their work covers tourism promotion, investment, export assistance and culture. In 1987, a Centre for International Studies was opened in Barcelona, modelled on the Royal Institute of International Affairs in Britain, with support from the Spanish and Catalan governments. The *Institut Català de Estudis Mediterranis* assembles people involved in Mediterranean issues. Nor is there an effort to outflank the Spanish government or to compete against it in Europe or abroad. There were some early arguments about rights to engage in external policy and sign agreements with regions in other countries, although in 1993, the Constitutional Court recognised its right to operate abroad in the area of its own competences. Generally, however, Catalonia has sought to co-operate with Spanish representatives and relationships have depended more on tactics and alliances of the political parties at any time than on institutional factors. On a well-publicised visit to Morocco in 1994, Pujol defended Spain's right to the North African enclaves of Ceuta and Melilla, claimed by Morocco. Although he was received like a head of state, both Spanish and Catalan flags were flown. Indeed when, on one occasion, the Spanish flag was mislaid, the Catalans offered to take down theirs, so as not to cause diplomatic offence.

This international presence is aimed at the political affirmation of Catalonia as a nation; at economic development; and at culture. Catalonia's economy is highly dependent on trade, both across the border to France and in wider markets, and on inward investment. There is an almost missionary commitment in the Generalitat to the promotion of Catalan exports, with an annual prize awarded to the firm that has done most in this field. A magazine, *Made in Catalunya* is devoted to export promotion. This used to publish trilingually, in English, Castilian and Catalan, but the Castilian has been dropped, symbolising Catalonia's direct access to the outside world. As one of the largest tourist destinations in the world, Catalonia also devotes a lot of effort to tourist promotion. Another economic priority is both inward and outward investment, in an effort to internationalise the Catalan economy and link it into European, global and Mediterranean circuits.

Economic issues dominate Catalonia's links with the European Union. Here, as in other matters, the Generalitat seeks to work closely with private groups. The *Patronat Català Pro Europa*, a public-private body which lobbies for Catalan interests in Brussels as well as promoting information about EU policies and programmes within Catalonia, was founded in 1982, before Spanish entry into the EC. Recognising that regions or stateless nations cannot in themselves hope to influence EU policy, the Catalan lobby now works closely with the Spanish government, hoping to influence the Spanish negotiating position. The *Patronat Català Pro Europa* maintains an office in Brussels to monitor developments in the EU but, rather than trying to circumvent the Spanish effort, it works and shares information with the Spanish permanent representation. Catalonia has been less strident than the Basque Country in demanding a direct role in EU matters, although it has now added its voice to those calling for the application in Spain of the clause in the Maastricht treaty allowing subnational governments to represent the state. Meanwhile, the Catalan government has a list of priorities which it wants to achieve via the national government, on fiscal matters, the exchange rate and financial institutions (Generalitat, 1992). In practice, the main means for influencing the Spanish position in Europe is not any formal mechanism on German lines but party connections and networks. Pujol's privileged relationship with the central government after the national elections of 1993 and 1996 was crucial here.

Catalonia is very active in inter-regional networking. A Euro-region links it with the contiguous French regions of Midi-Pyrénées and Languedoc-Roussillon, to promote cooperation in communications, business development, education and training, agriculture, culture and sport, and the environment (Euroregió, 1991). A Pyrenean working group brings together French and Spanish regions along the border. The Four Motors of Europe – Catalonia, Rhône-Alpes, Lombardy and Baden-Württemberg – links four of the advanced regions within their respective countries to develop high technology (Borrás, 1993). Although Catalonia's technological prowess pales beside that of the other three, the Four Motors allows it to mix with them on equal terms as well as providing a theme for marketing and inward investment promotion. Catalonia been very active in the Europe of the Regions movement generally, including the Assembly of European Regions, the Committee of the Regions and the alliances of constitutional regions or regions with legislative powers, which are seeking an enhanced role in European policy making and implementation. Another important arena in economic matters is the Mediterranean and there are co-operation agreements with countries of the Mahgreb on forestry, tourism and other types of economic development. Efforts are made to promote Catalan investment in these countries, both to help Catalan firms and to encourage development in North Africa and so curtail pressures on immigration into Catalonia from outside Spain, a phenomenon that has become important since the 1990s (De Jouvenal and Roque, 1991). Outward investment is, among other things, a means for stemming immigration pressures and improving relations with the countries of the southern Mediterranean generally. Barcelona is the main centre for the EU's Mediterranean initiatives and, while this has been a matter for the Commission and the Spanish state, Catalonia has sought to support these efforts and to be involved. There are also links further afield. Agreements have been signed with Buenos Aires and the state of Illinois, and Pujol has visited the World Bank, the International Monetary Fund, as well as financial institutions in Europe (Petschen, 1992).

Culture is also part of Catalan external policy, although Catalonia cannot count on a substantial world community or major power of the same language. As in other fields, the Generalitat uses a semi-autonomous agency, COPEC, to promote its culture abroad. There are educational exchanges and support for Catalan language programmes within Spanish departments in universities around the world. The European Union has been persuaded to take an interest in minority languages (Siguan, 1996), largely at the prompting of the European Parliament. Much political capital is made out of the 1990 resolution by the European Parliament recognising Catalan as a European language, although this was not followed through with provision for translation of documents and proceedings into Catalan. In 1981 the Parliament adopted a Charter of Regional Languages and Cultures, later taken up by the Council of Europe (Labrie, 1993). The Generalitat has also worked to promote a stronger cultural policy in the EU, and looked for a place for Catalan culture within this (Gifreu, 1993). Although there has been little response, the Commission does make available a small amount of money for studies and pilot projects, and Catalonia was strongly behind the Bureau for Lesser Used Languages in Dublin. Catalonia is also concerned to protect its own language laws from European regulation under competition policy, which prevented it from requiring Catalan labelling on goods. Similarly it is concerned with World Trade Organisation rules. UNESCO is another focus of concern and, while Catalonia does not have an official representative in it, there is an active UNESCO centre in Barcelona, which is used to promote Catalan culture and political issues within the UNESCO structure as well as to bring UNESCO issues to Catalonia.

External policy is used also in the cause of nation building at home, by the reflection of its promotion abroad, and also to gain recognition in the world as more than a mere region of Spain. This explains Catalonia's taking out advertisements in North American newspapers at the time of the 1992 Olympics and again on the day of Saint Jordi in 1994 asking rhetorically, 'where is Barcelona?' – the correct answer of course being 'in Catalonia' and not, as most foreigners would have it, 'in Spain'. The travels of Jordi Pujol in Europe, the Americas and elsewhere, are an integral part of this. Political links are also important in Europe and the world. *Unió Democrática de Catalunya*, the Christian Democratic part of CiU, like the mainstream Basque nationalist party, has been very active in the Christian Democratic International. So again Catalan leaders are playing a complex game, maximising their influence in Spanish politics, while taking every opportunity to play in the international arena.

Policy

Catalonia's economic development strategy combines a 'bourgeois regionalism', the promotion of a territorial economic interest in partnership with the local business elite, with a nation-building project. There is a strong focus on economic development as part of nation-building, tied to the definition of Catalan national character, with some efforts to tie business and, to a lesser extent, unions into the strategy. CiU is essentially in favour of a liberalised market economy but the Christian Democrat and nationalist strands to its ideology also produce and emphasis on social solidarity. There is no real effort at regional corporatism, a concept damaged in any case by association with Francoism, but there is instead a focus on looser forms of concertation. Economic interventionism is officially ruled out as inconsistent with market principles. Industrial subsidies are not employed to any great extent by conscious policy decision, although in any case under EU regulations, Catalonia is not a region in which large-scale subsidisation would be permitted. Instead, there is an emphasis on encouraging innovation and the emergence of industrial clusters, though no attempt to determine what these should be, and a general preference for the 'new regionalism' of light intervention, steering and the development of human capital, entrepreneurship and research and development. Technology transfer design centres are fostered by the government, but run at arm's length by companies which must pay their own way. Firms similarly are expected to pay for services received from the government. Policy is delivered through a series of agencies with private participation rather than directly by government.

There is a strong emphasis on internationalisation of the Catalan economy, notably through COPCA, an agency with offices in 33 cities around the world. This is also a light structure, dependent on local agents in the countries concerned and responding to demand. The ideology of social co-operation allows some degree of concertation, within the limits of a competitive market economy, but stops well short of regional corporatism. Employers' and labour organisations are too weak and too tightly integrated into their state counterparts to permit this, and there in no interest on the part of the government. Yet there have been important tripartite initiatives in labour relations, with the establishment of an industrial tribunal to mediate labour disputes. In 1998 labour market policy was transferred to the Generalitat and at this time a *Consell de Treball de Catalunya* (Labour Council of Catalonia) was formed with tripartite representation to advise on labour relations. These all represent steps towards a distinctive Catalan model of industrial relations, building on the perception that labour relations are generally better there, that employers are more responsible, workers more work-oriented and labour relations less politicised. On the other hand, both unions and employers are rather tightly controlled by their parent bodies, and the state still has important functions in this area. Nor, significantly, do labour negotiations and agreements take place in Catalan. Most are registered in Castilian and then translated into Catalan.

Territorial planning is quite well developed in Catalonia, aided by the monocephalic structure of the region, focused on Barcelona and the main transport routes to Europe and to the rest of Spain. Francoist planning was based on expansion of heavy industry, with state-sponsored mega-projects and little attention to coherent urban planning, accompanied by rampant land speculation and corruption. Since the transition there has been an effort to develop better land use policies, to control urban sprawl, to improve services and to improve social integration. The city of Barcelona has been transformed under the leadership of its local council, with the Olympic Games of 1992 being used as an opportunity to attract new development and rehabilitate whole zones of the old city. The Olympic works themselves were behind schedule and the whole programme was bedevilled by conflict between the Generalitat and the city corporation over control and who would get the credit, but everything was ready for the day and the general organisation is often contrasted favourably with the contemporary World's Fair in Seville. A land agency, the *Institut Català del Sol*, is active in assembling parcels of land for residential and industrial development, with powers of compulsory purchase. It then plans the development of the new zones, to ensure a rational use of space and the provision of housing for various income groups. Again, the strategy avoids direct public ownership, using co-operatives to provide social housing. Certainly, there have been corruption scandals and accusations of patronage in urban planning and land use policies, but generally urban and regional planning has worked well in Catalonia. Given the complexities of the matter and the multitude of actors and interests involved, this does suggest a willingness to cooperage in pursuit of agreed ends and to deliver on undertakings.

The Generalitat has pursued an active language normalisation policy with the aim of making Catalan the main vehicle of social communication. Its use has been extended in the schools, where almost all elementary and large parts of secondary and tertiary education are in the medium of Catalan and in the universities, especially in the humanities and social sciences. Yet there is no question of its displacing Spanish. Rather the idea is that eventually all children should have a command of Catalan, Castilian and a third language (normally English or French), so being able to function at home in their own language while also operating in the Spanish and European arenas. In order to avoid language becoming a mark of ethnic segregation, the law declares that there should not be separate Catalan and Spanish schools, but that parents theoretically have the right to choose either language of instruction. In practice, this means that Catalan prevails, with immersion classes for those who have come from non-Catalan family backgrounds. Catalan is the language of public administration in the autonomous government and the municipal governments, but it is still little used by the Spanish state administration in Catalonia or in the courts. There is an extensive policy of encouragement and subsidisation of Catalan in the media, publishing and the arts. The Generalitat's own radio and television stations, TV3, Canal 33 and *Catalunya Ràdio*, broadcast in Catalan, as do local radio stations. Such evidence as we have suggests that Catalans are happy to listen to broadcasts in either language, with a slight preference for Catalan. Spanish tends to predominate in newspapers in Barcelona, although in the hinterland there is a thriving *comarcal* press in Catalan and without any government subsidy (Folch-Serra and Nogue, 2001). Among the metropolitan dailies, *Avuí*, subsidised by the Generalitat, is close politically to CiU, but has only about a tenth of the combined market of the three main Spanish papers, *El País*, *La Vanguardia* and *El Periódico*. Since 1997 *El Periódico* has a Catalan edition whose editorial content is identical with the Spanish one and it seems that about half the readers opt for this (McRoberts, 2001) which still means that the great bulk of newspaper reading is done in Spanish. There are subsidies for books in Catalan in the form of a commitment by the Generalitat to purchase a specified number of copies of each publication and there are also subsidies for plays in Catalan.

While the first language law of 1983 caused little controversy, except among some die-hard Spanish nationalists, the second law, of 1998, did provoke opposition. This did not involve a social confrontation but rather took the form of mobilisation by groups of Castilian-speaking intellectuals and civil servants on the one hand, and by business people on the other. Ironically, the strongly nationalist *Esquerra Republicana de Catalunya* also declined to support the law, because it did not go far enough into the world of business and commerce, complaining that Catalan was in danger of becoming the modern equivalent of mediaeval Latin, used in schools and government, but less and less in commerce. At the same time, Catalan faces a challenge in metropolitan Barcelona, Catalonia's gateway to Europe and the world.

Catalan has thus made considerable advances as a language of public, as opposed to merely private, use and as a vehicle for building a sense of common identity. The percentage of the population able to understand it rose from 81 per cent in 1981, to 90.6 per cent in 1986, to 93.8 per cent in 1991, with the main increases in the metropolitan area of Barcelona. Speaking ability has increased and most young people are now able to write it. It has proved a powerful tool in region or nation-building and the fostering of common purpose. Whether this extends to forging a common territorial identity on economic and business matters is another question. Outside the family firms in the small towns, Catalan is used rather little in business and commerce and employers have been unenthusiastic in extending its use in the economy, regarding it as a burden. Given the strong social and political support for the language, they have been cautious in overt criticism of language normalisation, accepting the political necessity of co-operating, but they have resisted requirements to label their products in Catalan or to project Catalan abroad. This may stem from a perception that Catalan is seen negatively in the rest of Spain and could damage their market prospects and that it represents an additional cost, an unnecessary one given that anyone who can read Catalan also reads and understands Castilian. Wage negotiations tend to be conducted in Castilian and contracts to be written in that language, with a possible subsequent translation into Catalan. The Generalitat, with its sensitivity to the business community, has tread warily in this field. It has negotiated accords with large firms to encourage the use of Catalan but has avoided the sort of regulation found in Quebec (Keating, 2001a).

In cultural policy more generally, the Generalitat claims exclusive competence and complains that this is not respected by the Spanish state. It believes firmly in an active cultural policy but, in line with its attitude to social intervention generally, does not see this as a matter primarily for public provision and direction on French lines. Rather it seeks to encourage Catalanist organisations within civil society, with provision of subsidies where necessary. This has not prevented a series of disputes over what constitutes Catalan culture and whether producers operating in Catalonia through the medium of Spanish can qualify for public support, encouragement and subsidy.

The main instruments of social policy are still in the hands of the state, restricting Catalonia's ability to establish its own social model but, within the limits of its powers, the Generalitat does pursue a broadly Christian democratic vision. With the devolution of active labour market policy in 1998 it sought to frame a distinct Catalan model of industrial relations based on class compromise and arbitration. It used the limited devolution of income tax to improve deductions for children. In the run-up to the election of 2000, the Generalitat announced that it would improve payments for pensioners out of its own resources if the state would not provide a national policy with state funding. There is also something of an emphasis on social housing, through housing associations, government support and requirements for low income housing in new developments.

There is some linkage between Catalanism and environmentalism, as the image of the region is tied to some degree with the rural landscape, but this is not a particularly prominent theme. An analysis of national election manifestos showed CiU placing less emphasis on environmental issues than either the Socialists or the successive centre-right and conservative Spanish parties (Weale et al., 2000). On the other hand, Catalonia does pride itself on being an environmental leader, part of a deliberate strategy for improving its image and positioning itself alongside the more successful northern European regions (Börzel, 1999). A good environment is also an asset for the crucial tourist industry. So Catalonia has innovated on a number of issues, being first region to introduce charges for waste water (Weale et al., 2000). It has tried to transpose European regulations directly into its own legislation ahead of the requisite Spanish law, to give itself a comprehensive set of environmental laws and reinforce its image as a direct partner of the EU. Its record in actually implementing these laws, however, is much less impressive (Börzel, 1999). Small businesses who are so important in Catalonia are much less good than big firms in complying with environmental requirements and it seems that, in a clash between environmentalism and maintaining growth in the small firms sector, the Catalan government will opt for the latter.

GALICIA

Galicia in Spain

Galicia's economic prospects are dominated by its peripheral location, both within Spain and in Europe. It is off the main land trade routes, and its maritime trading prospects in Spain's era of greatness were long stymied by the monopoly of the American trade held by Cadiz, while Lisbon, down the coast, captured the Portuguese imperial trade. Galicia's economy developed in a dependent mode, with an emphasis on raw materials, notably wood and granite, to be processed elsewhere. Francoist development plans reinforced this model, adding massive hydro-electric schemes to provide power for the industrialisation of other Spanish regions. There is a sharp division between the coast, where Europe's largest fishing fleet operates, and the hinterland, dominated by thousands of tiny and poorly commercialised farms. A similar cleavage exists between the large cities, with a substantial presence of state servants and military personnel, and the countryside. Yet there is some industrialisation, notably a productive Renault factory at Vigo. Added to the region's natural disadvantages at the time of the transition was a poorly developed infrastructure, including roads, railways, ports, airports and telecommunications. There is no metropolis corresponding to Barcelona and a considerable rivalry between La Coruña and Vigo. Santiago de Compostela, inland, is the political capital, a centre for public administration, education and pilgrimage. Galicia, like other poor regions of Spain, has shown some convergence with the norm, going from 67 per cent of average Spanish GDP per capita in 1955 to 83 per cent in 1996 although in the earlier period this was achieved largely by the outmigration of labour from low productivity enterprises and farming, with the population stagnating. Both labour productivity and overall factor productivity have been the lowest in Spain (Pérez et al., 1996).

EU membership has increased the peripherality of Galicia and poses challenges to its traditional industries. Fishermen have come into conflict with those of other states over access and face problems of stock depletion. Traditional industries and agriculture face competition from Europe and the imposition of quotas, notably in milk and steel, while the farmers fail to get the same benefits as the large producers of northern Europe from the Common Agricultural Policy. Galicia's GDP per capita is just 64 per cent of the EU average, about two thirds that of Catalonia, although living standards are brought much closer to the Spanish average though transfer payments. Galicia is still dependent on traditional sectors, with 17 per cent of Spain's employment in agriculture and fishing, against 6 per cent in industry, 5.8 per cent in services and 7.0 per cent overall.

Culture and Identity

Survey evidence shows that Galegos have rather weak territorial political identities at all levels. The 1996 survey showed them below the Spanish average on identification with local, provincial, regional, Spanish and European levels, in contrast to Catalans, who scored higher than average on everything but the Spanish level (Moral, 1998). They were only half as likely as Catalans to see their region as a nation but tended to agree that regionalism had always been strong in Galicia, another example of the projection of the collective image which does not quite correspond to the individual perception. It is still common to attribute Galicia's backwardness to ingrained features of Galician culture and these are reflected in the auto-stereotypes of interview respondents. The Galician peasant is described as individually or family oriented, without entrepreneurial ambition and unwilling to co-operate in the greater social good – features recalling Banfield's 'amoral familism' in Italy. This in turn has been attributed to the fragmented pattern of landholding and inheritance, to the historic domination of the Church, and to the failure of the state effectively to penetrate the countryside. Galician business leaders are said to be lacking in innovation, poorly trained in management and unwilling to specialise. Customers still expect one firm to provide a complete range of products and there is an unwillingness on the part of firms to co-operate in research, exports and marketing. Galicians themselves are prone to repeat these views in response to surveys. In the 1992 CIS survey (but not in the earlier 1976 one) they attributed economic inequalities to regional character rather than natural advantages, although unlike the Catalans they recognised the importance of investment, state policies and capitalism (García Ferrando et al., 1994). Galegos neither see themselves nor are seen by others as being as entrepreneurial as the Catalans, having an image of conservatism and being tied to the land (Sangrador García, 1996). Yet they are seen as more entrepreneurial than people in most other parts of Spain, and more so by outsiders than by themselves, perhaps reflecting the success of Galego business people outside the country and their lack of success at home. Once again, we have evidence of the power of auto-stereotypes as a mechanism for rationalising people's condition. The Galego stereotype is consistently interpreted in a negative way, as a means of coping with failure.

Language is indicative of the problem. Galego is the only one of Spain's minority languages spoken by almost the entire population. This, however, is a reflection of the lack of immigration rather than the health of the language, since there is a sharp diglossia in use. Galego is used much more in the countryside than in the cities, more among the lower than the middle and upper classes and more in familiar than in formal settings (Real Academia Galega, 1995). Given its concentration in the least literate sections of the population, its use in written communication is very small. Unlike Catalan, it has suffered social disdain and the upwardly mobile have traditionally avoided using it. Social progress is still equated with speaking Castilian and there is a tendency for urban and upper class people to be less favourably inclined to Galego and its extension in education and public life (Real Academia Galega, 1995). In work, there is a tendency to use Galego with co-workers but Castilian to superiors (Real Academia Galega, 1995). So, unlike Catalan, Galego cannot readily be used to construct an imagined community seen as dynamic, integrated, modern and European.

Political Leadership

Political traditions and practices have served to perpetuate these traits. There is a definite sense of distinct Galician identity (García Ferrando et al., 1994; Moral, 1998) but this is not as strongly politicised as in Catalonia and not linked to a shared project for autonomy in Spain and Europe. The 1992 CIS survey showed that Galicians were slightly less likely than the average region to demand more powers for the autonomous community (García Ferrando et al., 1992). Politics is localist and territorially fragmented (Maíz, 1996) and levels of participation in elections at all levels has traditionally been low. Turnout for the referendum on the statute of autonomy was only 29 per cent and participation in regional elections has been the lowest in Spain. Voting tends to be seen in narrowly instrumental terms, being highest in local elections in places where *cacique* influence is strongest and it can be presented as part of an individualised transaction, and lowest on where elections are fought on more abstract issues (López Mira, 1996). Clientelism has a long history and was well established in the nineteenth-century, helped by the territorial and political fragmentation of the society and the centralisation of power. The notables, or *caciques* survived the turbulence of the early twentieth century and persisted under Francoism, as Galicia, unlike Catalonia, was a stronghold of the dictatorship. This pervasive clientelism is another indication that it would be wrong to describe Galicia as individualist since that implies a degree of self-sufficiency and independence that does not exist. Rather, the client system stifles the capacity for both individual and collective self-expression while favouring the production of divisible goods. Unlike Italian clientelism, the Galician variety operates at the collective rather than the individual level. Patrons do not generally command individual-level services like pensions or the ability to manipulate tax assessments, but depend on local collective benefits like roads, bridges and public works projects, delivered through local collaborators. This has created a pattern of political dependency mirroring the economic dependency of the region and militating against autonomous political mobilisation.

The system has survived because of the fragmentation of Galician political life and the failure to mount an effective opposition or alternative project. The autonomous government has been dominated since it was set up by the Spanish Conservative *Alianza/Partido Popular* (PP) under the leadership, since 1989 of Manuel Fraga, former Franco minister and unsuccessful leader of the national opposition. The Galician PP is a combination of two rather distinct elements. A centralist, *españolista* element, dominated by the Madrid leadership, has little time for Galician particularism and is increasingly inclined to a form of economic and social neo-liberalism to which the national PP has gradually evolved; it is strongest in the cities and in the province of La Coruña. The other element is more rooted in the rural world of traditional Galicia and espouses a traditionalist and somewhat anti-modern type of regionalism, associated with folklore and resting on networks of clientelism and patronage. Neither element has a project for an autonomous model of Galician regional development and modernisation. The Socialist Party, previously the main opposition, has declined amid factionalism and conflicts among its urban leaders and is no longer a serious contender for government. This has left the *Bloque Nacionalista Galego* (BNG) as the official opposition in the regional parliament.

Nationalism has a long history in Galicia, going back to the late nineteenth century, but it never achieved anything like the ideological hegemony it has had in Catalonia. It has been highly fractious, with no party ever able to establish its dominance over the nationalist camp. In contrast to Catalonia, there is no large 'bourgeois regionalist' party dedicated to modernisation and integration into Europe. It is not that Galicia lacks such traditions. There has historically been a liberal, modernising nationalism, going back to the last century and associated in the years before and after the Civil War with the legendary Castelao. In the 1980s, the *Coalición Galega* sought to occupy this space, teaming up with the Catalans in the Roca operation, but it failed to thrive and was marginalised when the Galician PP adopted a regionalist rhetoric, incorporating the regionally-inclined members of the middle class (Máiz, 1996). The *Bloque* itself is a coalition of parties, including traditional Marxists, post-communists, social democrats, centrists and a variety of nationalist and regionalist options. Its political line has been rather demagogic and opportunist and it lacked a clear vision of Galicia's place in Spain and the new Europe. While in the other historic nationalities, there is a strong relationship between being competent in the local language and supporting more autonomy, this link is absent in Galicia (García Ferrando et al., 1994) suggesting that nationalism/regionalism has failed to bridge the domains of culture, language, politics and social mobilisation. Language remains associated with a conservative traditionalist regionalism or, for a minority, with a radical rejectionism, rather than a modernising, European message.

Galicia has found itself marginalised in Spanish politics, since the local PP tends to be shut out when the Socialists are in power and taken for granted when its national counterparts win; when there were minority governments in Madrid it has less influence than Catalonia, with its ability to swing votes in the national parliament. Its financial dependence further reduced its power to mount an autonomous project. The Galicia PP was opposed to the concession of the 30 per cent of income tax which the Catalans got from Madrid, while the BNG supports fiscal autonomy but only in the long term. Recent years, however, have shown signs of change in Galician politics. Electoral turnout increased from 47 per cent in 1981 to 64 per cent in 1997 and the gap with other regions has narrowed. A more modernising regionalism has emerged, focused on the institutions of the autonomous government and civil society. The BNG has modified its line on both socio-economic and nationalist issues, making huge political gains as a result and has elaborated a series of policies across the board (BNG, 1998). Exposure to European influences has introduced further modernising themes.

Institutions

Galicia has autonomous government institutions similar in form to those of Catalonia but their evolution and performance is quite different. While

Catalonia, under a modernising nationalist elite, has sought a break with the old regime, Galicia has for most of its autonomous history been run by the post-Francoist *Partido Popular*. It still reflects the traditions and practices of *caciquismo* that dominated Spanish politics in the Restoration Era (1875-1920) and which persisted under Francoism. These clientelistic networks, indeed, were the prime targets of the early Catalan movement, which broke them at the turn of the century. Institutions also serve to maintain the old hegemony in Galicia and stifle movements for change. The dominance of the PP in the regional government meant that there was no big change in personnel from the Francoist era and only now is a new generation of officials, better trained and more oriented to change and development, coming into the administration. The Xunta (regional executive) itself is organised to reflect the factional interests within the ruling party, with a lot of duplication, fragmentation and personal fiefdoms.

Administration is extremely complex, with a plethora of programmes for similar purposes, serving the needs of clientelism and distributive politics. While Catalonia has sought to outflank the Spanish provinces, putting in place its own local administration, the provinces of Galicia have remained a key level for intermediation and distribution. Each is run by a PP 'baron', who thus channels both state and regional government patronage and keeps the local mayors in line. These institutions correspond poorly to the organisation of civil society and popular perception. The barons, with their territorial power bases, are also key actors in Xunta politics, with rights of appointments to ministerial and official posts. This, combination of access to, and patronage from, both state and regional administration, enables the barons to maintain control and depress levels of popular mobilisation and participation. There is a gradually evolving programme to establish decentralised planning on the basis of 53 *comarcas*, but progress has been slow given the resilience of traditional networks.

Economic development is entrusted to an agency IGAPE, intended to be more creative and entrepreneurial than the regular government departments with their bureaucratic traditions. Its tasks include awarding industrial incentives, in co-operation with the Spanish central government; promotion including inward investment; and innovation and training programmes. SODIGA is a risk capital society, taking stakes of up to 20 per cent in firms for up to seven years. INESGA is a strategic investment fund with the banks. Yet other programmes tend to proliferate for specific sectors or needs. In 1997, for example, the opposition criticised the establishment of a new public investment agency, designed to get around public spending restrictions by a form of creative accountancy that would allow it to issue debt which would be repaid by the Xunta after the year 2000. This put the agency beyond parliamentary control or scrutiny while providing yet another fund to be shared out in small clientelist operations across the region.

Correspondingly, the autonomous administration of the Xunta has a poorer image than its counterparts in Catalonia (or the Basque Country and Navarre). The 1992 survey showed that 39 per cent of Catalans, as opposed to only 26 in Galicia, considered the autonomous administration to be the most efficient level. In Galicia, 33 per cent, against 19 per cent in Catalonia, thought that the autonomous administration wasted money – the figures for central government were 43 and 32 per cent respectively. In Galicia 19 per cent thought that the central administration was less corrupt, about three times as many as in the other historic nationalities and more than anywhere else except Madrid (García Ferrando, 1994).

Unlike Catalonia, Galicia never produced a vibrant commercial and industrial bourgeoisie. The middle classes found employment in the state bureaucracy, the military or, if they entered the private sector, in the banks, while dynamic elements found outlets in internal or overseas migration. The failure to develop an entrepreneurial class was not due to lack of capital since, like many traditional societies, Galicia has had a high savings ratio, boosted from the eighteenth century by remittances from emigrants, but this money was usually placed elsewhere (Beiras, 1995). Landholding until 1926 was organised on precapitalist lines, encouraging the proliferation of small holdings (*minifundismo*) and subsistence farming (Maíz, 1996). Social relations within Galicia are polarised, with a fragmented class structure and a large social distance between the urban middle class, small farmers and the small industrial proletariat.

Galicia has long suffered from high levels of emigration, to South America until the mid 1960s and thereafter to Europe (Costa Clavell, 1976). Between 1964 and 1991, some 312,000 people left (Pérez et al., 1996). Other indicators can be ambivalent or misleading. Activity levels have usually been among the highest in Spain and unemployment between 1964 and 1991 was only about half the Spanish average. By 1995 it had risen to 17.2 per cent, still below the rate for Spain (22.7 per cent) or Catalonia (19.9 per cent). These statistics, however, disguised low productivity and capitalisation levels outside the extractive industries. Total factor productivity over the period 1964-91 was a little more than half than of Catalonia (Pérez et al., 1996). As employment was shed in small farms and fisheries, activity rates declined so that by the end of the 1990s they were at the Spanish average while unemployment fell more slowly than elsewhere in Spain, and was thus higher than Catalonia. Galicia thus appears as a poor periphery dependent on externally owned and extractive industries, and on small-scale farming, lacking an industrial base or a dynamic business class. There is much here that is consistent with dependency theory or 'internal colonialism' (Lafont, 1967) but the explanation for economic backwardness and the lack of dynamism is much contested. Galegos abroad are often noted for their business success and the wealthy emigrant returning to endow his home town is a staple figure in local lore. Yet the social and political structure does not seem to favour entrepreneurship at home.

We do not have the data on associations and participation for Galicia that exist, however, patchily, in Catalonia but, while there is dense network of groups at the level of the parish (Beiras, 1995) there appear to be fewer public interest or policy-seeking groups at regional level. Business is divided by sector and location, with the granite producers, the fishermen, the farmers and the industrialists having rather little in common. Most associations are local and descended from the old *gremios*, or guilds, with a rather defensive mentality. There is a regional employers' association, the *Confederación de Empresarios de Galicia* (CEG), founded in 1981 as a confederation of provincial and sectoral groups, which seeks to develop a regional vision. Most of the business of negotiating labour accords and delivering member services is done at the provincial level, with the CEG concentrating on dealing with the Xunta and on providing regional services. Relations within it have long been rather tense and in 2000 there was a crisis when it was alleged that funds given for training programmes had been diverted into the CEG's own accounts. These events precipitated the resignation of the president, Antonio Ramilo, formerly mayor of Vigo under the Franco regime and later a member of parliament for the *Alianza Popular* (predecessor of the present PP). Shortly afterwards, a similar crisis exploded in the provincial employers' association of La Coruña. Like those in other sectors, respondents in the business community complain about the lack of dynamism in some sectors, about conservative attitudes and an individualism that precludes co-operation in innovation and change.

Galicia has three main trade unions, UGT, CCOO and the *Confederación Intersindical Galega* (CIG), which was founded 1994 out of previously fragmented nationalist unions. CIG, which is rather smaller than the other two, is largely confined to metals and services and is strongest in the rural inland and more traditional provinces. UGT is, like its Catalan counterpart, Spanish in orientation and rather anti-nationalist. CCOO, also as in Catalonia, is a separate 'national' union affiliated to the Spanish CCOO, and is more sympathetic to the Galician national theme than is UGT. CIG, for its part, is close to the ideas of the *Bloque Nacionalista Galego*, although not formally linked with it. It is committed to self-determination for Galicia in the framework of a Europe of the Peoples, is keen on promoting the Galician language and has fraternal links with the Basque nationalist unions LAB and ELA. In the short run, it seeks to make Galicia the framework for all labour relations issues and laws. CIG adopts a militant and confrontational stance towards both government and business and is not interested in corporatist deals. This has created a lot of tension with the other unions, although these have also had problems between themselves. Along with the lowest trade union density in Spain (estimated at 8.1 per cent in 1995: Escobar and van der Meer, 1995), this has meant that there is little concertation in Galicia. There is a certain degree of collaboration, through the *Consejo Económico y Social* and its working groups. Most contact and work, for example on training schemes, however, is carried out at the provincial level. There has been some imitation of the Catalan experience, in establishing a *Consejo Galego de Relaciones Laborales* and a mediation tribunal for industrial disputes but this experience is rather recent.

There is evidence for a lack of capacity for large-scale social mobilisation in Galicia. Álvarez Corbacho (1995) has demonstrated that, while taxes and expenditures per capita in the large cities are equivalent to those elsewhere in Spain, the smaller Galician municipalities refuse to tax themselves at the same level. This not only reduces their own source revenue but because central grants are linked to fiscal effort, it reduces their transfers from the centre as well. This practice is attributed to a disinclination to undertake projects for collective good and a reliance, instead, on clientelism and divisible goods. Instead of putting in place rigorous urban planning policies, municipalities permit sprawl, hoping to expand the property tax base as an alternative to increasing rates. Population in the countryside is widely dispersed and local road systems rarely connect with each other. Social networks are closed and there is a high degree of dependence on personal contacts and family connections. On the other hand, these networks themselves do represent more than mere individualism and there are plenty of voluntary associations, notably at the level of the rural parish and a tradition of co-operativism from the early twentieth century (Beiras, 1995). Many of the stereotypical qualities of the Galician peasant can be turned around and seen as virtues (Mella, 1992). Reflectiveness, formerly a euphemism for insecurity, is now seen as a positive trait. Lack of dogmatism, formerly a mark of dependence on outside views, may be portrayed as openness. Social equilibrium, formerly synonymous with stasis, may now permit measured change. What is lacking is a system of social mobilisation at the regional level corresponding to the needs of modern development, and to explain this we need to look at symbolic integration and leadership, at institutions, and at policy.

External Relations

Galicia's projection in Europe and abroad has been hampered by its poor image as a rural periphery and by the lack of a clear vision of the region in the world. The leftist parties of the BNG have tended to take the anti-European line that was common in many peripheral regions until the 1980s, when the Europe of the regions theme led to a reappraisal. The European Community was condemned as a capitalist and imperialist operation against the interests of the Galician people. This allowed the BNG to capitalise on the serious problems of adaptation of the Galician economy and on the crisis in the fishing industry, which could be blamed on the Common Fisheries Policy. Since the 1990s the BNG, as part of its move to the centre, has been less hostile to Europe and, while it opposes the actual structures and policies of the EU takes a much less stridently anti-EU line than before. In 1988/9 there was a debate over whether the BNG should present candidates for the European Parliament, given its fundamental opposition to the institution. Eventually it was decided that absenting themselves would be irresponsible and called for unity around a single candidate to represent Galicia. Their programme called for a minimal reform, which would give each nation (including Galicia) direct representation with a right to veto any Community action that was against its interests. By the 1994 European elections, the line had moderated to the extend that the BNG list could be headed by Carlos Mella, a moderate who had been a minister in the brief coalition government of 1987–89 between the Socialists and the liberal nationalists (and which had not included BNG).

Manuel Fraga, on the other hand, took up the Europe of the regions theme shortly after coming to office and has been very active on the European regional circuit. His regionalism is distinguished sharply from nationalism, being placed firmly within the context of the Spanish state and envisaging the regions as an entrenched third level of government (Fraga, 1991). Galicia has an office in Brussels and has been active in the Committee of the Regions, the Assembly of European Regions and bodies like the Atlantic Arc. The Euro-region linking Galicia with the North of Portugal has opened up economic and transportation links and changed attitudes by positioning Galicia as part of a thriving Atlantic region rather than a peripheral part of the Spanish continental economy. As noted below, Europe may prove an important force in opening up the Galician political system and undermining the old networks, but so far the adverse affects of European policies in sectors like fisheries, milk and shipbuilding have worked against promoting the sort of European vocation that Catalonia has forged.

As a result of emigration, Galicia has a large diaspora in Latin America, many of whom have been successful in business and provide potential economic opportunities as well as political linkages. Fraga has courted them assiduously and the emigrant vote (which is kept for life) is largely cast for the PP. In recent years, the nationalists have been following the same route, with nationalist leader Xosé Manuel Beiras also making trips to the Americas. Fraga, as an elder statesman of Spanish politics, is also a frequent visitor to other parts of the world, keeping up a family friendship with Fidel Castro (their fathers emigrated to Cuba together) and daring to visit Ghaddaffi in Libya to the consternation of the Spanish government. This is all part of the strategy of region building, but one kept within the strict limits of Spanish nationalism, presenting a marked contrast to the forward strategy of CiU in Catalonia.

Policy

There is a huge effort in industrial development policy in Galicia and IGAPE is committed to innovation and change. Yet policy, overall, tends to the traditional. Spending on infrastructure has been very high, as elsewhere in Spain in the 1980s, bringing roads, telecommunication and airports up to European standards. There is a massive and largely indiscriminate programme of investment subsidies, up to the high limits laid down by the EU for the most needy regions (60 per cent of the investment over most of Galicia and 50 per cent in the rest of the region). These are largely financed by the state and the EU, although there is some cost to the region itself. While these grants are generally automatic and demand-led, investment in infrastructure follows a political and clientelistic logic (Alvarez Corbacho, 1995), controlled by the provincial barons and their underlings. All this makes it difficult to impose strategic priorities, whether territorial or sectoral. There are three airports with aspirations to international status, and there is competition between the main seaports. Land use planning and infrastructure projects are constantly frustrated by dispersed land ownership and unwillingness to alienate family property. Some strategic planning is provided by the need to produce the Community Support Framework for EU aid, but this is poorly integrated into other policy instruments. There is little policy innovation, but a constant tendency to look to Catalonia and to try and follow developments there. So the Catalan accords on labour market policy were followed by a similar initiative in Galicia. Tripartite concertation is weakened, however, by the weakness of representative political, business and union organisations at the regional, as opposed to the provincial level. Assistentialist policies have also characterised Galicia's approach to the restructuring of agriculture and fisheries, with a continuing problem of over-capacity. European rules though have begun to limit these.

All this would suggest that the factors which caused Galicia's underdevelopment in the past are being perpetuated, with the region trapped in a cycle of dependency. Yet in so far as these factors are the product not of primordial cultural traits but of institutional factors and political leadership, together with external circumstances, then there is scope for change. Such change would not mean the imposition on Galicia of an external model of development, but a programme to tap the inherent strengths of the region and to address its weaknesses. There are some signs of change. European integration is supported by almost everyone, although its actual effects are widely deplored. This has strengthened the neo-liberal wing of the PP, with their discourse of competitiveness and fiscal discipline, against the traditional regionalists. Europe, through the structural funds programmes, has also favoured public-private partnership and a shift in emphasis of policy from hard infrastructure and investment subsidies to human capital and training. It has encouraged policy evaluation and impact analysis. It has also sparked a debate on the position of the region within Europe, with the nationalists adopting a more positive attitude and the PP becoming more active in the Europe of the regions movement (see above). Europe has also provided much of the planning framework for Galician development policy, through the need to establish Community Support Frameworks and Galicia has as good a record as the rest of Spain in absorbing Structural Funds, better than the regions of southern Italy or Greece.

Rural depopulation is gradually undermining the power base of the traditionalists. The opening of the Portuguese border has had some major effects. Competition from lower wage labour in Portugal has undercut Galician industry, while Portuguese capital has entered in considerable quantities. Portugal, which has had one of the highest growth rates in the EU in recent years, also offers an example of modernisation and change, although few think that the Portuguese model, based on low wages, can either be transferred directly or even survive unchanged in the longer term. Another external example is Ireland, an even more peripheral part of the EU which has enjoyed remarkable growth and with which Galicia has long been recognised as possessing cultural and historic affinities (Keating, 1988). There has been a steady institutionalisation of the Xunta (Maíz and Losada, 2000), with an improvement in the quality of officials and better policy capacity. Electoral participation has steadily increased and elections have become more competitive. There is an emerging nationalist alternative to the PP power bloc, gradually acquiring a realistic programme for government. There are great efforts to increase the region's international connections, both in Europe and in Latin America. Like Ireland, Galicia has a large diaspora in America, whose success in business belies the simplistic ethnic stereotype, and there is an effort to mobilise them in order to gain trade opportunities and both inward and outward investment. The Galician employers' organisation represents some of the more dynamic economic sectors and, despite its fractiousness. is active in promoting a regional vision while both it and the Xunta have begun to pay more attention to fostering good business practice, entrepreneurship and inter-firm cooperation.

There is a policy of linguistic normalisation, less ambitious than in Catalonia and without the nationalist motivation, which seeks to raise the status of the language while extending its social use. This has had some success, but there is still resistance, with the more modernising elements in society, including young people, still regarding it as an obstacle and insisting that it is more useful to gain proficiency in English. Galego is promoted in the schools, although alongside instruction in Castilian and there is encouragement for broadcasting and publishing in the language. The autonomous government operates in Galego and the municipalities are also supposed to do so, although not all in practice do. There is also an argument about the relationship with Portuguese. More conservative regionalists insist that Galego is a separate language, placing it within the Spanish context. Others, including many nationalists, think of it as a close relative of Portuguese, offering the prospects of wider diffusion. Lest this lead to a feeling that Galego is mere dialect of Portuguese, they insist that the language originated in Galicia, spreading southwards. There is a slow but consistent enhancement of the status of Galego, enabling it better to be used as a vehicle of modernisation, although it still lacks the prestige of Catalan.

As in Catalonia, there has been less emphasis on social policy since this is mainly a state responsibility, although there is a Plan for Support for the Family, aimed at assistance for large families.

CONCLUSION

The comparison of the two regions shows that location and resource endowment are still important factors in development, but that historical legacies, cultural endowments and social practices are important in constructing a development model. Yet cultural stereotypes and primordialist theories greatly over-simplify matters. Both regions have cultural and economic resources and a 'useable past' that can be pressed into service. Catalonia has its traditions of diffused authority, shared sovereignty and pactism, but Galicia has its relative social cohesion, an egalitarian ethos in the countryside and dispersed property ownership, which could be used as factors in a virtuous development model in the new economic order (Mella, 1992). There is a much sharper contrast in the stereotypes attributed to each region (Sangrador García, 1981, 1996) than in actual attitudes. In both cases, the region has emerged as a significant *référentiel*, the framework for governing institutions, electoral orientations, civil society and public policy on development. Both are still embedded in state politics, but with an opening to Europe. Their institutionalisation, however, has taken contrasting forms as have their development strategies.

The cases also show that institutional arrangements matter. Both regions have similar formal structures of government, as autonomous communities on the 'fast track', yet institutionalisation has taken different forms. Clientelism in Galicia is buttressed by the party system, by the administrative structure and the distorted pattern of political competition. Institution-building in Catalonia has taken a different form, representing more of a break from the old regime and from Spanish state practices, though not entirely free from clientelist elements itself. The idea that Catalonia is inherently associational but Galicia is not does not really stand up to examination. Catalans are not great joiners, many of its associations are of dubious representativeness and the network of business associations is highly diverse and poorly integrated. Galicia is no better but it does have a network of groups and co-operatives. Nor does the individualist stereotype of the Galician help a great deal. Catalans come out in surveys as rather individualist, while Galicians look to institutions and elites for leadership. What matters is more the linkage between government and civil society and the opportunities for groups and associations to influence policy, and the incentives for them to adopt positive-sum attitudes. Institutionalism may be a better guide here than cultural reductionism. Catalonia can be seen as an example of the strength of weak ties (Granovetter, 1973) in which a common identity does not preclude innovation and policy can be provided through steering and encouragement rather than direction. Galicia's ties are of the stronger sort, with a highly localist tradition and a web of mutual obligations based on clientelism and patronage.

Leadership is critically important in this matter, as it is in building the 'imagined community' at the right spatial level. A selective use of history is part of this as is the use of language and cultural policy to present a self-image and identity. In both cases, as in many regions, symbols of identity, notably language, are stronger in the countryside than in the cities, which are at the forefront of modernisation and globalisation, but this is much more pronounced in Galicia. Catalonia has associated its traditions, its language and its culture with a modernity that respects tradition. Galego and Galician culture are still seen somehow as an obstacle to modernity. Yet even in Catalonia there are limits to the use of the local language as an instrument of modernisation and internationalisation and it is notable that Catalan has made much less progress in the world of commerce than in other fields. An additional aspect is the projection of success stories. Catalonia has some serious structural economic problems and social strains; its membership of the Four Motors group of advanced technology regions comes close to being a bluff. Its economy is increasingly dependent on multinational capital as the old indigenous industrial elite declines. Yet it has successfully projected itself as a leader of an emerging Europe of the regions, while Galicia continues to labour under a negative auto-stereotype.

In economic development, Catalonia has the easier task, given its favourable location and higher standard of living and some of the policy differences reflect EU and Spanish rules, for example on the amount of subsidy that can be given to investment. Yet allowing for these, Catalonia has a more selective and less assistentialist approach to development. Services to firms are charged for and those that are not used are closed down. More emphasis is placed on private sector leadership, reflecting the existence of a local business elite. While Galician policy can hardly be described as dirigiste, there is a much heavier emphasis on government initiative and public funding. Catalonia is also more in line with contemporary development thinking in its emphasis on human capital, technology and innovation, while Galicia retains the traditional emphasis on physical plant. Consequently, development remains dependent on continuing subsidies, with little capacity for self-sustaining growth.

In both cases, the challenge is to move to a modernising regionalism, in opposition both to traditionalist regionalism and to a global neo-liberalism which would dissolve the region as a framework for public action altogether. This involves a conjunction of institution-building, cultural policy and economic development. Again, this has been more successful in Catalonia, but the limited deployment of Catalan in business life shows the limits to this strategy. It would be a great simplification to describe Catalonia as a successful region and Galicia as a failure. Both face the same challenge in building a development model and both have their strengths and weaknesses when looked at in a European perspective. What they do show, however, is that regions are not merely policy-takers, subjected to a single global model of development, but that different strategies, mobilising social and cultural resources, are possible.

4.   Belgium: Flanders and Wallonia

CONFLICT AND FEDERALISATION IN BELGIUM

Belgium formally and constitutionally became a federal state in 1993. In May 1995 the parliaments of Flanders and Wallonia were elected directly for the first time (the Brussels region already had an elected parliament since 1989), with the second elections in June 1999. Yet already in 1971 a first major revision of the Belgian Constitution had defined, albeit rather theoretically, the existence of the regions of Flanders, Wallonia and Brussels and of the French, Dutch and German language communities. The 1971 reform was in turn the result of a process of a societal and party-political regionalisation that had been going on for several decades. The creation of the Belgian regions is the consequence of a gradual territorialisation of the conflict between Dutch-speakers and Francophones going back to the creation of the Belgian state in 1830. The Belgian regions are clearly not historical regions or communities. They are the products of a conflict and of its solutions that occurred within the context of the modern Belgian State.

The two regions we are looking at here, Flanders and Wallonia, have their roots in the same reform of the Belgian state, but contrast in the way in which they have been defined and in the way in which they search for a way to identify themselves in the new political and economical context of the late twentieth century. The origin of Flanders is the defence of the Dutch language, which offers it an obvious identity. The gradual conquest of autonomous political institutions and the growing economic strength of Flanders have transformed it into a region that proudly combines this now assertive identity with its economic performance. Flanders is probably the European region in which the belief in a culture-driven development has been pushed towards its most extreme forms.

The Walloon region has a slightly different origin. As soon as the Francophone reaction to Flemish emancipation focused on the southern part of Belgium, as its homeland, it took a very strong economic dimension. Wallonia does not claim autonomy for linguistic or cultural reasons, but to be able to protect and re-develop its economy. There is no obvious cultural element in the Walloon process of region building, though the search for cultural markers to be added to the territory and to its economic definition is never very far away. The linguistic definition of Flanders furthermore puts Wallonia in a difficult position, since the French language does not coincide with the Walloon region. There is a third Belgian region, Brussels, that is also predominantly Francophone. When adding culture to economy, Wallonia faces a difficult problem of defining its exact territorial boundaries. For Flanders the combination and coincidence of territory, culture and identity is easier, though also disturbed on the margins by the presence of the Brussels region.

When Belgium was created in 1830 after seceding from the northern part of the Netherlands, one of the reasons to do so was the use of language. The other, even more important at that time, was religion: the Dutch population was mostly Protestant, while the Belgians, either Dutch or French speaking, were Catholics. The Dutch language of the northern Low Countries was not the language of the elites in the Belgian part of these Low Countries, and the newly created Belgium thus became a Francophone country. The very limited degree of democracy at that time did not take into account the fact that a large share of the Belgian population, actually a small majority, did not speak this language, but spoke a Flemish dialect (the common people) and Dutch (some of the elites), be it in a less standardised and unified way than in the Netherlands, where Dutch had been standardised for a couple of centuries. Yet the use of language rapidly became a political issue in the new Belgium, leading at the end of the nineteenth century to the official recognition of Dutch as a second Belgian language, spoken by the population of the northern provinces, but not of the elites of the north, who predominantly spoke French.

From 1918 on, when universal male suffrage started to translate into politics the existence of a Dutch-speaking majority, the language issue became fairly salient. A Flemish movement claimed full formal recognition of the Dutch language, but also, among other things, the right to organise education in the language of the people. This led from the 1920s on to the territorialisation of the conflict, because the claim of the right to use Dutch referred of course in practice only to the Flemish part of the country. A generalised bilingualism was never a real option. Belgium was thus divided in three linguistic territories: the Dutch one in the north, the French one in the south and a bilingual one. That bilingual territory was needed to account for the capital city of Brussels, a former Flemish-speaking city and geographically located in Flanders, which had expanded and had gradually become French-speaking throughout the nineteenth and twentieth centuries. The limits of the three territories were defined from 1920 onwards on the basis of a language census, to be organised every ten years. The higher social status of the French language however led to assimilation and pushed the language border in one direction, allowing for the further expansion of the bilingual area of Brussels into the former unilingual Dutch territory.

The conflict reached a high point in the early 1960s. There was not only the problem of the language censuses; the region of Flanders was now becoming economically stronger, after having been for a long time rural and backward. The south of the country, being one of the oldest industrial areas of Europe, was confronted with economic decline, and felt that the now Flemish-dominated state would not be willing to help them out.

In the early 1960s there was a near consensus on the need to reform the old unitary state institutions. One could see a mutual distrust of the Belgian state, and the acceptance of the idea that decentralisation might be the solution. The preferred options differed between the north and the south, however, in a way that marks Belgium's constitutional structure to this day. The Flemish side, given its history of linguistic struggle, defended devolution to language communities, which were seen as cultural institutions. This solution would imply that Brussels be included in the Flemish community, since it is historically a Flemish city and since Flemish people still live there. The Walloons defended autonomy, for economic reasons, for the southern region, in order to have the necessary powers to redress a declining economy. The Brussels Francophones, who are not Walloons, feared the Flemish domination and claimed a full regional status for Brussels, which would allow the Francophones to keep and to use their clear majoritarian status in the city. On the table were thus fully incompatible demands for devolution towards two language communities and for devolution towards three regions. The solution finally consisted of combining the two perceptions, not by finding an impossible middle way, but by doing both, by creating a double federation of both regions and communities.

At first sight the double character of the federation may seem awkward, because it involves a double distribution of competences. Yet there is a very easy logic behind it, in the sense that competences related to individuals (mainly state services) were given to the communities, while competences that involve a more territorial logic have been attributed to the regions. Both major communities are competent for community matters in Brussels, offering services in their respective languages for the inhabitants of the Brussels region. The regions and communities have received many competences, leaving few tasks for the federal level, the main ones being social security, justice and defence, for some technical matters in economic policy. The fiscal role of the federal state is however quite important. The regions and communities have a very limited taxing power, and the bulk of their budget is provided by the redistribution of tax income collected by the federal state (Deschouwer, 2001).

In this chapter we look at the two major regions of the Belgian federation: Flanders and Wallonia. That means that we have one region, Flanders, that is at the same time a language community and that expands territorially, but only for community matters, to the Brussels region. The Walloon region is confined to its regional territory and has only limited competences in community matters. It is linked, but not identical, to the French Community that expands into the Brussels region, where the French Community matters have been decentralised to a Community Commission taking care fairly autonomously of these matters in Brussels. This is an important institutional difference that we will have to take explicitly into account when assessing the way in which a region can rely on cultural resources. The institutional difference reflects a clear choice for a different self-definition within the Belgian context, and reflects the complex and cumbersome combination of language and territorial decentralisation. Flanders has an obvious cultural (linguistic) *raison d'être*, in contrast to Wallonia, which does not even have the formal competences to deal with cultural matters.

Flanders and Wallonia have more relevant differences, although it took some time before they were perceived as such. Most obvious are the social and economic differences. A number of areas in what was to become Wallonia were among the first in Europe to industrialise. The Flemish provinces remained for a long time mainly rural, except for some industry in the major cities like Ghent and Antwerp. In other words, in the nineteenth century the economic centre of the country was concentrated in the Walloon industrial basins. Yet the financial centre of the country was located in Brussels since all the holdings controlling Walloon industry since the 1830s had their seats there (Saey et al., 1998).

From the end of the nineteenth century, the old industrial centre in Wallonia gradually declined because the port of Antwerp and its hinterland attracted most of the investments in new economic sectors (Saey et al., 1998). In 1901 coal was discovered in Flemish soil (Limburg) and coalmines emerged after World War I (Witte et al., 1990). By 1930 the seats of the major industries and financial institutions were concentrated in the Antwerp-Brussels-Clabecq axis, constituting the new economic centre. Rural areas in Flanders and Wallonia still formed the periphery while the old economic centre in Wallonia had been reduced to a semi-periphery, joined by newly or re-developing areas in Flanders and Wallonia (Saey et al. 1998). Many of these newly developing businesses in Flanders were medium and small enterprises, in contrast to the large industrial factories of Wallonia. This gave rise to the creation of an endogenous, mainly Catholic, Flemish leading economic class whose interests did not coincide with the interests of the mainly Liberal Francophone financial bourgeoisie (Witte et al. 1990). The economic upheaval of Flemish areas and the decline of traditional Walloon industry boosted the Walloon movement (Kesteloot, 1998). Despite the slow but steady improvement of Flanders' economy since the 1880s it was not until the sixties of the twentieth century that Flanders finally caught up with Wallonia. It was also only then that employment in the industrial sector started to decline (Quévit, 1978: 112–113).

The consequence of a different societal and economic composition of the two regions is a very different party-political landscape. The regional cleavage reinforces and is itself reinforced by both the economic (class) and religious differences between the north and the south of the country. The consociational nature of Belgian politics, its pillarised or vertically segmented society and the deep penetration of party politics in both public administration and the civil society, has a very visible regional dimension (Deschouwer, 2002). Flanders is the region of Christian democracy, of the Catholic pillar with all its active auxiliary organisations, of a strong Christian-democratic trade union. Flanders has often been referred to as the 'CVP-state', which points at the electoral strength of the Christian-democratic party and even more at the dominant position of Christian organisations in Flemish civil society, which at have survived the electoral decline of the party.

Until the early 1960s the Christian democrats controlled more than 50 per cent of the Flemish vote. Even after a number of quite dramatic losses (especially in 1965, 1968, 1981 and 1991) they remained the strongest party. In 1968 the Belgian Christian-democratic party split in two autonomous unilingual parties, which reinforced the power of the CVP in Flanders. It became not only the largest party of the region, but also, given the demographic weight of Flanders, the largest party in Belgium. Only in 1999 did it lose its leading position, and thus the leadership of the region and the country.

The Walloon region on the other hand is dominated by the Socialist Party. Here the socialist pillar has its strongholds, the *Parti Socialiste* (PS) controls local politics, where it has strong ties with the dominant socialist trade union, and is involved in a dense network of organisations that offer services for the citizens from the cradle to the grave. The PS has also declined at the polls, but less dramatically than the CVP in Flanders, and the PS has been able to stay in office, both in Belgium and in Wallonia. It is interesting to note however, that in 1999 in the French Community (which also includes the Francophone votes in Brussels) the Francophone Liberal Party (PRL) became, by a small margin, the largest party. The competing definitions of the 'south of Belgium' – either the linguistic reference to the French community or the more purely territorial reference to Wallonia – are reflected in party politics. In a partitocratic country, it is difficult to grasp the real meaning of what is going on without explicitly looking at the dynamics of party politics.

Although the two regions have a different party system, and are linked in a different way to the party politics at the federal level, the absence of a truly Belgian party system confronts them both with a number of awkward problems. Most important probably is the lack of visibility of the regional level of policy making, and that is a very relevant feature for the processes of region building that we want to describe. So far the parties have tried to keep regional and federal coalitions 'congruent', that is to produce the same coalitions at all levels. This seems to be the best possible way to manage the multi-level game by actors that are only present and visible at the regional level. So far the regional and national elections have been organised on the same day, which allowed the parties indeed to play the game this way (Versmessen, 1995; Deschouwer, 2000). Yet it also means that in their communication to the population, in the discourse they use in campaigns and in the way in which they distribute and reshuffle their political personnel constantly between the different levels of politics, they present the regional and the federal levels as a single political game, as one single reservoir of power for policy making. After the second election of the regional parliaments in 1999, none of the three regional prime ministers had been elected at the regional level, or even presented as a potential candidate for that position. So, paradoxically, the strange double party system does not provide extra visibility to the regions.

With two major language groups, each having their own party system and thus also their own public opinion and their own forum for public debate, one can actually say that there is no real political centre in Belgium. Federal policy making involves dealing with the different sensitivities in both sides of the country. The media will report on details of their own side, and refer to the other side as the single Flemish or Francophone position. The solution at the federal level will involve and will be interpreted as an agreement between the two sides so that 'the centre is where the other is.' Federal politics looks very much like inter-regional politics and is obviously conducted or opposed by regional parties.

If the centre is where the other is, the two major regions and communities of Belgium seem to be very much locked into each other. That has important consequences for the way in which they see and define themselves. The two major regions and communities only exist because the other exists, and thus need each other to define themselves. That is often done in a negative way: the other is what we do not want to be; but by looking so often at each other, they might of course also imitate each other, take over the good ideas and strategies of the other.

FLANDERS

Culture and Traditions

Our unit of analysis here is the region of Flanders. Yet Flanders defines itself in the first place as a language community, including both the region of Flanders and the Flemish community in Brussels. Brussels is also a region in the Belgian federation, and for matters devolved to the regions Flanders has only competences within the territorial boundaries of the Flemish region. This situation seems ambiguous, but in practice it is less so. The difference between the Flemish region and the Flemish Community is the relatively small group of Dutch-speakers in Brussels, who account for some 15 per cent of the Brussels population, and a mere 3 per cent of the Flemish population of Belgium. The Flemish Community can easily function as a region with a fairly clear territorial definition.

If the term Flanders is today a rather non-contested concept, this is the result of the mobilisation for this entity since the 1850s. The current meaning of Flanders, referring to the linguistic-territorial collectivity, to the Dutch-speaking population of the north of Belgium, has slowly come into existence as the result of the Flemish Movement. The terms Flemish and Fleming are actually much older and at the time of the Belgian independence referred to all the Germanic dialects and to the speakers of them. Neither term yet had the territorial connotation that Flanders has acquired today. Yet already in the second half of the nineteenth century its activists had expanded the term Flanders beyond the old medieval county or to the two provinces of East and West Flanders, but it would take many decades for this broader meaning to become spread more generally. At that time the long and glorious history of Flanders was not seen as competing with the history of Belgium. On the contrary, the heritage of Flanders was seen as being at the core of the Belgian history (Tollebeeck, 1994; De Schryver, 1988), much to the annoyance of many current Francophone and Walloon historians (Hasquin, 1996). It is not surprising therefore that a separate and collective presentation of the five current Flemish provinces in the history books only occurred just before World War I (De Schryver, 1988).

If Flanders is nowadays associated with a rich cultural heritage, this is to a large extent the result of a conscious cultural policy conducted by the Flemish government. It could however only be successful in combination with the current strong economic position of Flanders. For more than a century the image of Flanders was one of rural backwardness. The thousands of poor and 'uncivilised' Flemish peasants (thus speaking a Flemish dialect) who emigrated south to work in the Walloon industry did a lot to reinforce that image (Quairiaux and Pirotte, 1978). For a long time the cultural reference of Flanders, the language, thus denoted low status, referring to backwardness, to 'poor Flanders' (*arm Vlaanderen*). Today this cultural reference to the nineteenth and the first half of the twentieth century has almost disappeared. The history of Flanders now rather uses historical reference points that relate directly to trade and economy, and to glorious cultural products. The medieval history of the county of Flanders, of its cities Ghent and Bruges, of its famous painters and of course of its then prominent place in the world as a trading region, allows it to draw a direct line between that glorious past and the strong position of Flanders today as a trading nation, as a nation looking at the world, and as a nation that can still be proud of its cultural identity and cultural products. Culture is indeed now seen as an important economic asset (see also below).

If the standardised Dutch is today the official lingua franca of the Flemings, and not a standardised Flemish vernacular, this is again the result of the mobilisation by the Flemish Movement. This took off in the nineteenth century as a romantic literary movement that turned later on into a political movement, demanding the recognition of Flemish/Dutch on an equal footing with French in the Flemish provinces. The promoters of a Flemish 'popular' language initially disagreed about which idiom to advocate, but they finally opted for the standardised Dutch as it had been developing in the Netherlands since the seventeenth and eighteenth centuries, and not for a standardised Flemish vernacular (Vandeputte et al., 1986). This did however not mean that the Flemish dialects disappeared. Standardised Dutch has indeed become the *written* language of the Flemings and this written version is quasi identical to the Dutch of the Netherlands, but the *spoken* language has remained different. Today most of the Flemings still speak, depending on the context, either a very local dialect or a form of 'general Flemish'. It is only during the inter-war period that such a 'general Flemish' (*schoon Vlaams*), differing lexically and grammatically from the standard Dutch, started to be used by some Flemish intellectuals at home. Before, it was solely spoken at official occasions (Goossens, 1975). This 'general Flemish', nowadays often called an in-between language (*tussentaal*), is not one single language. It is more like a continuum between the standard Dutch and the variety of local dialects (Taeldeman 1999; Goossens 2000). The use of this *tussentaal* further expanded with the gradual increase of political and cultural autonomy for Flanders. Everybody understands the standard Dutch, since it is the official language of education and of the Flemish media. But the 'home based' soap operas on television, one of the major assets in the competition between public and private channels, have in the past decade given the Flemish *tussentaal* a very prominent position in the media.

This ambiguous and sometimes even reluctant use of the standardised Dutch language can only be understood in the context of the ongoing relations with, and the obvious vicinity of, the Netherlands. The Flemish Movement fought against the unilingual French or French-dominated Belgian state, but the choice for Dutch as an alternative was in the beginning not an obvious or easy one. Dutch was the language of the country out of which Belgium seceded, and Dutch was also the language of Protestantism. Furthermore Dutch, in the standardised version developed in the Netherlands, was not the language spoken in the north of Belgium. In the early days of the Flemish Movement the Netherlands were geographically close, but politically and culturally rather distant. The Netherlands themselves also kept their distance. Since World War II, however, the Flemish elites have been trying to achieve a larger cultural integration with the Netherlands. By arguing that Flanders and the Netherlands belong to the same cultural community, they wanted in the very first place to achieve an upgrading of the Flemish image vis-à vis the French culture. Later on in the 1960s and 1970s, and in the context of a growing European integration, the linguistic link with the Netherlands was more and more used as an argument in the push for cultural autonomy for Flanders within Belgium. It is not surprising to see that the predecessor of the current Flemish Parliament, created after the constitutional revision of 1970, was called the Cultural Council of the Dutch Cultural Community of Belgium (*Cultuurraad van de Nederlandse Cultuurgemeenschap van België*). The reference to the Netherlands had for the Flemings mainly an internal Belgian function. The Netherlands, however, made sure not to get involved in this intra-Belgian linguistic quarrel, and did not share the Flemish idea that language and culture are fundamentally linked to each other. The only formal agreement reached between Flanders and the Netherlands is the creation of a linguistic union (*Taalunie*) in 1980. Meanwhile the political autonomy reached by Flanders has produced a shift in discourse from *Dutch* to *Flemish* culture (Steen, 1999).

Did this cultural and political emancipation of Flanders create something like a Flemish identity? That is a tricky question, and it has led to heated political and academic debates. Many social science theories would assume that this identity has indeed come into being (Deutsch, 1972; Anderson, 1991; Gellner, 1983). From the available research however it is not easy to formulate a straightforward answer (Kerremans and Beyers, 1996; De Winter and Frognier, 1999; Maddens et al., 1994). Intuitively the Flemish Dutch seems to be the most evident ethnic marker to differentiate oneself from the Walloon/Francophone and Dutch neighbours. If consciousness is added to the language (attachment or devotion to it), then only 20 per cent of the Flemings report a weak linguistic consciousness (Maddens et al.,

1994). Many do however believe that Flemings are essentially different from the Walloons, that they have a different culture. Previous research among Flemish and Walloon elites and population (Van Dam 1997; De Winter and Frognier, 1999) and our own research do confirm the general acceptance of this perceived cultural differentiation. The elites refer often to the cultural divide – after all it is the great divide between the Germanic and Latin Europe – as a legitimisation for the strive to more autonomy, though the latter argument is not shared by a large majority of the population.

Central in the auto-stereotyping of the Flemings is their work ethic: they are workers, not thinkers. This is not the Protestant spirit but the Catholic one, in which suffering hard and being able to suffer is crucial. Walloons also generally stereotype the Flemings as such. Flemings furthermore see themselves as dynamic and pragmatic (Van Dam, 1997). They are however often criticised for being very locally rooted, for having a high degree of *campanilismo*, for not wanting to move too far away from home to find a job, or for commuting over long distances in order to be home every day. This contrasts with the positive image of the Flemish openness that is mostly supported with the argument of multilinguism. Reference is often made to the relatively good knowledge of foreign languages by the Flemings, even if one is very much aware of the fact that the mastering of French is declining rapidly (Van Dam, 1997). Research conducted in 1999 revealed that 57 per cent of the Flemings are able to have a conversation in French, and 51 per cent in English (De Standaard, 20 May 1999)

The official discourse says that all the inhabitants of Flanders are Flemings. Yet when the Francophone minority of the area around Brussels is referred to, the discourse becomes more ambiguous. This Francophone minority is the Achilles heel of the Flemish identity. These Francophones are very much oriented to Brussels and to the French culture, and do not necessarily feel the need to learn and to adapt to the official language of the region, which is often not the dominant language at the very local level. Flanders perceives this as a lack of respect, which can easily be linked to the long history of non-adaptation of Francophones to the linguistic reality of Flanders. All Flemish governments so far have given a very limited and restrictive interpretation of the linguistic rights given in 1963 to the Francophone minority in a small number of municipalities around Brussels and along the language border, the so-called 'facilities' in administrative and educational matters. The Flemish governments want to safeguard the 'Flemish character' of the linguistically mixed municipalities around Brussels, by discouraging the migration from Brussels to that area and by encouraging Flemings to settle in the Brussels periphery (Beleidsnota De Vlaamse Rand, 1999-2004). For most of the Francophones, supported unanimously by the Francophone political elites and press, this policy is perceived as an unacceptable discrimination against the Francophone minority in the Brussels periphery. In these highly symbolic matters there is no common ground for a rational debate.

If identity is defined as a national consciousness (attachment to the nation and state), then a Flemish identity is the weakest among the younger age groups (Maddens et al., 1994). Furthermore we can see in the 1990s that in opinion polls the proportion of Flemings identifying themselves exclusively or primarily as Flemings is decreasing, after decades of increase. De Winter (1998) finds 27 per cent of strong Flemish identifiers. At the level of the population one can thus not see an increasing identification with Flanders. Opinion polls also show that the Flemish population does not demand a higher degree of Flemish autonomy and even prefers a re-centralisation of competences to the Belgian level. Demands for more autonomy are stronger among the better educated and among those who show a real interest in politics (De Winter, 1998). Yet the vast majority of the Flemish population has a very poor knowledge of Belgian and Flemish politics and political institutions (Cambré et al., 1997).

Political Leadership

As the result of the disintegration of the Belgian political parties, all Belgian parties are regional, and therefore Flanders has its own and separate party system. Christian democracy was long the dominant force and obviously took the leadership of the Flemish executive: Gaston Geens from 1980 to 1992 and then Luc Van den Brande from 1992 to 1999. A turning point came in 1999, when after new and heavy electoral losses the Christian Democrats were overtaken by the Flemish Liberal Party (VLD), now the largest party in an increasingly fragmented landscape. With its 22 per cent the VLD cannot dominate Flanders as the old Christian democrats did, but it is in a position to lead it. The same party also took office in the Belgian federal executive, including the post of Prime Minister. This puts the VLD in the same awkward position as the CVP before: it is the largest party of Flanders and thus leads the region, but at the same time this regional party has to fill in the Belgian leadership. That is a very typical double role that needs to be played by the Flemish political leadership, and that creates tensions within the leading party. Defending the region means often to go against the interest of the federal level, where a colleague of the same party is responsible for keeping the peace between the regions and communities. With Luc Van den Brande as the Flemish Prime Minister, pressing hard for more autonomy, this meant regular open conflict with the Belgian Prime Minister Dehaene. After Van den Brande the Flemish executive opted for a lower profile, but the tension between the two levels and thus within the leading party remains in-built and unavoidable.

Unlike Wallonia, Flanders still has outright regionalist parties, defending a larger autonomy or even independence. Of course all the parties, given the fact that they only mobilise within the region, are to a large extent regionalist, in the sense that they defend in a very natural and obvious way the interests of the Flemish region. From the 1960s the *Volksunie* was the main party demanding more autonomy and pushing the other parties in the same direction, to the point that they fragmented along linguistic lines. The Volksunie always faced a strategic dilemma: participating in the incremental reform of the state, or defending a full and pure autonomy and in 1978 suffered a breakaway of its militant wing in the form of the *Vlaams Blok*. The Volksunie was eventually dissolved in 2001, because it was unable to keep together the radical and more moderate positions concerning further state reforms.

While the Flemish population does not strongly identify with the region, political actors all to a great extent use the region as their point of reference. When the Liberal party changed its name in 1993, it opted explicitly and consciously for *Vlaamse Liberalen en Democraten* (*Flemish* Liberal Democrats). The Christian democrats went further when they changed their name in 2001, and became CD&V or *Christen-democratisch en Vlaams* (Christian democratic and *Flemish*).

Most elites do indeed defend a larger degree of autonomy, especially fiscal autonomy, but not a final break-up of the Belgian state. Flanders might eventually be able to survive economically without Brussels and without the weaker Walloon partner, but this is not seen as a desirable evolution. The Flemish elites think that a sort of Europe of the regions is, in the long run, a feasible and interesting evolution (Van Dam, 1997), though there are also many doubts about the exact and concrete institutional translation of this wish. Very few defend or accept the idea of an active cultural policy on the part of the European Union. They fear that this will lead to the disappearance of the cultural diversity and thus of the very cultural wealth of Europe. If Europe has to integrate culturally, then this will be the result of spontaneous evolutions and the spillover effects of increasing economic integration and increasing mobility. Social integration through social rights and protection is perceived as a more important goal to be realised by the EU in an active way. Many see the democratic functioning of the European institutions as the most urgent problem, especially in view of the further enlargement. The increased cultural heterogeneity that this will produce is not seen as a major problem – at least if one finds the adequate institutional set-up to deal with it – since Europe has to limit itself to the drafting of a general regulatory framework. Most

Flemish elites envisage some kind of confederal Europe of the regions, with a large degree of cultural autonomy for the member-regions.

The Flemish government has always been a very active and visible policy maker. The formal institutions of Flanders (government, parliament, and administration) have now to a large extent taken over the role and function of the old Flemish movement (Bouveroux, 1998; Deschouwer and Jans, 2001). They actively and – in the current institutional set-up also obviously – defend the interests of Flanders. The societal Flemish Movement, with its major yearly rituals and feasts, has become marginal and deeply divided, only getting media attention because of its glorious past and because of the current weakness and ongoing strategic quarrels.

Institutions

The Flemish Movement has always emphasised the need to foster its own elites and the key role these should play in development, a theme that remains today (Van Dam, 1997). Like the Quebec movement, with which it has historic ties, it believed that the region would only be able to develop if it would have its own cultural, political and economic elites, displacing the Francophone elites of the nineteenth century. As Flanders modernised and advanced economically, an important part of the new economic elites identified with the Flemish movement. As early as 1926 the Flemish Economic Union (VEV – *Vlaams Economisch Verbond*) was created by the first generation of Flemish entrepreneurs and the movement was reinforced after the Second World War (Witte et al., 1990). Today the VEV is an important pressure group, and keeps an eye on the degree in which the Flemish political elites defend the Flemish region both in Belgium and on the international scene. Its study centre monitors Flemish policy and it is generally very much respected for the quality of its analyses.

The VEV is a strong defender of an active role not only for the Flemish region, but for the regional level in general and it is prominent among the economic and political actors who have fully endorsed the idea of 'new regionalism'. It accepts the 'Eurocultures model' defended and spread by the Europe of Cultures 2002 Foundation and sees Flanders as a cultural region, in which societal factors plays a central role in steering and thus also explaining economic development. A strong regional identity, good practices of formal and informal social networking and a clearly formulated goal for the region are necessary inputs for regional economic growth. That is why the VEV itself wants to develop and defend these practices. It warns the Flemish political elites that Flanders might be doing well, but that it still needs to work actively to realise the right societal conditions for a sustainable regional development: 'regional identity, societal consensus,

communication, international orientation, trust ... have to become the
parameters of our social-economic actions for more welfare and more well-
being' (VEV, 1999). The VEV bases this conclusion on a comparison of 14
regions and smaller countries. Flanders, it says, seems to be lagging behind
because it still cherishes an inferiority complex compared with successful
regions like Bavaria and Catalonia, which are much more self-confident.
Flanders also needs to improve its administrative capacity and transparency,
the efficiency of its social partnership, its image abroad, and its long-term
policy vision. This is an ambitious programme, and the VEV plays the role
of the watchdog, reminding the Flemish government of its crucial task of
societal, cultural and thus economic region building. The most central point
in the VEV's view is the need for a broad consensus between all the social
and economic actors for the future development of Flanders. In 1999 it
called for a Flemish Conference to create this consensus. Although the
Flemish government supports the idea, so far only a 'scientific think-tank'
has been put into place, led by a former president of the VEV and by Karel
Van Miert, socialist former European Commissioner.

Since 1945 Belgium has an institutionalised system of deliberation and
consultation between trade unions, employers and the state.
Decentralisation of most economic policy has led to the creation of separate
Flemish institutions for social and economic interest mediation. In 1980 the
VESOC (*Vlaams Economisch en Sociaal Overlegcomité*) was created, in
which the Flemish government and the Flemish wings of trade unions and
employers organisations meet. If an agreement is reached in the VESOC,
the Flemish government will in principle execute and implement it. This is
an exact replica of the Belgian model. Federal interest mediation is,
however, still needed for matters and in sectors that pertain to federal
competences. Negotiations at the federal level are quite difficult, because of
the increasing differences in policy between the north and the south and
Flanders, again especially the VEV, often defends the idea of a fully
decentralised social partnership. The socialist trade union, which is very
strong in Wallonia, is blamed for sticking to old models and vested
interests.

For the trade unions, this situation presents difficulties. The trade unions
have regional wings, but are still Belgian organisations that need and want
to keep a coherent position. The socialist trade union, defending (like the
Walloon elites in general) the unity of the country, is therefore perceived in
Flanders as an impediment to a smoother consensus seeking. The socialist
trade union is also absolutely against the idea of devolving parts of the
social security system, as demanded by Flanders.

Flanders clearly has its own distinct civil society. We already mentioned
the total separation of the parties and thus of political debate and

competition. The media, including newspapers, magazines, radio and television, are all homogeneously Flemish. They use Dutch and cover only the Dutch-speaking part of Belgium. This distinct Flemish society is directly linked to the new Flemish regional and community authorities, since these are the source of the bulk of the policy outputs and especially of all the services offered to the population: education, culture and arts, sports social welfare, public transport, economy. Social and cultural organisations in Flanders will generally have the term 'Flemish' in their name. This is partly the result of the fact that former Belgian (and thus Francophone or bilingual) organisations were split up, generally on the demand of the Dutch-speakers. While the Francophones generally keep the 'Belgian' name or a neutral name, in Flanders the organisation becomes explicitly Flemish. Good examples are the radio and television companies. The former Belgian public broadcasting company BRT (Belgian Radio and Television) has been split up in two separate organisations: VRT (Flemish Radio and Television) and RTBF (Belgian Radio and Television – French Community).

Policy

The Flemish economic policy is a mix of what we have earlier (Chapter 1) identified as a 'nation-building project' and 'bourgeois regionalism'. Its origins go back to the early days of the still incomplete Flemish autonomy in the 1980s, when Prime Minister Gaston Geens launched his 'Flanders Technology' campaign (Schramme, 1999), but it was the governments led by Luc Van den Brande that really defined the new orientation. They stopped using public money to rescue declining enterprises and sectors like ship building or mining. Instead they focused on reinforcing the 'growth power' of the economy by stimulating an 'entrepreneurial attitude' focused on the new economy, and by fostering innovation. Also stressed was the need for endogenous development instead of relying on innovation from outside.

The 1990s were an important period for region building in Flanders. The political leadership of Van den Brande, and his deep belief in the need to put Flanders on the map and to produce a strong and winning combination of identity and self-confidence, of institutional strength and of active international promotion of the image and product of Flanders, gave a dynamic impulse to the still young autonomous institutions. This very assertive attitude did, however, face criticism, especially on the use of culture and identity as an economic asset and export product. The strong Flemish position of Van den Brande also made relations with Wallonia and with the federal level rather tense. After Van den Brande and his Christian democratic party lost power, the discourse was softened indeed. References to culture and identity are less prominent in the governmental strategy, but mainly economic policy follows the same line and is still inspired by the idea that Flanders as a region needs to develop and to finds its place in Europe and in the world.

The official story is that the Flemish economy is going through a phase of structural renewal, that the innovative strength of the Flemish enterprises is still too weak and needs to be reinforced. Flanders needs new centres of knowledge that can play a prominent role on a world scale. Since the economy of the twenty first century will be based on knowledge and brains, these commodities – rather than capital, one of the major beliefs of Van den Brande – need to be 'anchored' in Flanders. Education and formation should be better matched with the needs of the economy and, according to the official governmental story, Flanders therefore needs a more integrated 'region-based' management of the regional economy. The huge fragmentation of actors at the sub-regional level has to be 'streamlined', in order to bring all the 'live forces' together. The government wants to realise a number of infrastructure projects by setting up public-private partnerships. Culture is one of the explicitly mentioned growth sectors, which means that Flanders has to organise events of high quality and try to develop the Flemish design market (Beleidsnota Economie, 1999-2004).

Flemish policies and plans, including the demand for a more autonomy are now based and legitimised with market-oriented arguments. An autonomous Flemish policy, it is argued, would be better (more efficient, more effective, more client oriented) than the old Belgian policy style, and it could still be improved further if Flanders would have more competences organised in larger blocks. The lack of fiscal autonomy as an instrument for economic policy making is seen as a particular problem. Since Flanders and Wallonia are objectively different in economic terms, it is argued, policy must be differentiated. A uniform or unitary policy is seen as bad for both Flanders and Wallonia.

Not only is there now a less emotional and more business-like language in the way Flanders is presented and defended, the government has also moved away from one of the central ideas of Van den Brande on the relation between culture and economy. For Van den Brande the economy is culturally driven; values and norms do play a crucial role in the way a region can develop. This discourse, which had almost reached the status of a dogma in the 1990s, is no longer defended in such an absolute, straightforward and simple way.

Flanders has a clear political project, intimately linked to its economic policy and performance. Things are going well in Flanders, and the political elites take credit for this as the result of their deliberate and conscious economic policy. In general this has a more liberal flavour, certainly more liberal than the Walloon economic policy. The state should play a limited role as an enabler and facilitator. This attitude, and the difference with Wallonia became very visible when the federal level asked the three Belgian regions to participate in the new airline company to be the successor of Sabena, after this national company when bankrupt. The Flemish region refused to participate, saying that investing in an airline was not a core function of the state. The region was however willing to participate in the airport infrastructure, making economic activity by private companies in and around the airport possible. It was of course an important factor that Brussels airport is located outside of the city and on the territory of the Flemish region.

Policy continues to emphasise the Dutch language as the sole medium for communication and integration between Flemings (Beleidsnota Cultuur 1999-2004) but over time this has shifted in emphasis. While at one time, there was an absolute insistence on standard Dutch, leading to a certain insecurity on the part of Flemings, there is now more tolerance for Flemish dialects or *tussentaal*. There is still, however, a debate over the use of Dutch, standardised Flemish and dialects and whether Flemish region building should emphasise the first or the second. Linguistic policy was initially aimed at the dominance of French among elites, hence since 1973 a Flemish decree obliges all communication between employer and workers in firms located in the region of Flanders to be conducted in Dutch. The same goes for the communications between these firms and the Flemish administration. Now there is growing concern about the advance of English, especially in the world of business management and the same rules are applied here. This provision, protecting workers from the need to have to speak the language of their employer, is generally respected, and does not seem to harm investments in Flanders. In practice, English is informally used in many international firms, and a recognition that has indeed become the 'lingua franca' of economic life. For external relations though the use of English is widespread and not problematic at all. Yet a written communication in French in Flanders is absolutely out of the question. The history is still too close for being pragmatic about the use of French in Flanders.

Relations with the French community remain tense and problematic, particularly because of the continuing debate on the statute of the Francophones in the Brussels periphery, but the Flemish government has tried to normalise the relations with the Brussels and Walloon region. This is clearly a difference in style compared to the more nationalistically-minded governments of the 1990s, when on both the Flemish and Walloon side the tone of speeches was rather aggressive and rude. On the substance of the state reform and of the competences to be given to the regions,

Flanders has however not changed its demands for further regionalisation. It wants fiscal autonomy, the competence for organising parts of social security (health insurance and child aid), and a renegotiation of the existing financial equalisation rules.

The assertive attitude of the Flemish region in economic matters, does not find a counterpart when it comes to presenting or defending environmental policy. In this area the results are rather poor, and the practice of intensive livestock breeding (pigs and chicken) has caused some trouble. Drastic measures have to be imposed in order to reduce the number of pigs and to avoid excess manure to further pollute the soil. For one full decade now consecutive Flemish governments have produced so-called 'manure plans', aiming at reducing the size of the enterprises and the number of animals in general (De Rynck, 2002). These plans always caused animated debates and fierce refusals from the side of the agriculture organisations. The major one – the *Boerenbond* – was and is intimately linked to the Christian-democratic party and has always been able to put enough pressure on the party to avoid too stringent rules. But since the removal from power of the Christian democrats, things have not progressed. Environmental pressure groups and the agricultural organisations defend radically opposite views, and the government tries to find a middle way, which is in this case too slow a route to a cleaner environment. So productivist considerations have continued to dominate policy making, with no real accommodation to ideas of sustainable development.

External Relations

The Flemish region-building project has its roots in the Belgian history, but today it is very much oriented to the outside world, projecting Flanders as a region of Europe and using the European theme in turn to define the modern Flanders. An ambitious programme for the future of the region, produced again by the Van den Brande government, was entitled 'Flanders – Europe 2002', showing how the Belgian level had lost its symbolic relevance. Flanders is indeed very active on the international scene, and has been looking for partners to defend its view of a very culture driven regional development.

The Europe of Cultures 2002 Foundation is one of the most visible results of this Flemish project. It was established as a non-profit association under the Belgian law, and received a permanent secretariat in the Warande, a meeting place for the Flemish economic and political elite in Brussels. The Foundation brought together more than twenty 'cultural' regions and states, and organised many meetings and conferences, all focussed on the central theme of cultural identity as a motor for regional economic development. Although formally an international foundation, it was very much if not predominantly anchored in the Flemish region. The reference to 2002 is a reference to the seven hundredth anniversary of the 'battle of the golden spurs' on the 11th of July 1302. This battle, represented as the Flemish people defeating the French army near the city of Kortrijk, has given modern Flanders its national holiday. As in many such cases, the modern meaning of the battle is the product of nineteenth century romantics, notably Hendrik Conscience, and the historical Flanders of the time comprises only a part of the modern Flemish region. The Foundation was financed, supported and kept alive by the government of Flanders. Its programme was exactly the kind of story that Flanders wanted to tell the world and to share with other similar regions and small nation states. After the departure of Van den Brande, the Foundation did survive until 2002, but its strong link with the Flemish government is gone, which reflects the more moderate and less culture driven discourse of the post Van den Brande period.

Culture and identity play a strong role in Flanders' projection in Europe and the world, and have been linked to economic performance to foster an image of dynamism and creativity. The Van den Brande government had introduced 'cultural ambassadors', Flemish artists with some international reputation who received hefty subsidies to promote the glorious and dynamic image of Flanders abroad. The idea was that by showing the world the artistic and cultural capacities of Flanders, its economic capacity would also be appreciated. This too was moderated by the succeeding Liberal-led coalition, which abolished the cultural ambassadors, but cultural policy is still explicitly situated in a European and global perspective (Beleidsnota Cultuur, 1999–2004). Much attention goes to the Flemish 'cities of art' (Ghent, Bruges, Antwerp and Brussels). The political discourse links the glorious past, in both arts and trade, of the cities to the entrepreneurial spirit of the medieval Flemings to the current economic and cultural dynamic of Flanders. The official discourse thus now says that culture is not an economic product, but at the same time still connects explicitly the cultural to the economic development of Flanders.

Van den Brande believed that it was not enough for Flanders to be a star region in Europe, but that Flanders had to be politically present in, and also outside, the EU. It is not enough for the EU and the world to be represented in Brussels, which is the capital city of Flanders, but Flanders had itself to go to the world. 'Flemish Houses' were opened in Vienna, in The Hague and in Paris to bring together the diplomatic mission, the foreign trade service and the tourist service. Yet 'selling' Flanders to the world is not an easy job. There is some confusion about who is doing what. Belgium and the Belgian economy abroad are promoted both by the federal embassies and by the autonomous administrations for international trade of the three Belgian regions. Beyond Europe Flanders, like Wallonia, has problems of name recognition, although Brussels is slightly better off in this respect It has thus sought to expand its influence, especially in Europe, by co-operating with 'similar' regions (Beleidsnota Buitenlands Beleid 1999–2004), in consortia such as the Constitutional Regions or the Regions with Legislative Power that were formed to press for more regional input into EU policy making at the time of the treaty revisions of the late 1990s and early 2000s.

WALLONIA

Culture and Identity

The term Wallonia as the common denominator for the southern part of Belgium is even younger than Flanders for the north (Henry, 1974). Although there was never a medieval county of Wallonia or any similar reference point to be used, at the time of Belgium's independence the terms Walloon and Wallonia did exist and referred to the Roman dialects and the speakers of them. This is a situation quite similar to that of Flanders but the slower development of the process of Walloon identity-formation is notable. Belgian Francophone historians started to pay attention to the region as a whole only after World War II. The 1960s saw a real boom in the publications on Wallonia, coinciding, not by accident, with the real breakthrough of a Walloon political movement (Hasquin, 1996). This Walloon movement had remained very marginal until World War I and its influence on the political parties is negligibly small even until 1940 (Vagman, 1994).

The origins of the movement date back to the end of the nineteenth century, which is fifty years later than the Flemish movement. The first Walloon Leagues were created in Brussels, and to a lesser extent in Antwerp and in Ghent, by unilingual Francophone civil servants who felt threatened by the advance of Dutch in public life (Zolberg, 1974; Wils, 1993; Kesteloot, 1998). The movement is thus clearly a reaction against the first successes of the Flemish Movement. In the early years, there was no territorial basis for the movement, which was focused on the Francophones as a group and the defence of French as the main language of public life in the unified Belgian state. Although the defence of the Walloon cultural heritage was emphasised, there was no question of defending the distinct Walloon dialects or erecting them into a separate language; rather the emphasis was on the role of standard French.

The idea that 'Flemish Walloons' or 'Flemish Francophones' on the one side and 'Walloon Walloons' on the other side had different interests to defend, started to be mentioned in the early twentieth century. The linguistic laws of 1921 are seen in this respect as a milestone. These laws, regulating the use of language by civil servants, for the first time defined the area where French or Dutch would be the official administrative language, and which local municipalities would receive a bilingual status (Murphy, 1988). The language law of 1932 reinforced the principle of language being rooted in territory. This produced a further differentiation between the Francophone Walloons and the Francophone inhabitants of Brussels (many of whom were Flemings who had been assimilated to the French pole), and led to a gradual emancipation of both the Walloon and the Brussels wing of the Walloon Movement (Kesteloot, 1998).

If the notion of class plays today a prominent role in the Walloon identity, this has very much to do with the great strikes of 1960–61. These were in the first place the action of Walloon workers feeling threatened by the closing of the now unprofitable coal mines that were mainly located in Wallonia (Witte et al., 1990). Already from 1930 on the economic problems of Wallonia were playing a more important role in the discourse of the Walloon Movement, but until 1960 this was not taken over by the Walloon elites or by the Walloon population. A possible explanation for this ignorance of the coming problem is probably the fact that the economic balance between Flanders and Wallonia only changed to the advantage of the former from the 1960s on (Quévit, 1978). The closing of the Walloon coalmines was the catalyst. The idea that the Belgian state, and thus the Flemings who were starting to dominate it (*l'état Belgo-Flamand*), was to be held responsible for the Walloon decline rapidly spread as the basic credo of the Walloon Movement and now also of the Walloon elites and population. The great strikes of 1960–61 forged the link between the Walloon Movement and the Walloon labour movement, making the latter an essential ingredient of the former. At this point the Walloon Movement clearly stopped being a movement for the defence of a cultural identity. The strikes of 1961 marked the beginning of a movement defending the economic future of a territorially defined region.

These strikes were an attempt to protest against the economic policy plans of a centre-right government. The socialist trade union (strong in Wallonia) went for a general strike, but the Christian Democratic trade union (strong in Flanders) was rather reluctant to engage in this extreme type of action and the strikes failed because the workers in Flanders did not follow the movement. This led to a sharp awareness that Wallonia would have to deal with its problems alone, and that it therefore needed its own institutions for its own economic policy. These major events thus triggered the further regionalisation of Belgium, but did not produce an overarching Walloon identity.

The Walloon Movement never saw the defence of a Walloon culture and language as a primary goal, and never mobilised the population for it (Destatte, 1998). The Walloon *patois* are therefore less alive than the Flemish dialects. Standard French is the official language, though there is a characteristic and correct Belgian way of speaking French (Klinkenberg, 1999). The difference between Walloon French and standard (Parisian) French is however less pronounced than the linguistic disparity between Flemish and Dutch. Furthermore the difference is also less recognised because the official ideology stating that Walloons speak 'real' French is very dominant. The centralising effect of Paris has been and still is extremely strong, also because Wallonia is geographically so close to this centre of French language and culture (Klinkenberg, 1999). For years Francophone Belgian elites defended the principle that there were no differences between French culture in Belgium and in France (Fontaine, 1998). The discrepancy between the official rhetoric and reality has also led to a considerable degree of linguistic insecurity among Francophone Belgians. This did not disappear with the increasing political autonomy of Wallonia, unlike in Flanders, because of the complex institutional position of region and language on the Francophone side in Belgium. Confronted with a unified Flemish community, the idea of a unified French culture, still referring to the big partner in the south though stressing the Belgian context now, had to be valid for both Walloons and Francophone *Bruxellois*, so excluding a separate Walloon culture.

Since the end of the 1970s however there has been a certain Walloon cultural renaissance (Fontaine, 1998). Folk happenings again attract crowds, theatres staging plays in Walloon dialects are having success, old Walloon songs are being dug up and there is some interest for the preservation of the Walloon dialects. Although the older generation still speaks the local *patois*, the middle generation only understands them, while the younger generations are largely unfamiliar with them. The Walloon *patois* have also very much been Frenchified (Klinkenberg, 1999). Yet there are now courses in Walloon, although proposals to introduce Walloon language courses at school have thus far not been realised. Those defending the preservation of the Walloon language explicitly say that this should be seen as a collective enrichment, and not as an indication of closing oneself off (no *repli sur soi-même*). Others stress that what is important for the creation and institutional recognition of the Walloon identity is not the knowledge of the old popular languages but of Walloon history (Klinkenberg, 1999; Destatte, 1998). Even more important is the recognition of a Walloon cultural distinctiveness in the media, television in particular. Defenders of the Walloon identity feel that the Francophone public broadcasting company RTBF is too much a Brussels affair.

Yet all this is a matter of internal debate in Francophone Belgium. The 'single French culture' is still the official discourse, and is defended by the French community authorities. The majority of the Walloon elites adhere to this discourse and reject the idea that they have to go and look for a cultural identity in the Walloon history and tradition (Van Dam, 1997). The Walloon Movement of today, supported by a small number of intellectual elites, defends very much the typical Walloon difference, but has not been able to mobilise for it. It blames the institutions and especially the fact that Wallonia as a region has no cultural competences. Wallonia therefore lacks the policy instruments for building a Walloon identity (Destatte, 1998). Flanders, with its fusion of region and community, can more easily link region building with identity building or identity defence.

Walloons see themselves and their culture as open, tolerant and creative. Contrary to the Flemings, the Walloons are rather 'thinkers' and not 'workers'. To the Flemish capacity to organise they oppose the Walloon creativity, and also their *savoir-faire*. To the Flemish self-defence and closure they oppose their own tolerance. The fact that Flanders has a strong xenophobic right-wing extremist party and Wallonia not, is often seen as the proof of their own tolerance. Walloon elites often also refer very proudly to their grand industrial past, to their technological realisations of that time and the spreading of them all over the world (Van Dam, 1997).

Walloon elites very much stress the importance of multilinguism for economic development. They are aware of the fact that this multilinguism is still higher in Flanders, but they are confident that the younger generations are closing the gap. Figures for 1999 show that only 18 per cent of the Walloons is able to have a conversation in Dutch, and 26 per cent in English (De Standaard, 20 May 1999). Their knowledge of Dutch is certainly not yet at the level of the knowledge of French in the previous Flemish generations, but since the knowledge of French in Flanders is rapidly declining, they believe the gap will soon be closed. In any case, they insist that knowledge of other languages than French is crucial to be more open and receptive to the world, because English now outranks French on the international scene. The *Francité* must however remain an important and relevant network of countries and regions, helping to keep the use of the French language at a sufficient level.

One cannot say that Wallonia is today really a 'nation in the making'; it lacks both the elitist and the popular elements of it. As in Flanders but more so, the majority of the population identifies in the first place as Belgians. Only 12 per cent of the Walloon population in 1995 declared that they felt only Walloon or more Walloon than Belgian and the vast majority of these strong Walloon identifiers belong to the middle or working classes (De Winter and Frognier, 1999). While Flanders has a small militant fraction wanting full independence of the region, no such thing can be heard in Wallonia (Maddens et al., 1998). Only 19 per cent of the Walloon population defend a larger Walloon autonomy. Even if social security is excepted and can be guaranteed as a fully federal competence, only one third of the population would eventually support more Walloon autonomy. At the elite level nobody wants an independent Wallonia, and certainly not one without Brussels. Even strong Walloon regionalists believe that the tactical alliance between Brussels and Wallonia has to be maintained in the present circumstances, even if this means a cultural dominance of Brussels over Wallonia. An expanded autonomy for Wallonia (and for Flanders) can only be accepted under very strict conditions. The major one is that further regionalisation should not mean an economic and financial weakening of Wallonia.

This is however not unproblematic. Since Flanders does push actively for a larger autonomy, and since Wallonia is economically weaker and more vulnerable, many Walloon politicians who would indeed like to see a more autonomous Wallonia are kind of trapped in the alliance between the Walloon region and the French community. Cultural autonomy for Wallonia would mean the breaking up of the link with Brussels and thus a weakening of the alliance. The Flemish demands, and the rejection of them for their 'nationalist' flavour by many Francophone elites in Brussels and Wallonia, means that many demands for some Walloon specificity are immediately labelled as 'nationalist' and the term of nationalism is an absolute taboo in Wallonia, since nationalism is seen as a (bad) Flemish habit. The Flemings are believed to be nationalist and even racist and intolerant. The Walloon Movement struggles with this general discourse and tries to prove that it is indeed possible to mobilise for a Walloon non-nationalist identity (Destatte, 1998). The frequent use of the term *Communauté Wallonie-Bruxelles* instead of *Communauté Française de Belgique* is certainly a concession to the Walloon regionalists, though they do not see this as a sufficient step.

Political Leadership

Like Flanders, Wallonia has its own political parties and its own party system, but it is very different from the Flemish one. The most striking difference is the clear dominance of the Socialist Party. Until the early 1960s, it controlled a majority of the Walloon votes. Today its score is down to 30 per cent, but that still leaves it in the leading position. One reason why the Socialist Party remained that strong, is that it has incorporated the old Walloon regionalist parties so that, in contrast to Flanders, there are no regionalist parties in Wallonia.

There is a further asymmetry. Since the Belgian parties fell apart along the linguistic divide, there are Flemish and *Francophone* parties, the latter covering both the Walloon region and the Brussels region (with only a 15 per cent minority of Dutch-speakers). This makes matters more complex, since the political debate and party competition occurs within the French community, and not only in the Walloon region. The Socialist Party is certainly the leading party of the Walloon region, but in the French community the Liberal Party is the strongest, due to the strength of the Liberals and the relative weakness of the socialists in Brussels.

Leaders of the Francophone parties have a double role to play: they represent both the French language community and the regions of Wallonia and Brussels, of which only the Walloon region is homogeneously Francophone (except for the 50,000 German-speakers in the east of Wallonia who have their own community institutions). While in Flanders the institutions of the region and of the community have been fused, they remain separate on the Francophone side. There is a never-ending debate about whether one should give priority to the community logic (keeping the Francophones united) or to the regional logic (allowing for a different dynamic in Wallonia and in Brussels). The Socialist Party has the more prominent Walloon regionalists, while the Liberal Party tends to defend the community logic, not least because its strength is based on its position in Francophone Brussels.

While the Flemish political leadership has been strong and fairly personalised, with only three Prime Ministers since the early 1980s, the Walloon leadership has displayed a fairly high level of turnover. A very high turnover can also be seen for the members of the government, who easily switch between region, community and federal level.

The institutions of the Walloon region have only partly taken over the role of the Walloon Movement, which was always less important and less socially rooted than its Flemish counterpart. Some of its demands remain unrealised, and the complex institutions of region and community do not allow the Walloon government and administration to go unambiguously for the defence of the region as such. Yet the relatively small but active intellectual core of the Walloon Movement does have an influence on Walloon politics and policies. A good indicator of this is the impact of the *Wallonie au Futur* congresses (1987, 1991, 1995 and 1998) on the discourse of Walloon politicians (Destatte, 1998).

The Walloon government is gradually playing the role of active leader of the region, and does so in an increasingly European perspective. The aim is that before 2010 the Walloon GDP should reach the European average.

Today this is 88 per cent of the average (against 114 per cent in Flanders). A number of Walloon sub-regions still suffer deeply from the industrial decline and qualify as Objective 2 regions. The real Walloon problem is the province of Hainaut, which has European Objective 1 status, marking it out as a poor European region, although the funds will be phased out by 2006. Despite the European money that was poured into the province, it remains in very bad shape.

The Walloon government is clearly the first actor trying to really mobilise the *forces vives* of Wallonia. It has launched a 'contract for the Walloon future' (*Contrat d'avenir pour la Wallonie* – see also below). Yet the implementation of the CAW – so it says – cannot be left to the government alone. The whole Walloon society has to be mobilised. Everybody has to participate and one has to do it together. One should therefore get over sub-regional divisions (*sous-régionalismes*). These are indeed important. Provincial references, but also reference to lower levels of identification are often heard when Walloons refer to their *pays*. It explains why the government wants to stress the need to think in terms of the region as a whole. It is not easy, because these sub-regionalisms are also fairly strong within the political parties, and especially within the Parti Socialiste that is very deeply rooted in the local and provincial politics of Wallonia.

The government thus wants to play an active role, but not by dominating the scene. It wants to be only one of the partners of the region-building process, in constant negotiation with the other social and economic actors. Yet the major criticism against the project has so far been the very high profile of the government and its tendency to take the real leadership. The trade unions have already expressed their discontent and fear for the ending of the traditional social-economic negotiation and bargaining.

The research of Van Dam (1997), conducted in 1994–1995, showed how Flemish and Walloon elites had at that time a slightly different perception of the role of the state. At the Flemish side a more restrictive or Liberal vision of the state prevailed, while the Walloons defended a more active state, especially as long as the Walloon economy remains depressed. Although there have been visible evolutions in these attitudes, the stereotype of the 'state oriented' Walloons is still very present in Flanders.

The CAW only deals with matters for which the Walloon region has the competences. This excludes once more matters related to culture and, very important in this respect, education. These are competences of the French community, with which there has been no negotiation under the CAW.

Institutions

The class cleavage has dominated politics in Wallonia for more than a century and it still deeper and more important than in Flanders. The Walloon (socialist) trade unions have thus a long tradition of radicalism, making the conclusion of agreements between workers and employers more difficult than in Flanders. Criticism of the radicalism of Walloon trade unions is not new, but it acquired a different meaning in this context of the Walloon future contract CAW.

Promoters of Walloon autonomy were to be found among the Walloon captains of industry between the World Wars (Kesteloot, 1998). In 1945 the Walloon Movement, supported by the major Walloon companies, created the *Conseil d'Economie Régional* (CER) (Quévit, 1978). As in Flanders, the employers have their own Walloon organisation: the *Union Wallonne des Entreprises* (UWE), but its position in the region is quite different. The Flemish VEV has always had very close relationships with the dominating Christian-democratic forces, and has good relations with the Liberal Party. One can say that the VEV belongs to the core of the Flemish Movement, that it has been at the origin of the economic consciousness of Flanders. That is not the case for the Walloon UWE. The leftist and trade unionist origins of the modern Walloon Movement puts the UWE much further away from the core of the political leadership of the region.

As a regional organisation however, it does play a role and increasingly so in the creation of a conscious regional economic thinking and planning. The UWE organises and defends Walloon enterprises, and acts as a powerful pressure group that monitors the economic policy of the Walloon government. Like the Flemish VEV, the UWE asks for an active regional development policy, but its regional project differs from that of the VEV. The UWE does not at all adhere to a 'Eurocultures' model, but produces a more pragmatic economic discourse. When it criticises Walloon policy, it does not refer to a lack of identity and self-confidence, but to the need of economic reconversion of the remaining old steel industry, the need for diversification, the need to attract foreign investments. The government therefore needs to guarantee a 'friendly' environment for investors, a good area development planning, a drastic simplification of administrative procedures. Interestingly, the UWE warns against sub-regionalism, against the internal competition between sub-regions in Wallonia. Some areas – mainly the centre area – are indeed in deep economic trouble, while the territories close to the German, the French and the Flemish borders are performing much better. The message of the UWE is that Wallonia has to think in terms of Wallonia as a whole. That is the recipe for sustained growth and development.

Van Dam (1997) showed how for the Walloons the perception of the role of their elites is less important than in Flanders. Her Walloon respondents have the feeling that a Walloon elite identifying with the region and mobilising for it is still in the making and that the crucial networks are rather sub-regional than regional. This seems however to be changing, but it shows again how the process of region building in Wallonia, for the several reasons we have discussed, lags behind Flanders.

There is no clear and separate Walloon civil society like there is in Flanders. Again this is due to the fact that the framework of public debate is the French community. There are certainly a lot of Walloon organisations and activities, some also organised or sponsored by the official Walloon authorities, but the media are organised along the community lines. Newspapers, magazines, radio and television are mainly based in Brussels and cover what happens within the French community of Brussels and Wallonia. This constant ambiguity is a major obstacle for the development of a coherent and project for the Walloon region alone.

Policy

As noted above, the Walloon government wants to reach the average European GDP level in 2010. In order to achieve this, the Walloon government has presented, after a broad societal consultation and with active input of academics, an ambitious development plan called *Contrat d'Avenir pour la Wallonie*. Except for the concern with Wallonia's presence and influence on the European and worldwide scene, this contract still comes close to what we have labelled a 'social democratic' development strategy (Chapter 1). This is not too surprising when one is aware of the enormous weight and influence of the Parti Socialiste in Wallonia. The liberal partner, which joined the government in 1999 and now controls the department of economy has, however, been able to pull the Walloon official discourse a little bit more in its direction. Furthermore the influence of Europe becomes much clearer in the most recent policy plans and accompanying discourses.

In order to realise sustainable growth the Walloon economy – so says the official story – must become more dynamic and try to strengthen social cohesion in the Walloon society. Wallonia is a social region, relying on the equality of chances. Yet this equality is not realised today, because the region has a far too high rate of unemployment, especially among youth. The Walloon unemployment rate in 1999 was more than twice as high as in Flanders (13.1 against 5.6 per cent). Youth unemployment was 31.5 per cent against only 14.2 per cent in Flanders. By 2010 the ambition is that Wallonia's activity rate (today 50 per cent) should reach European levels of

60 per cent. That means the creation of 16,000 extra jobs per year, with a policy focused on training. The younger generations should acquire an entrepreneurial spirit (*esprit d'entreprise*) and more generally a spirit of success and solidarity (*culture du succès et de la solidarité*). Intensive language courses and special programs, especially oriented to the new technologies, have to enable the young Walloons to find their way into and on the labour market. The government says it wants the emancipation of each Walloon citizen in the society of knowledge (*société de connaissance*). For the development of this 'integrating knowledge society' (CAW, 1999: 21). R&D, the development of new technologies and networks between research institutes and the economy are absolutely crucial. Terms like innovation and renovation are used over and over again in the CAW. The whole plan also adopts the logic of endogenous development, based on the Walloon small and medium-size enterprises.

The task for the Walloon region is not easy. It is still confronted with a high level of unemployment, and with the devastating effects of the declining and disappearing old industry. Relaunching the machine by relying on a very different model of economic development will take time. The Walloon government also wants to speed up the development of the sub-regions now receiving European money. The planned reduction in funding from 2006 created some sense of urgency that can really been felt in the CAW project, which aims to lessen dependency through a new spirit of enterprise and innovation. Earlier elite research (Van Dam, 1997) showed that the Walloons seemed at that time rather confident that the region would recover sooner or later. The Walloon crisis was part of an international crisis, and that would not last forever. Though there still is some optimism around, one can hear quite some awareness that it might almost be too late and that one has to act without delay.

External Relations

Wallonia has grown closer to Flanders in its acceptance of the fact that the regional level is a crucial instrument for policy making, and that regions have a role to play on the international and especially on the European scene. Flanders and recently also Wallonia engage in international relations and networks of regions. Both are very active in the network of 'constitutional' regions that reflect about their role and place in the future European institutional framework.

Wallonia is thus increasingly presenting itself to the international scene. Its style is very different from the Flemish one, with more references to the culture in Flanders and a more economic discourse in Wallonia. Like the other Belgian regions, Wallonia has received extended international powers for all the competences that have been devolved to the regions. That means that policies like the promotion of exports and the attraction of investments are in the hands of the regional administration. There is a department of foreign relations of the region (*Département des Relations Internationales* – DRI) and an organisation for the promotion of export (*Agence Wallonne de l'Exportation* – AWE). These administrations present Wallonia to the world in English, and that seems a very natural thing to do.

On the international scene, the institutional tension or ambiguity between Walloon region and French community is also present. The French community is also very active on the international scene, and seeks to develop contacts with foreign partners, many of which are Francophone. Africa therefore receives special attention. The French community is present in the world with its own institution: the *Commissariat Général aux Relations Internationales* (CGRI), which deals mainly with cultural matters. Often the community and the region act together, concluding agreements in which there are both cultural elements for the community and economic elements for the region, but the combination of the two, that is much more normal and obvious on the Flemish side, is not seen by everybody as an advantageous combination. 'A *vernissage* (an exhibition opening) is not an economic contact', says the Walloon minister of economic affairs. It is not enough to be present with your cultural products. If you want to export or to attract investors, you have to focus on that aspect specifically.

The advantage of acting together with the French community though, is that the community and the region can be presented as the *Communauté de Wallonie-Bruxelles*. This explicit reference to Brussels opens more doors than only the reference to Wallonia, a small region in the south of Belgium. Wallonia has been able to attract Ryanair to the airport of Charleroi, and Ryanair is a growing company that offers good opportunities to show the Walloon hub to the world. But since the city of Charleroi is not well known (and if it is, it is known for its high unemployment and high crime rates), the airport is simply called 'Brussels South'.

CONCLUSION

Flanders and Wallonia are an interesting pair for comparative analysis. Both are constitutional regions that have received extensive competences within the newly built Belgian federal state. Both are engaging in a process of active region building, but they do so in a very different way. As such they offer show that there is not one single way of region building, that institutional opportunities, economic conditions, culture and identity can be used and combined in many different ways to produce a more or less coherent thinking and consequent policy making that refers explicitly to the regional territory.

In terms of institutions and competences, Flanders and Wallonia are different. Flanders, as a fusion of a region and a community, comes close to an independent state, though it lacks the fiscal autonomy really to go its own way. As a community it extends to Brussels, which for regional matters has its own government, but the Flemish presence in Brussels is so small that it does not really harm the definition of Flanders as a territorially based region. The community logic though defines the identity of Flanders: it is composed of the speakers of the Dutch language in Belgium. The Francophone minority living in the area near Brussels is again a disturbing, but not fundamentally harming, feature in this respect.

Wallonia functions in a much more complex institutional environment. Besides the Walloon region there is the French community. Not only is there a different definition (a territorial versus a linguistic), but the two institutions are formally separate, which means that Wallonia as a region alone has less competences than Flanders as a region-community, and it means especially that Wallonia lacks the instruments for conducting a cultural policy. Cultural identity in the south of Belgium is defined as the counterpart of the Flemish identity, and thus refers to language and language defines the community, not the Walloon region.

The two Belgian regions are economically very different. Wallonia has a long history of industrial development, and since the 1960s basically of economic decline and of difficulties attracting and developing new kinds of industries. Flanders modernised after World War II, and rapidly became the more prosperous region of Belgium. Flanders proudly exports its economic success, and has produced a discourse that links its current combination of economic success and emancipated identity to a medieval past of part of the region with a tradition of international trading and high quality cultural products. Flanders has a region-building discourse that is very much culture driven, although the high profile of the 1990s has been tempered more recently. Wallonia is basically in search of economic recovery, and defines itself rather as an economic territory with a great tradition of industrial and economic innovation and a potentially good future. Both regions are able to use and knead the history and the available cultural symbols to define or redefine the region in today's globalising economy.

Although the two regions are different, and engage on different paths of region building, they are intimately linked to each other. There is no real centre in Belgian politics. The federal decision making is to a large extent confederal, requiring negotiations and agreements between the two language groups, which each have their own civil society and own party system. The way in which one region is defined or defines itself, affects the definition of the other. They each exist because the other exists. Although they both try to develop their own autonomous route, they cannot avoid each other.

In this bilateral and confederal relation, Flanders is in a stronger position. Its unified region-community institutions, its clear identity and its economic strength makes it press hard for more autonomy, especially in fiscal matters. It is already using the small margins that are available to reduce its taxes and to raise the level of services offered to the population. Wallonia is not able to follow. Not only is there historically less pressure for more autonomy, its economic position today means that it cannot afford it. But being confronted with a richer neighbour creates quite some tensions. Every move by Flanders is seen as an attempt to break the national solidarity. Every reluctant reaction from Wallonia is seen in Flanders as the proof that Wallonia wants to rely on Flemish subsidies. Even if the federal state would help Wallonia to offer the same advantages as Flanders, the problem would not be solved. Federal money is not neutral federal money. The proportion of the Belgian GDP produced in Wallonia is 24 per cent, while its share of the Belgian population is 33 per cent. Economy is thus the nightmare for Wallonia, while autonomy remains mainly the Flemish dream.

5.   France: Brittany and Languedoc

CENTRALISATION AND REGIONALISM IN FRANCE

France has long been regarded as the archetype of the unitary state (Hayward, 1983) and it is true that the dominant tendency within the French state has been towards centralisation and uniformity. French political and administrative elites, trained in the *grandes écoles* like *Sciences Po, Paris* and the *Ecole Nationale d'Administration* (ENA), are imbued with the ideology of conceiving France as the one and indivisible Republic. Sociologists such as Michel Crozier and Jean-Claude Thoenig have shown, however, that, in practice, central-local relations in France are much more complex than this simple picture would suggest (Crozier and Thoenig, 1983). Prefects, instead of being governors ruling over territories dominated by the central state, have been intermediaries between the local society and the state and involved in a complex set of relationships with local 'notables' (Machin, 1977). At the same time, this system of mediation, dubbed the 'honeycomb' system, was more a means by which the centre incorporated and controlled the periphery, rather than recognition of the autonomy of the latter. A dominant feature of the French system has also been uniformity in both policy and administration with regional variations in regions such as Corsica being granted only grudgingly and with great difficulty (Loughlin and Olivesi, 1999).

The key levels of government in this complex system of intergovernmental relations, before the 1982 decentralisation reforms, were the central government in Paris, the *départements*, and the large and medium size cities, although Paris has been pre-eminent among the cities (Hoffmann-Martinot, 1999). There has been a tier of regional administration since the 1970s but this has been the poor cousin of sub-national government in France. Part of the reason for this is the official Jacobin ideology of the French state, which since the nineteenth century, has been opposed to regionalism and regionalisation, as these were associated in the past with reaction and opposition to the Revolution and the Republic. This hostility was especially manifested against those regions with a strong identity such as Brittany, Corsica and Alsace, characterised by distinctive languages and cultures which the French state made every effort to suppress although never quite succeeding in doing so (Gras and Livet, 1977; Loughlin, 1989).

Regionalism, as an ideology and political movement, never quite disappeared in France and, since World War II has experienced a revival under various forms, first as economic or functional regionalism (Hayward, 1969), then as cultural regionalism, finally as political regionalism (Loughlin, 1989). These different forms of regionalism made varied demands on the French state. The more extreme demands of separatism or a quasi-federal autonomy concerned only a few regions – Brittany, Corsica, the French Basque country, Occitania – and quite small numbers of people within those regions, although the political violence used in some cases, especially Corsica, ensured that the effects of their actions was out of proportion to their numbers.

Regional balance in France, encapsulated in the title of the geographer Jean-François Gravier's book *Paris et le désert français* (1947) became, by the 1960s, a cause of concern among influential members of the French political and academic elites. Active regional policy started in the early 1960s in a highly centralised mode. The aim was to address the underdevelopment of much of rural France (including Brittany and Languedoc-Roussillon), to integrate them into the national economy, and to prepare for European competition. DATAR (*Délégation à l'Aménagement du Territoire et à l'Action Régionale*) was staffed by a new generation of technocrats and aimed to by-pass the existing class of territorial notables, as well as the field services of central bureaucracies such as the *Ponts et Chaussées*. The aim of integrated regional policy and planning was encapsulated in the term *aménagement du territoire*, almost untranslatable into English. Growth poles were designated and the power of the state used to relocate large-scale industrial developments to the regions. The National Plan, the main vehicle for indicative planning, gradually took on a stronger regional element. Within some regions, new dynamic social forces emerged among business people, farmers, trade unionists and academics, the famous *forces vives*, and in 1964 the state sought to co-opt these into the centralised planning system through the CODER (*Commission de Développement Economique Régional*). The experience was a mixed success and many of the more progressive people abandoned the CODER in disillusionment at their lack of power in the face of the central state (Phlipponneau, 1981).

Efforts to link state regionalisation with bottom-up regionalism continued with De Gaulle's referendum of 1969, the failure of which led to his resignation as president. His successor, Georges Pompidou, opted in effect to hand the regions over to the old notables in the reform of 1972 in the form of the *établissement public régional* – an administrative entity with functions mainly related to economic planning and development. They were indirectly elected from the local governments of the area and their boundaries paid little attention to culture or historic territorial identities. Thereafter the initiative moved to the left, which in its period in opposition became more interested both in political decentralisation and bottom-up models of economic development. Following the Socialists' victory in the presidential and parliamentary elections of 1981, a large programme of decentralisation was launched (Keating, 1983; Loughlin and Mazey, 1995). The regions would henceforth have regional governments elected by universal suffrage and would become full *collectivités territoriales*, that is, with the same legal status as the *départements* and *communes*. They would also have the main role in regional planning and economic development, taking the initiative from below. Regional development plans would be harmonised with national strategies through planning contracts and regions would assume many of the powers of the state in according grants and subsidies.

The 1982 reforms were concerned more with *decentralisation* than *regionalisation* and even less with *regionalism*. Their initial aims were to bring about administrative streamlining and to enhance democracy by bringing administration closer to the citizen. Nevertheless, at least part of the reforms was concerned with strengthening the regional level. The problem was that decentralisation and regionalisation were not wholly compatible in that the former also upgraded the departments and communes, whereas full regionalisation demanded a clear choice between the department and the region. The new region was weakened still further by using the departments as the electoral constituencies of the regions, delaying the regional elections until 1986, and holding them on the same day as the parliamentary elections.

Decentralisation brought about real changes in the French politico-administrative system, although the results were not quite along the lines of the original aims of the reformers (Verpeaux, 1999). The first commentators on the reforms identified the main winners as the mayors of the large cities, the prefectures and, to some extent, the traditional notables (Rondin, 1985). While this analysis is still largely justified, it probably underestimates the way in which the new region, despite the difficulties of competing with the departments and the large cities and the obstacles of the regional electoral system, has slowly carved out a niche for itself in the French politico-administrative system. Some regions, at least, have managed to do so.

But this patchy nature of regionalisation indicates one of the most interesting consequences of the 1980s reforms which is the ending of the uniform character of the French political system and the introduction of a de facto asymmetry. Some regions, such as Rhône-Alpes and Brittany, have managed to exploit the new situation to their advantage. Others, such as

Centre or Languedoc-Roussillon have failed to do so. Furthermore, the twin processes of decentralisation and regionalisation are continuing. The Jospin government set up a commission under the chairmanship of Pierre Mauroy, who had been Prime Minister in 1981–2 and oversaw the initial reforms, to examine the question. Even if the results of this commission were extremely disappointing for those who sought further decentralisation, it is an indication that French decentralisation is a process and not just an event (Rapport Mauroy, 2000). The peace process in Corsica and the Jospin government's bill which gives the island a greater degree of autonomy and some limited legislative powers, have also contributed to a wide debate in France on the question of the state's territorial organisation (Loughlin and Olivesi, 1999).

Given the existence of strong cultural regions in France, it might come as a surprise that in fact it is the state that has final responsibility for cultural policy, although it shares this with the regions and other local authorities. Some regions have gained a foothold in this policy area by including culture under *aménagement du territoire* for which they do have responsibility. This highlights one of the problems with the word 'culture', which is defined differently by these various agencies and by different policy actors and pressure groups. For the French state, at least since the time of André Malraux as Minister of Culture (1959–1969), it means both the propagation of the French language and civilisation, and highbrow culture such as theatre, opera and classical music. However, another definition of culture is held by cultural activists in regions such as Brittany and Languedoc-Roussillon, where there exist non-French languages and cultures and whose histories do not coincide completely with the official history of France. These minority cultures and languages have been traditionally derided and suppressed by those agents of the state (particularly in the Ministry of Education) who believe in the superiority of the dominant French language and culture. This long-standing contempt reached its apex during the period of the *trente glorieuses* (1950–1980), when minority languages and cultures also seemed to be obstacles to the then dominant paradigm of regional economic development (Loughlin, 2000). This led to clashes between regional cultural activists and state representatives and were an important element in the increasingly vociferous regionalist movements of this period. The interpretation given to the term culture has practical implications in the educational, juridical, broadcasting domains as well as sign-posting and street names.

Even within the more mainstream statist definition, a problem has been to decide whether culture falls within the jurisdiction of the Ministry of Education or under the Ministry of Culture and what is the relationship is between these two ministries. There are also problems within the field services of the latter. With regard to the meaning of one of its responsibilities, *le patrimoine*, for example, it is difficult to know whether this refers only to buildings such as castles and abbeys, or also to customs and practices (Négrier, 1998a). These problems of institutional overlapping and of definition have led to difficulties for regions in elaborating coherent and effective cultural policies. Furthermore, the part of the regional budget devoted to 'culture' is quite small and covers a wide range of issues (see below).

This is the context necessary to appreciate the situation of our two case studies, which illustrate admirably the asymmetrical character of today's French system of territorial politics and administration. These two regions have basically identical political and administrative institutions but differ in their historical backgrounds, the strength and coherence of their identities, their economic performances, their political cultures, and their relationship with the French state. While Brittany can be characterised as a region with a coherent history, a strong identity and a successful economic history, Languedoc-Roussillon is a region with a chequered history, fractured identity(ies), and a problematic economic performance. In Brittany, despite internal political differentiation and conflict, there exist regional political, cultural and economic elites who have been able, at least since the 1950s, to work together around a regional development project. In Languedoc-Roussillon, the political, cultural and economic elites are deeply divided and incapable of putting together such a project. The remainder of this chapter will examine how and why there have been such contrasting outcomes, despite the existence of identical institutions. By controlling for the similarity of the institutional and state settings, the relationship between regional culture and regional social and economic development can be more easily analysed.

BRITTANY

Brittany in France

A major difficulty in discussing the Breton region is whether to limit oneself to the four départements (Côtes-d'Armor, Finistère, Ille-et-Vilaine and Morbihan) of the current *Région* or to include the fifth department (Loire-Atlantique) of the historic region. Analyses of Brittany which deal with its historical political, cultural and identity aspects, usually take the historic region with the five departments as the unit of analysis (Favereau, 1993; Monnier, 1994; Le Coadic, 1998; Nicolas, 1982). There is a great deal of justification in this approach as there exists a strong desire in the fifth department for reunification with the rest of Brittany. An opinion poll taken in September 2000 showed that 63 per cent of those living in the boundaries of the region and 71 per cent of those living in Loire-Atlantique were in favour of reunification (Armor Magazine, November 2000). Studies of regional policy and economic development (Morvan, 1997) and documents emanating from the regional council itself (Région Bretagne, 1997, 1998) usually limit themselves to four departments although there are some exceptions (Le Faou and Latour, 2000). In this chapter, we shall use the four department region as the unit of analysis unless otherwise indicated.

Culture

Brittany, like Corsica, is one of the most stereotyped of French regions, thanks largely to the works of nineteenth French authors such as Balzac (1829), Victor Hugo (1874) and Flaubert (1885). The picture of Brittany and Bretons painted by such authors was rarely flattering. Often there is an explicit or implicit contrast between French culture, civilisation, and state, conceived as progressive, enlightened, rational, and in every way superior to the region, which is seen as backward, superstitious (priest-ridden), alcoholic, speaking an idiotic and barbarous language, and in every way inferior (Le Coadic, 1998). In the period between the two wars, Brittany is symbolised for many French people as a particularly stupid and backward woman in the form of a cartoon character called Bécassine (the name is taken from a bird which was often found scratching the ground near churches), whose stories appeared in a number of French newspapers. Occasionally, Bretons themselves might agree with some of this description but give it a positive gloss, so that 'idiotic stubbornness' becomes 'intelligent determination' and 'priest-ridden superstition' becomes 'fidelity to one's religious traditions', but it was basically the same stereotype assimilated by the Bretons themselves.

This began to change in the last quarter of the twentieth century as the Breton economy became a success story and people of the post-materialist generation began to seek, in a neo-romanticist way, new natural paradises. In a 1991 SOFRES poll on *L'image des régions vue par les français,* 80 per cent of respondents replied that they had a lot or quite a lot of sympathy for Bretons, who came top in this regard among the French regions (quoted in Le Coadic, 1998). When asked which among a number of traits best described the Bretons, the top four were: hard headed (43 per cent); hard workers (22 per cent); genial (21 per cent); welcoming (19 per cent), of which the last three are quite flattering and the first could be seen as term of affection (but previously it had the more pejorative meaning of stubbornness). Bretons themselves have a sense of being different from the rest of French people but, at the same time, identify with France. The sense of difference is perhaps somewhat based on the stereotypes outlined above, but there are a number of more concrete characteristics that account for the feeling of differentiation.

Although Breton culture is wider than language, an important identity marker is the existence of Breton, a distinct Celtic language, once widely spoken, as well as a dialect of French called Gallo, although both the language and the dialect have lost ground in recent years to French. The Breton language has been a source of contempt and derision for Parisian French people. An indicator of this contempt is seen from the fact that one of the few words to pass from Breton in to standard French is the word *baragouiner*, meaning 'to speak gibberish'. This comes from two Breton words bara (bread) and gwin (wine), which are the words spoken by Breton peasants on their way to Paris and seeking a meal on the way. Because the French Government refuses to include a question on language use in its census forms, accurate figures of the numbers of speakers are difficult to obtain. In the 1950s, it was claimed there were a million Breton-speakers. This is an exaggeration but not too far off the mark. Francis Gourvil, in a study carried out in 1952, found that 700,000 people used Breton as their daily language, 300,000 more understood it and 100,000 were monoglot Breton-speakers. A study in 1983 revealed that 800,000 understood Breton and, of these, 600,000 spoke it with varying degrees of fluency. These figures are roughly the same as those of the INSEE office in Brittany who, in a 1990 study, concluded that 450,000 understand the language and 300,000 speak it. Finally, a recent study financed by the general councils of Finistère and Côtes d'Armor arrived at somewhat similar figures: 250,000 speak the language; 650,000 understand it (Favereau, 1993). Although the global figure of those who claim to understand the language is fairly constant, the number of speakers has experienced an important decline.

A number of factors explain this decline: the almost unremitting hostility of the French state to minority languages exemplified in the republican school tradition of Jules Ferry; the decline of the rural society which was its stronghold until the 1950s; and the low status of the language denigrated by French and some Breton elites as a peasant *patois* with little literary expression compared to, for example, Catalan or Occitan (with its history of medieval troubadour literature). This decline was accelerated during the period of the *trente glorieuses* when a perceived economic imperative made Breton-speaking parents switch to French when speaking to their children. It is remarkable that, despite these difficulties, the Breton language has survived at all. Today, a clear majority of Bretons, including those living in Loire-Atlantique, do feel an attachment to the Breton language and would very much like to see it flourish (Favereau, 1993),

The European dimension has, in recent years, become a factor in the linguistic issue (Le Faou and Latour, 2000: 113), although, the Région has had no strategy for exploiting it. It tends to be individuals or private associations who are involved at the European level, for example, through the European Bureau of Lesser-used Languages or through the minority language group in the European Parliament but they find it difficult to exploit these European sources of support because of the complicated administrative procedures for applications and their own lack of expertise. Nevertheless, Europe has been influential in a more indirect manner. European integration has contributed to loosening the tight grip of national governments over activities in this domain. As a result, regional actors have looked outside the nation-state both for inspiration from, and practical collaboration with, similar groupings elsewhere. Breton cultural activists have been inspired by the Welsh and Irish examples of, respectively, successful linguistic development and the promotion of a wider cultural agenda through music and dance.

The Catholic Church is also a marker of a broader Breton identity (Le Coadic, 1998). Although the high levels of attendance at Sunday Mass have declined since the 1960s, nevertheless it remains higher than in France as a whole. Furthermore, according to recent surveys, a large majority of Bretons remain attached to Catholic expressions of values such as community solidarity, the importance of marriage and the family, honesty and integrity. Breton Catholicism, however, has been a complex phenomenon. In some parts of Brittany, there was an alliance between the *curé* and the *château* and the Church was then a reactionary and backward-looking force. But, in other parts, Catholicism produced, in both its clergy and laity, some of the most dynamic and modernising figures in Breton society. In the 1950s and 1960s, Catholic movements such as the *Jeunesse Agricole Chrétienne* (JAC), advocated modernisation of the countryside through the application of the principles of solidarity and co-operation. This ideology became an important mobilising tool in the 1950s as Breton elites were in the vanguard of the resurgent regionalism in France in the form of the CELIB (*Comité d'Etudes et de Liaison des Intérêts Bretons*), although this was not an exclusively Catholic movement but drew on the wide spectrum of the *forces vives* of Breton society.

A superficial reading of Brittany's political orientation would simply place it on the right of the political spectrum, relating this to the strong influence of Catholicism and to its situation as part of the *grand ouest* of France. It is true that until the 1980s, when the Socialist Party made important gains in the region, right-wing parties were predominant and this was indeed related to the strong position of the Catholic Church in Brittany.

This general picture needs, however, to be nuanced by a more judicious political sociology of the region which reveals a much more complex political profile (Monnier, 1994).

Political Leadership

First, the predominant political tradition in Brittany is *centrisme* with a strong component of Christian democracy and this is indeed related to the position of the Catholic Church in Brittany (Ford, 1993). Analysing sixteen elections and referendums for the period 1945–1993, Monnier found that the centrist vote in Brittany was 22.1 per cent, in the West as a whole 20.5 per cent, against 13.6 per cent in France as a whole. In the immediate post-war period, this Christian Democratic tendency was incarnated in the *Mouvement Républican Populaire* (MRP). With the demise of this party in the 1950s, *centrisme* moved somewhat to the right and allied itself with parties such as the neo-Gaullist *Rassemblement Pour la République* (RPR). This right-wing drift of Bretons was to some extent a reaction against the excessive attacks on the Church and especially on Catholic schools by the anti-clerical left (Monnier, 1994). But Breton *centrisme* could also shift to the left once these attacks were toned down as happened with the formation of the new Socialist Party of Mitterrand in 1971. Many left-wing Catholics and organisations such as the previously Catholic *Conféderation Française du Travail* (CFDT) also rallied to the left in the 1970s and 1980s. In Brittany, the Rocardian (supporters of perennial presidential hopeful Michel Rocard), current of the Socialist Party, sympathetic to decentralisation and *autogestion* was particularly strong. So the new Breton socialism of the 1980s owed much to the *centriste* traditions of Breton political culture.

The second point that needs to be made about Breton politics is that, despite presenting a rather homogeneous and somewhat caricatural picture to outside observers, internally it is territorially variegated (Monnier, 1998). Some of the territories within Brittany have always voted conservative, while others have socialist and communist traditions. The conservative territories correspond largely to those regions with a strong Catholic presence, while the left-wing territories are mostly towns with a working class presence or rural and coastal areas, which experienced dechristianisation in the nineteenth century.

There is a strong tradition of regionalism in Brittany and several political parties and movements have been formed, known by the general term EMSAV (Nicolas, 1982). In the period between the two world wars, these parties adopted either an autonomist programme seeking to revise Brittany's position within the French Republic or were outright nationalist, seeking independence. During the Second World War, a small number of autonomists sympathised with the Vichy regime while others collaborated with the Nazi occupants. In general, these movements were on the right and, sometimes even on the extreme-right of the political spectrum. After the war, Breton regionalism took the form first of economic (or functional) regionalism and, in the form of the CELIB, had a great deal of success (see below). Equally successful has been cultural regionalism, with a vast flourishing of cultural groups and associations of all kinds. Political regionalism has had less success, at least in electoral results. A number of regionalist and nationalist political parties appeared in the 1960s and 1970s. The first was the *Mouvement pour l'Organisation de la Bretagne* (MOB), a classically *centriste* organisation seeking greater autonomy for the region. The *Union Démocratique de la Bretagne* (UDB) split off from the MOB as a Marxist variant of autonomist regionalism. There have also been a number of clandestine armed groups such as the *Front de Libération de la Bretagne-Armée Républicaine de la Bretagne* (FLB-ARB), largely inspired by the Provisional IRA's campaign in Northern Ireland. The FLB-ARB was dismantled in the 1970s but there are still individual sympathisers and small political movements, such as *Pobl*, which demands Breton sovereignty, and *Emgann*, an outright separatist group, have succeeded it. What is striking with regard to political regionalism in Brittany is its lack of electoral success. The UDB has managed to have a small number of councillors elected at the municipal level but has never breached the regional or departmental councils. At least one reason for this is the moderation of the mainstream parties, such as the Socialists, the UDF and even the Breton RPR, which have assimilated some regionalist themes in their party programmes. If a Breton elector has to choose between an outright regionalist candidate such as the UDB or a mainstream candidate with a regionalist discourse, he or she will choose the latter (Monnier, 1998: 348).

   Most of the political parties in Brittany have a strong identification with the region and are willing to collaborate to bring about its development. The ideological differences of left, right and centre and even of regionalism, are less important than the well-being of the region itself. The general pattern of relationships among the various groups is of collaboration rather than conflict although this unity may mask important divisions within the region. But these tend to be forgotten when it is necessary to present a positive image to the outside world, whether this is the French state, the international business community or simply tourists and consumers of Breton products. This approach clearly draws on strong traditions of identity but also of now rather submerged elements such as Catholic social teaching which emphasises collaboration and the common good rather than an individualist ethic.

Institutions

The regional Council operates within a complex politico-administrative system involving the field services of the state, the departments and the communes, including medium-sized towns such as Rennes and Nantes. Any particular policy sector will involve all of these levels of government although the actual configuration of actors and the relative dominance of any one level will depend on the policy sector in question. In the field of culture in general and regional culture in particular, for example, the state is represented mainly by *Direction Régionale des Affaires Culturelles* (DRAC) of the Ministry of Culture and the Rectorate of the Academy which is dependent on the Ministry of Education. The region, the departments and the towns also have their cultural policies supported by their own budgets. Sometimes, these policies are carried out by the agency or collectivity acting alone, sometimes in conjunction with the others. The general picture that emerges with regard to the Breton regional and local authorities is of a certain amount of harmony in key areas such as culture and economic development although there is also some rivalry as well, for example Rennes and Nantes have long disputed the position of being the region's capital.

The region, since its council was elected in 1986, has slowly affirmed its position within the politico-administrative system through a strategy of expanding its powers to the fullest extent within what is legally permitted (Morvan, 1997). A distinction should be made between *compétences énumérées* and *compétences extensives*. The former are what are designated in the legal texts and include the 'traditional' regional competences such as planning, economic and infrastructure development. In Brittany, there has traditionally been harmony between the region and the other local authorities in these areas. Over the years, new competences in the fields of secondary and higher education and training were added as new decentralisation laws were passed.

The region, however, under the leadership of its first two presidents, Marcellin and Bourges, did not limit itself simply to these enumerated areas but adopted (with little hindrance from the central state) an increasingly generous interpretation of the concept of the region's *intérêt général* which they saw as including urban planning, the environment, social and sporting affairs, and culture (Morvan, 1997). The budget devoted to these activities was never more than a tenth of the entire regional budget but Morvan sees the region as more significant than its institutional and financial limitations might suggest. According to this former president of the region's economic and social council, it has developed a *pouvoir de gouvernance régionale* through the exercise of five key functions: a) as a policy entrepreneur, initiating ideas and policies which would not have happened had it not existed; b) as a facilitator of groups and individuals bringing them to behave in ways propitious for their future development; c) encouraging a partnership-based approach in various policy areas; d) co-ordinating groups to form networks in order to maximise the results of their activities; and e) through economic, social and cultural concertation encouraging dialogue among elites in these areas. Morvan highlights the role of the economic and social committee in carrying out the last function. This rather optimistic picture by one who is admittedly an insider, needs to be qualified by referring to critiques of the administrative region from the more regionalist and radical groups within Brittany. What the picture does reveal, nevertheless, is the dynamic and evolving nature of the new system of regional governance inaugurated in 1986 and the potential for a particular region to exploit the new situation's ambiguities. As the region affirmed itself as a key actor in the politico-administrative system, it passed from being simply a conduit through which state subsidies were channelled within the territory to an economic entrepreneur and investor in its own right.

Brittany is characterised by a rich fabric of associationalism, largely deriving from its Catholic traditions but also from other traditions such working-class socialism and communism, as well as its farming and fishing activities. This can be seen even in the cultural activities of the *fest noz*, which involve the entire community in dance. Although it might be argued that this communitarianism was a myth, since Brittany has also been riven by conflict, it is a myth that has tended to become reality. The CELIB successfully exploited it in the 1950s and 1960s with the slogan *L'Union fait la force* as did the Catholic *jacistes* (members of the JAC) during the same period. Today, the myth has largely transformed itself into a feature of the strategies employed to bring about regional economic and cultural development. It is now natural for groups, even those with opposing ideological positions, to come together to achieve their ends. A representative of the Breton CFDT summed up the idea of *l'esprit breton*, arguing that 'there is a culture of concertation, a practice and a habit, that is more important in Brittany than elsewhere', pointing to examples such as the building of the Rennes Metro where concertation has produced concrete results.

External Relationships

Relations between Brittany and the outside world have been mainly in the form of cultural contacts and exchanges or events such as the Festival Interceltique. The region is also part of some interregional associations and not least the Arc Atlantique whose headquarters are in Rennes. The European Union is a source of funding for culture and the arts in general (Kaleidoscope in the arts, Raphael for patrimoine, Ariane) as well the other structural funds, which may have a cultural component. Furthermore, the EC founded, in 1982, the Bureau of Lesser-used Languages which has assisted with the adoption of a number of activities projects in Brittany such as the *Premières rencontres interrégionales langues et culture* in 1990, the publication of a Breton-language dictionary and various activities in the Diwan *lycées* (Le Faou and Latour, 2000: 113). Nevertheless, Brittany has not yet developed a strong extra-regional or international set of activities, although it is generally thought that this ought to be part of its strategy of regional development (Morvan, 1991). The region tends to look to its Celtic cousins for inspiration and the example of the Celtic tiger is a strong stimulant while the recent devolution of a Scottish Parliament has also sparked the imaginations of those Bretons seeking to develop such as a strategy.

Policy

Some authors have spoken of *le miracle breton* (Le Bourdonnec, 1996; Morvan, 1997). By this they mean the transformation of Brittany from economic backwardness and isolation after the Second World War to being the leader within France and in Europe in many areas of economic activity. This transformation was brought about by a number of factors, not least the activities of the CELIB, a movement that developed after the Second World War with a programme of economic regionalism (Hayward, 1969; Nicolas, 1982). The CELIB, consciously and with great success, drew on the Catholic corporatist traditions of Breton identity outlined above encouraging industrial decentralisation away from Paris and the development of an agrifood industry. Bretons travelled to Northern Europe and studied the Dutch and Danish forms of intensive agriculture and imitated them with success, making Brittany the leading agricultural region of France with 10 per cent of the French population employed in agriculture and producing 15 per cent of total French agricultural output (Le Bourdonnec, 1996). Many of these entrepreneurs were contemporaries and were formed in the Catholic youth movements of the 1950s and 1960s such as the JAC (*Jeunesse Agricole Chrétienne*) thus giving the Breton *milieu d'affaires* a certain degree of coherence. Some of the key figures were: Pierre Marzin, 'father' of the telecommunications industry who became managing director of the *Centre National d'Etudes des Télécommunications* (CNET), in Lannion; Yves Rocher, an ardent Breton and lover of plants; Louis Le Duff, the founder of *La Brioche Dorée*, a fast-food chain; Emile

Leclerc, founder of the supermarket chain; and many others.

This transformation of Brittany's economic performance has been very much an expression of the dominant economic models of the *trente glorieuses* based on Keynesianism, mass-production in smoke-stack industries and, in the agricultural sphere, the application of similar factory-type methods of intensive production. Today the Breton model is in difficulty as these forms of production have been criticised on environmental and safety grounds. Furthermore, the neo-liberalism of the 1980s, which dominated the Uruguay Round of the World Trade Organisation (WTO) and which has forced significant reforms of the EU's Common Agricultural Policy (CAP), are forcing a rethink of Brittany's agricultural production sector (Poussier, 1997; Région Bretagne, 1997).

Currently, many Bretons are seeking an alternative model of regional development, one which will both respect the environment and promote Breton culture. Sectors that are now targeted are telecommunications, tourism, and leisure activities associated with the sea such as thalassotherapy. Brittany, the second most popular tourist region in France, now emphasises cultural tourism. Interestingly, this process of conversion is also drawing on the same traditions that underlay the earlier economic miracle: a strong sense of communal identity and the capacity to work together for the sake of the region. But now the emphasis is on the quality of life of Breton society with its low crime rates and general sociability (Le Bourdonnec, 1996).

Culture, too, has become part of the new paradigm of regional development with an explicit link being made between the two phenomena from the early 1990s (Le Bihan, 1993). *Coop Breizh*, which was founded by the Breton cultural movement at the end of the 1950s to publish books and records, was already well placed to exploit this new approach. Today, it ensures around 80 per cent of Breton cultural productions and has become a major economic actor within the region with a continually expanding output. In 1995, the region and three regional daily newspapers (*Le Télégramme*, *Ouest France* and *Presse Océan*) supported the setting up of the association *Produit en Bretagne* to encourage both Bretons and non-Bretons to consume regional products. This association grouped together a number of companies found in the five departments: 62 from agribusiness, 9 distributors, 3 banks and one transport company. The success of this strategy may be gauged by a survey in 1997 which showed that 94 per cent of Bretons preferred to buy Breton products and that products bearing the logo *Produit en Bretagne* had increased their sales by between 10 and 30 per cent (Le Télégramme, 22 December 1997). There was also an attempt to promote a positive image of Brittany to the outside world on the basis of the quality of the region's products and of its environment. By 1998 the number of adherents of the association had progressed to 103 (Le Télégramme, 29 May 1998). Other initiatives along the same lines are *Création Bretagne*, which in 1998 had 17 members, and which promoted Breton exports on the international markets (Le Télégramme, 20 July 1998).

By the mid-1990s, the strategy moved from simply promoting the notion of 'made in Brittany' to one which incorporated more explicitly the cultural and linguistic dimension into marketing the product with the creation by *Produit en Bretagne* of a *Collège des biens culturels* alongside the *collèges d'industrie, de services, de distributeurs et de biens d'équipment* (Le Télégramme, 10 December 1998). The cultural college consisted then of fifteen companies involved in the production of music, books and photography. 'The cultural image is promising with the juxtaposition of a Breton identity with a rich cultural creativity to a society that is increasingly geared to the consumption of leisure' (Le Télégramme, 10 December 1998). Yves Rocher, the Breton perfume manufacturer, founded and presides the *Club Bretagne 21ᵉ siècle* whose honorary president is Joseph Martray, one of the founders of the CELIB. This Club makes the link between culture and economic development even more explicit and was behind the setting of the *Diorren,* an association of Breton-speaking business leaders, which, in 1998, numbered around 30. The aim was to promote the use of the Breton language in companies as well as in professional life. In May 2000, the *Klub Embregerezhiou Breiz* (Club of Breton Businesses) was founded by Breton-speaking company directors to make the link between the world of work and the Diwan schools to provide employment opportunities in Breton for pupils leaving the Diwan schools. Other associations include the *Club des Trente,* which groups some of the most powerful economic actors of the region, and the *Institut de Locarn,* set up by Jean-Pierre Le Roch, founder of Intermarché, and Joseph Le Bihan, a Breton-speaking professor at the Haute Ecole de Commerce in Paris. The Locarn Institute sees itself as a Breton think-tank of the new regionalism (see Chapter 1) and has a membership of 120 companies and associations (La Tribune, 21 September 1999). In practice, all of these associations have overlapping memberships and there is a great deal of consensus and collaboration among them as well as with the members of the region.

It is clear that many of these initiatives emanate from the business and cultural policy communities. What is not always clear is their relationship with the political and administrative institutions of the state and the region. We saw above that problems of institutional overlapping and of definition have made it difficult for regions to elaborate coherent and effective cultural policies. The DRAC's mission is to support culture in general and its director argues, with some justification, that it is difficult to distinguish between specifically Breton and non-Breton culture, when what is culturally produced in Brittany (for example plastic arts or orchestral music) might be classified as regional culture. Furthermore, the DRAC supports a number of activities which might be considered as part of a traditional Breton culture, for example traditional music or heritage sites. Nevertheless, Le Faou and Latour (2000: 119) conclude that despite these efforts by the DRAC to justify its support of Breton culture, 'it is nevertheless the case that the state administration within the region does not place a strong emphasis on specifically Breton culture'. This is also true of the teaching of the Breton language which falls under the responsibility of the Ministry of Education. There are three systems in place for teaching the Breton language: a) *l'initiation* (beginners); b) partial immersion; and c) total immersion. L'initiation involves introducing Breton language and culture to pupils in primary and secondary schools and, in 1998–9, involved 18,769 pupils (of whom 15,558 were introduced to the language). Partial immersion, available since 1982 only, means bilingual classes in regular French-language schools. Total immersion is the method used by the Diwan schools where it is possible to complete primary and secondary education totally in Breton. In 1977, when the first Diwan school was set up, there were 16 pupils. In 2000, there are 2,251 at all levels from nursery to the lycée (Le Faou and Latour, 2000). Education in the Breton language has been possible mainly through parents' and teachers' associations putting pressure on the French state which remains reluctant to support them through financial assistance, although in 2001, the socialist Minister of Culture, Jack Lang, proposed integrating them into the national education system. This was opposed by the 'lay' movements (*les mouvements laïques*) ferocious defenders of the Jacobin unitary state who brought the case to the Conseil d'Etat. It should also be pointed out that it is the private (that is, Catholic) educational sector, strongly represented in Brittany, which has been the most open to developing these initiatives.

The four departments of the region have also developed their own policies toward the culture and language, although not all in the same way or to the same degree. It is not surprising that Finistère, the most Breton-speaking part of the region, has the strongest set of policies in this regard. Out of a total budget allocation of 85 million francs in 1998 to culture in general, 17.2 million or 20.2 per cent went specifically to 'Breton culture'. This included assistance to teaching the language in schools as well as to adults, cultural activities and road signage. The *Diwan* schools received 3.48 million francs (Le Faou and Latour, 2000). In 1999, the department initiated a policy of supporting cultural associations through the signing of conventions. Côtes d'Armor comes next with an allocation of 4 per cent of its budget to Breton culture although allocated across a different spread of activities. Morbihan only began a specific policy towards Breton culture and language in 1998 while Ille-et-Vilaine has yet to develop a coherent policy but, instead, supports individual local projects. This is also the case of the fifth department, Loire-Atlantique, despite the large number of Breton cultural associations within its boundaries. The towns, too, have developed cultural policies and, as in the case of the departments, the strength of these varies in accordance with the strength of the language in that area. Thus, Quimper has a strong set of policies including financial support to the Diwan schools, to the cultural associations and to a policy of bilingual signage.

With regard to the region, culture is one of the areas where it has attempted to develop a distinct policy to some extent independently of the central state (Morvan, 1997) even if the part of the regional budget devoted to this area is quite small and covers a wide range of issues. In 1998, the region's allocation for *action culturelle* was 98.5 million francs out of a total budget of 3,125 million francs (Région Bretagne, 1998). The bulk of these allocations are devoted to supporting cultural activities in the sense of mainstream culture – theatre, audio-visual activities, dance. A small amount is allocated to supporting activities devoted to 'regional' culture, which includes festivals, shows and exhibitions. There has also been some support from the region for the Breton-language Diwan schools.

Support for the Breton language and culture by the region is largely channelled through the *Institut Culturel de Bretagne* (ICB) and the *Conseil Culturel de Bretagne* (CCB). The idea of the ICB goes back to the CELIB but it was only in 1974 that the newly constituted *Conseil Régional* decided to study the possibility of setting it up. It remained merely an aspiration until 1981 when the new socialist government gave the green light for it to come into existence as a regional institution (Le Nail, 1996). The *Institut*, originally based in Rennes but now in Vannes near Nantes, is at the centre of a network of Breton-language teachers, writers, researchers, architects and various cultural groups and societies. In 1986, a section of the Institute was hived off to form a separate *Office de la Langue Bretonne*, taking with it about six (half) of its full-time employees. The other main regional body promoting the language, the CCB, originated with an initiative from above, when, in 1977, President Valéry Giscard d'Estaing, announced that the government would sign with the regional council a *Charte culturelle de Bretagne* which 'aimed at supporting the survival of Breton culture in all its forms'. This *Charte* was addressed to all five Breton departments and the CCB was to become an umbrella organisation for most Breton cultural associations in these departments. It is composed of four 'colleges': representatives of local authorities; cultural associations and federations; institutions, and organisations concerned with the development of Breton culture; and, since 1999, public and private enterprises with a stake in the development of Breton culture. Although the ICB and CCB have a good relationship and work together very well, it is perhaps the CCB which best expresses the collaborative and communitarian approach of Breton society which we have emphasised in this chapter. Both bodies, are however, strongly contested by a number of civil servants responsible for cultural affairs at the regional level who would like to see them abolished.

Although, as we saw above, Breton culture in the wider sense is thriving, the language continues under threat of extinction, despite the fine efforts of the ICB and the CCB and the dedication of thousands of militants. The region with a few notable exceptions, has been criticised by these militants for its failure to develop a specific policy to safeguard and promote the language. For example, there is a certain reticence among Breton politicians to use the language in the council chamber even when they are competent speakers (Le Nail, 1996). There is no recognition of the language in official publications of the region nor is there is a policy of bilingual signage. The amount of the budget allocated to the language is extremely small. In 1996, out of a regional budget of 2.77 billion francs, only 70.75 million francs (2.9 per cent) were devoted to the Breton culture in general, of which 5.2 million francs went specifically to the language. It is true that if we add the 600,000 francs that pass through the Institut Culturel, the total share of the cultural budget devoted to the language reaches 9 per cent. The relative importance of the language, however, can be gauged by comparison with the budget for the Orchestre de Bretagne which, in the same year, was 7,687 million francs! (Le Nail, 1996). In 1998, the Breton region's allocation for *action culturelle* was 98.5 million francs out of a total budget of 3,125 million francs (Région Bretagne, 1998) but, again, this was largely devoted to general cultural activities rather than Breton culture in particular. Nevertheless, there have been improvements. In 1999, Jean-Yves Cozan, vice-president of the region and responsible for identity and culture issues, managed to increase the budget to 135 million francs (20.3 million euros) (La Tribune, 21 September 1999). This represented a 64 per cent increase in comparison with 1998. Furthermore, the regional president, Josselyn Le Rohan, has committed the region to supporting the language and culture as part of a more general programme of regional economic development (Le Faou and Latour, 2000).

We have already remarked that there has been an attempt by Breton cultural and business elites to link these two aspects. However, the much-vaunted Breton 'economic miracle' is now threatening some of the more attractive aspects of the image the region projects to the outside world. This has led to a new emphasis on environmental policy. The economic miracle of the 1960s did succeed in reversing the rural exodus of the previous years. Brittany produces today more than half of France's pork, 40 per cent of its poultry and eggs, and 12 per cent of its total agricultural production, with only 6 per cent of its surface area. But this economic success exacted a heavy price on the region's environment with the intensive use of artificial fertilisers and the pollution of its rivers and coastlines by nitrates and phosphates. Added to these internal causes was the pollution of the coast by the petrol tanker Erika in December 1999. For many years, the French state turned a blind eye to this problem and there was widespread evasion of environmental regulations by farmers and the agrifood industry. National and regional elites were satisfied that the results of the productivist model were good for Brittany but also for France as a whole.

This complacent attitude began to change in the 1980s as the French government began to adopt a more environmentally conscious approach and were particularly concerned with the problems in Brittany. Bretons, too, have become more conscious of this pollution of their environment and, indeed, are more so than non-Bretons. Surveys have suggested that Bretons are more likely than other French people to care about the environment. With the growing importance of the tourist industry and the generally favourable attitude of non-Bretons towards the region's products, it was vitally important to try to remedy the steady degradation of the environment.

Ironically, given Brittany's reputation as one of France's wettest regions, it is the seriously deteriorated quality of its water which has provoked an important mobilisation of political and administrative actors as well as the formation of environmental associations. Brittany is not only the region which produces the most processed pork, it is also the region which uses the most bottled water! One of the oldest environmental groups in Brittany is *Eau et Rivières de Bretagne*, originally founded in 1969 as the *Association Pour la Protection du Saumon de Bretagne* by fishermen worried about the deterioration of the region's fish stocks. Now they have a dozen full-time members of staff, about a thousand members and around 50 local associations.

This preoccupation with the quality of Brittany's water has led to the setting up of two policy programmes entitled *Bretagne Eau Pure* (BEP) followed by BEP II, which is primarily driven by the region but also involves a number of other partners including the EU, the state (in the form of the field service the *Direction Régionale de l'Environnement* – DIREN), the councils of the four Breton departments, and the organisation *L'Agence de l'Eau Loire-Bretagne* which includes the fifth department. The approach adopted by BEP has been to try to bring about a voluntary change among farmers and the agrifood industry to encourage them to a greater environmental sensitivity in productive methods. It has been generally acknowledged that the first BEP largely failed to make a dent in the increasing levels of pollution by these industries largely because the resources made available were spread right across Brittany. Now, BEP II has taken a more selective approach and it is hoped that a small number of successes, even if initially more limited, will spread through example (Décision Environnement, 1995).

The other major programme, run along similar lines, is *Bretagne Environnement Plus*. This programme was stimulated by the European programme Stride-Environment, which had involved 121 companies of the *Union Patronale Interprofessionnelle d'Armor*. *Bretagne Environnement Plus*, launched in 1994, grew out of this experience and formulated its aims as follows: to produce while respecting the environment; to use clean technologies, to manage waste, and to prevent and treat pollution (Le Monde, 8 August 1997). Again, like BEP I and II, this programme is based on the collaboration of public and private sector bodies, including the region, the state, the *Union Interprofessionnelle de Bretagne*, Citroën, and the gas and electricity utilities, GDF and EDF. Again, the approach adopted is based on conscientisation of the polluters and the reduction of pollution through voluntary co-operation (Décision Environnement, 1995).

These approaches show that Bretons seem to be drawing on their traditions of partnership and collaborative action to deal with the problem. The region set up *La Conférence Régionale de l'Environnement de Bretagne*, chaired by the regional president himself and made up of elected politicians, the regional and departmental prefects, representatives of associations, other qualified personalities as well as a scientific advisory board (Région Bretagne, 1999). The region has also developed an approach entitled *Contrat-Nature*, of which there are two types: *Contrat Nature Territorial*, which seeks to rehabilitate particular habitats; and *Contrat Nature Thématique*, which seeks to develop pluriannual programmes to protect species and natural landscapes right across Brittany (Région Bretagne, n.d.). The region will fund 60 per cent to a maximum of 500,000 francs for the first programme and 50 per cent to a maximum of 800,000 for the second.

Not everyone is happy with this promotion of a new model of sustainable economic development since, as one newspaper article put it, 'a whole approach to economic development is put into question'. There is thus a certain amount of ambiguity in the attitudes and policies developed by regional and local politicians towards the environment. One high official of the DIREN went so far as to claim that 'there really is no regional policy. The regional council adopts, for purely political reasons, a "hell for leather" approach in its activities with defining its priorities for number of activities (the regional politicians do not want to privilege one territory over another)' while the departments have no real environmental culture. According to this interlocutor, only the DIREN had an effective approach to these questions!

Whatever about these reservations and ambiguities, it does seem clear that the old Breton model has reached a crisis with its very success threatening the image which it has created. Some measures are being taken by the region and the departments in collaboration with a number of actors but it is doubtful whether these are extensive enough or sufficiently effective to reverse the degradation. For the moment, the outside world seems largely unaware of this problem and so the positive image of Breton identity held by them has not been seriously dented.

LANGUEDOC-ROUSSILLON

Languedoc-Roussillon in France

Languedoc-Roussillon is a more classic example of French regionalisation. As its name suggests, it is an almost entirely artificial region, cobbled together from five disparate departments (l'Aude, le Gard, l'Hérault, la Lozère and les Pyrénées-Orientales). One of our interlocutors, responsible for economic affairs, bluntly stated: 'Languedoc-Roussillon n'existe pas'! The region is marked by strong centrifugal tendencies. Geographically, it is pulled in different directions: the western part of Aude toward the neighbouring region of Midi-Pyrénées and its eastern part toward Provence-Alpes-Côte d'Azur; Roussillon, capital of P-O toward Catalonia in Spain; and Aude, in the east, (Genieys and Négrier, 1998). Culturally and linguistically, besides French there are two minority languages, Catalan and Occitan, but these have been more a source of dissension than collaboration among their militants. The religious history of the region has been marked by conflicts between Protestants and Catholics during the Wars of Religion, which today expresses itself in the conflict between left-wing Masonic republicanism versus the Catholic right, poignantly described in the autobiographical works of Marcel Pagnol. A principal task of the regional council has been to overcome these divisions.

Culture

Given the artificial nature of the region and the strength of these cleavages, it is difficult to speak of a specific regional culture and identity. It remains the case, however, that Languedoc-Roussillon shares the general culture of the south of France – the Midi. This is noted for its socialist, communist and radical traditions, which have given it the name of the *Midi rouge*. To some extent, this culture of radicalism was related to the republicanism of the

Protestant parts of the south. It was also a consequence of the kind of the kind of agriculture which predominated from the end of the nineteenth century until the 1960s. This was based on the mass production of cheap table wine in factory-type conditions using a large rural proletariat rather than the traditional French *paysan* small-holder (Lem, 1995).

The Midi of France generated its own myths and stereotypes. French is spoken with a certain accent, the pace of life is somewhat slower and more exposed to the beneficent rays of the sun than the North (a geographical reference which is, of course, relative and could be anywhere above Lyon or anywhere above Paris). The Midi is also allegedly characterised by a certain individualism and an emphasis on the local, rather than on a larger entity such as the region or even the state, which is seen as a distant enemy but also a source of benefits. The two archetypical figures of the Midi were the *viticulteur*, (as opposed to the *vigneron*) producing his low-quality wine, and the *notable* defending the interests of the *viticulteurs* through direct pressure on the French state (Gilbert, 1989). These two figures were *contestataires*, permanently in revolt. As Gilbert expresses it: 'Regularly, since the beginning of the twentieth century, the region [of Languedoc], with the notables leading, will put pressure on the state to play its role of support wine-growing or to protest if it thinks this support has not been sufficiently vigorous' (Gilbert, 1989: 17). This attitude of protest has sometimes been traced to a mythical *Homme d'Oc* going back to the period of the Cathars, Albigensian heretics forcibly suppressed in the thirteenth century but whose legacy of revolt has provided an important historical reference point in modern times.

All this changed from the 1960s, with the *grande transformation du Midi rouge* to quote the title of a recent special issue of a French academic journal based in the area (Pôle Sud, 1998). This refers to the change of the traditional system of mass wine production which collapsed and gave way to more specialised quality production and attempts were made to attract high tech industry into the region (Keating, 1985, 1986). Somewhat ironically, the 1982 decentralisation reforms profoundly modified the role of the *notables*. Traditionally on the left, they found their position threatened by the decentralisation reforms of the Socialist government at the centre as this meant, as far as they were concerned, a disengagement of the state and the drying up of the usual sources of benefits for their clients. This paved the way for the emergence of new elites, mostly from the right of the political spectrum. It also necessitated the construction of a new *imaginaire*. Gilbert (1989: 17) sums up the change: 'At the beginning of the 1980s, the region was faced with a number of political and economic developments which would turn upside down the stable relationships between a number practices (technical, economic and financial, etc.), strategies (political and institutional), and systems of representation …' all of which interacted and mutually reinforced each other. The coming into existence of the new region with the first elections in 1986 would add a further element of instability and tension as the right and extreme right took power in the council.

In effect, what emerged in the region was a struggle between modernisers, mostly on the right of the political spectrum but including some on the left, represented by organisations such as the *Jeunesse agricole chrétienne* (JAC) and the *Centres Départementaux des Jeunes Agriculteurs* (CDJA) and the traditionalists, mainly on the left, represented by the agricultural unions and the *Comités d'Action Viticole* (CAV). The former sought the development of a new kind of agriculture based on the principle of quality, the latter defended the traditional monoviticulture. At root, the modernisers accepted a version of the neo-liberal retreat of the state and advocated bottom-up, endogenous development, while the traditionalists wished to maintain the older system of heavy state intervention. Each tendency conceived the image and identity of the region in very different ways: on the one hand, a smart, proactive and dynamic image and identity based on the development of local resources; on the other, a dependent, reactive and static image based on the local development of resources handed down from above. Territory, too, is conceived differently in each model. For the traditionalists, it is the heavy 'matrix' within which actors operate, which determines the logic of their activities and which serves as a protection against outside interference. For the modernisers, it is a kind of background support which actors may use in a flexible manner as they respond positively to the economic, social and technological changes resulting from globalisation, Europeanisation and deregulation (Gilbert: 23-4).

Each of these models has been presented in a rather caricatural manner to emphasise the profound changes that have been operating in this region over the past thirty years. Each contains some truth but each exists simultaneously with the other although to some extent the new modern image is still in the process of asserting its domination over the traditional one. To what extent has it succeeded? There is little doubt that the old world of the traditional wine-growing areas of the Midi with their staunch left-wing defenders against the state has now gone forever, thanks both to the general economic transformation of agriculture and to decentralisation. There is also little doubt that a new class of political entrepreneurs has arisen projecting the new dynamic image. However, the modernising image is probably more characteristic of some parts of the region, especially the towns such as Montpellier which have a high concentration of research and development activities and which have attracted a highly qualified workforce from the outside. It is also found in those wine-growing areas which have switched to the production of high quality *appellation controlée* wines. Behind the stereotypes, then, is a highly complex situation of competing elites seeking control of the mechanisms of governance at the regional, departmental and communal levels, each trying to impose its vision of the region or locality.

These socio-economic changes have impacted on the region's political traditions. The *député du vin*, usually a radical or socialist was the archetypical political figure. The radical tendencies of the region were reinforced by the militancy of the winegrowers as in the revolt of 1907 or, in more recent years, the mobilisation of the peasants at Larzac (Touraine et al., 1981). The three departments in the east of the region – Gard, Hérault and Aude – were consistently on the left for most of the twentieth century, although in recent years both the right and the extreme-right have made inroads. The right, on the other hand, established a foothold in some of the towns such as Montpellier, where the *Union pour la Démocratique Française* (UDF) is dominant, and in the department of Lozère, where Jacques Blanc, *UDF-Démocratie Libérale,* has become the dominant force (Genieys and Négrier, 1998). Smaller political groups such as the ecologists and the extreme-right have, as mentioned above, established themselves in recent years in the region and have impacted on the political landscape.

Besides these dominant cultural traditions and images, there exist two minority cultures and languages with Catalan and Occitan existing alongside French. The situations of these two languages are very different. Occitan is allegedly spoken by 5 million people if one takes into account all its dialects from south-west France to northern Italy. It is also the inheritor of a rich cultural and literary history which goes back to the medieval troubadours and a society which was politically independent until conquered by the French monarchy from the thirteenth century onwards. Today, however, after several centuries of repression by the French state, it is regarded as a *patois* and hence marginalised and in danger of extinction. Catalan, on the other hand, although it is very much a minority language within Languedoc-Roussillon, benefits from its large and powerful neighbour across the border in Spain, the Autonomous Community of Catalonia. Catalan speakers north of the border benefit both culturally and materially from this association in a way their Occitan compatriots could not do. It is difficult to estimate precisely the number of speakers of these languages, given that there is a spectrum which ranges from daily use as a first language to understanding some words of the language. A survey carried out for the region in 1997 (Région Languedoc-Roussillon, 1998a) in the Catalan-speaking zone of Pyrénées-Orientales (Perpignan plus 46 smallish communes) estimated that 34 per cent could speak the language,

16 per cent used it often or on a daily basis, while 55 per cent could understand it. However, only a minority (48 per cent) are very or quite attached to the language, although 68 per cent are favourable towards bilingualism. Over half claimed that they could recognise features of Catalan culture, which are especially evident in: cuisine and gastronomy; the *sardane* (a form of dancing); local village festivals; the language; and Catalan music and singing. A similar survey was conducted on the Occitan language (Région Languedoc-Roussillon, 1998b). This covered a much wider geographical area with 131 communes including several medium sized towns. 19 per cent claimed to be able to speak the language although only 5 per cent used it on a daily basis. 41 per cent are very or quite attached to the language and 68 per cent are favourable towards bilingualism. A majority (56 per cent) thought they could recognise features of the culture: festivals and carnivals; shows based on local heritage; the language; media representations; and regional literature, stories and legends. With regard to this last marker of Occitan culture, it should be noted that the literary movement known as the *Félibrige*, based on the traditional language and culture, flourished in Languedoc from the end of the nineteenth century until the 1930s. It can be seen, therefore, that it is difficult to find a coherent regional culture in Languedoc-Roussillon except for the rather diffuse *culture du Midi*. Rather, there are several distinct cultures and languages with an important contrast between Catalan, which is generally regarded as dynamic and forward-looking and Occitan, characterised by conservatism and immobility (Hammel, 1996).

Political Leadership

It should be clear by now that Languedoc-Roussillon lacks an overall coherence in terms of its history, culture and identity. This is true also of its political makeup. While there existed strong political traditions as we have seen, these have been overtaken as a result of the great transformation of the region in the 1960s and 1970s. There is no regional political elite capable of developing and carrying through a regional development project in collaboration with the other local authorities as is the case in Brittany. The regional council, since it its direct election in 1986, has been dominated by the right, with Jacques Blanc as the most important leader. In effect, the targeting of the region was a deliberately strategy on the part of the right to counterbalance their weakness in three of the departments where the left has continued to be hegemonic. However, they have not been able to command an absolute majority in the regional council on their own and have turned to both the extreme-right National Front (FN) and to the greens for support. It is especially the rise and successes of the FN which has had an important effect on politics within the region, with its percentage score throughout the 1990s averaging around 17 per cent. This has given it a leverage in the regional council where Jacques Blanc has entered into a coalition with it to obtain the presidency. Finally, it is worth noting that, despite the existence of the two minority languages and the considerable regionalist mobilisations of the 1970s (Touraine et al., 1981; Keating, 1988), regionalist parties have never been represented in the regional council and, indeed, have had little impact on any of the levels of government. In the case of the Occitan regionalist movements, this is, to some extent, a consequence of the diffuse nature of Occitanism as well as tensions between the organisations representing the two language groups. It may also be because of the drift of regionalists towards the extreme-left which discredited them in the eyes of the electorate (Genieys and Négrier, 1998).

Institutions

The general picture that emerges of Languedoc-Roussillon is of a weak regional institution with a low capacity to develop and bring to fruition coherent policies even within those areas that have been devolved to it under decentralisation. Unlike Brittany or other French regions such as Rhône-Alpes, the region has failed to establish a dominant position vis-à-vis its departments and towns, and relations between the different levels have been conflictual. There are a number of reasons for this. First, there is the factor of partisan politics with the region led by the right-wing Jacques Blanc supported by the extreme-right Front National, while the majority of departments have been dominated by the left, and especially by the Socialist Party. Blanc has explicitly stated that he wishes to reduce the power and influence of this old guard in order to modernise the politics of the region: 'I wish to change the image of the region by casting aside the old Socialist shibboleths and embracing the new epoch' (quoted in Gilbert, 1989: 174). However, this is easier stated than done. The difficulty of the region establishing its hegemony over the other local authorities is illustrated by Blanc's experience in trying to set up a *Conférence des Présidents* (of the *conseils généraux*, the departmental councils) operating under the leadership of the region. Robert Capdeville and Gérard Saumade, presidents of l'Aude and l'Hérault respectively, forthrightly opposed this idea arguing that the departments should operate in an 'institutional space' independent of the region. In practice, the *Conférence des Présidents* constitutes an alternative overarching body substituting itself for the region. One occasion when there was almost a *union sacrée* between the region and the departments was in 1993 when the DATAR proposed that, within the context of the Latin Arc, some of the towns in the east of Languedoc-

Roussillon be linked to Marseilles (La Croix, 6 November 1993). This caused an uproar as it left the rest of the region excluded. Nevertheless, little came of the call to union and the different tiers reverted to their normal conflictual relations.

Added to this explicit opposition by the other tiers of government is the weak institutional capacity of the region which has difficult relations with central governments, even those of the right, largely as a result of the president's flirtation with the extreme right. It is indicative that, in March 2000, Languedoc-Roussillon was the one of the last French regions not to have signed the *contrat de plan Etat-Région*. These weaknesses have meant that the region has been absent from several policy areas, such as economic development and some aspects of cultural policy, where it does have a competence. This has allowed the departments, especially l'Aude and Hérault, and towns such as Montpellier and Nimes to occupy these policy terrains at the region's expense.

In contrast to Brittany, social relations in Languedoc-Roussillon have been traditionally both clientelistic and conflictual. The proletarianisation of the world of wine production meant a certain atomisation of the work-force and a continual battle against the forces of the state which it perceived as ranged against it. The *grands notables* of the left both represented and protected the population against the state while the latter periodically rose up against the state. With the *grande transformation*, this conflictual and individualistic culture remains but is now concentrated *within* the region as old and new elites compete with each other for control of the political structures of the region and the other levels of government. It also expresses itself in competition by the different parts of the region against each other: Perpignan and Nimes against Montpellier, Lozère against Hérault, Catalans against Occitans. In contrast to Brittany, there is no regional elite capable of generating and sustaining a mobilisation around the development of the region as a whole. Instead, there are mobilisations at the departmental and communal levels in competition with each other. The employers' organisations and trade unions are also weakly organised with the region and incapable of developing a common development project as in Brittany. The conflictual nature of society in the region has been exacerbated with the arrival of immigrants from North Africa and the racist reaction against them exploited by the *Front National*.

External Relations

Europeanisation has played a key role in the economic transformation of Languedoc-Roussillon. At first, though, the EC had a negative effect by introducing an element of economic competition from other the countries of

Southern Europe. Today policy actors and economic interest groups within the region see Europe as a source of financial assistance and avidly seek EU grants. At the regional level, Jacques Blanc has played an important role in this European orientation although there is a great deal of competition between the region and the departments and communes for EU funds. The region has also been active in developing cross-border links with its neighbours through the *Communauté de Travail des Pyrénnées* (involving three French regions; four Spanish autonomous communities and the state of Andorra) and the *Eurégion Catalogne/Midi Pyrénées/Langudoc-Roussillon*. According to one left-wing member of the regional council, however, most of these initiatives are *en panne* (broken down). It has also been argued that these external activities are a compensation for weakness *within* the region and the latter's lack of hegemony over the other levels of local government. Among the general population most inhabitants are today pro-EU, despite their previous hostility. For growers of good quality wines, Europe was appreciated because it controlled the mass production of low-quality wines. For the fruit-growers, there is the expectation that Europe will help bring about an important reconstruction of French agriculture. Whatever the arguments, these are massive changes of attitude compared to the hostility towards Europe shown by these groups in the 1980s.

This does not mean that everyone is a Europhile or that the old radicalism has disappeared. A (French) Catalan economic network, known as the G16, for example, is rather less positive towards Europe. This group thinks the EU is more relevant for large businesses rather than the small and medium enterprises which they represent. Furthermore, they think their interests are better represented in Europe by national politicians rather than European *députés*. Nevertheless, they, too, reckon that Europe 'should be part of their future orientations'.

Policy

There is one important similarity between Brittany and Languedoc-Roussillon. Both have been traditionally agricultural regions with a high percentage of the population employed in this sector. However, there are many differences in the kind of agriculture and in the changes that have occurred since the 1950s. Traditional Breton agriculture was composed of small farms which were replaced by large industrial-type units in the 1960s. In contrast, industrial-type wine production was dominant in Languedoc-Roussillon until it was replaced during the same period by higher quality *vins de table* and *appellation controlée* wines. Curiously, the reasons for the change were similar: the effects of the European Community's Common Agricultural Policy which encouraged Bretons into mass production while

Languedocians became unable to compete, especially after the accession of Portugal and Spain, with cheaper wines from Southern Europe (Touzard and Laporte, 1998; Gavignaau-Fontaine, 1998). There is practically no tradition of heavy industry in the region, with the exception of a few mining enterprises.

In Languedoc-Roussillon, the region and the localities were forced to reinvent themselves faced with these economic challenges (Smith, 1998). In a sense, the lack of heavy industry was an advantage, since this meant there was no need to deal with the consequences of its decline nor with serious environmental degradation. New economic sectors, based on small and medium enterprises and in the fields of new technology, services and tourism, could be developed. This has led to important economic growth in some geographical locations, especially in Montpellier and Nimes and along the littoral, but has meant a destabilisation in others (Genieys and Négrier, 1998). In national terms, the region has one of the largest service sectors and is the fastest growing in this field, with a record growth of those working in research, as well as being a leader in tourism. This new economy has meant that Languedoc-Roussillon has the fasted growing population, largely as a result of immigration, of all the French regions, although this also includes a number of retired people, migrating to the south because of its beneficent climate. Nevertheless, the internal imbalances of the region are clear from the fact that, despite these features of strong economic growth, the GDP of the region, at 195.7 million francs (1996) is below the average of the French regions as a whole, which means the existence of large areas of underdevelopment. These economic developments have had an important impact on the image of the region and, in fact, have contributed to the construction of a new more modern identity by key policy makers.

The region has responsibility for devising an overall economic strategy for the region and, like all of the French regions, is meant to do so in close collaboration with the state through the *contrat de plan État-Région*. In 1991, in the context of the preparation of the eleventh national plan, it set up a *Commission régionale de Prospective Stratégie 2000* to assess the strengths and weaknesses of the region and to devise a strategy for mobilising its resources (Genieys and Négrier, 1998). The Commission produced a document entitled *Stratégie 2000*, which advocated the development of those areas located away from the littoral and to produce a more balanced economic profile. According to this analysis, the challenges were: the production of quality goods; communications (telecommunications as well as transport links); social and territorial integration; intra- and inter-regional co-operation; intercommunality; co-operation with other European regions especially those in the Mediterranean and providing a hospitable welcome for new arrivals. To meet these challenges the document proposed a strategy based on three axes: training; competitiveness; spatial planning. What is striking in this wish list is its similarity with regional development models found right across Europe: the notion of the learning, innovative region, mobilising internal resources in order to compete, but also to collaborate with, other European regions in a broader international context.

In order to implement such a programme, the region must act in concertation with the state, the department and the communes, following the logic of the division of powers in blocks as a result of the French decentralisation reforms. Within this system the region was supposed to be the lead player. In Languedoc-Roussillon, this has manifestly failed to happen. In fact, there is a very confused situation in which distinct contracts are signed by the different partners independently of each other: between the state and the towns and even between departments and small communes (Genieys and Négrier, 1998). The co-ordinating role of the region has been extremely weak and even non-existent.

There is, thus, little evidence that the region has managed to develop a successful and coherent strategy of economic development for the entire region. Rather, while it has developed a number of initiatives, it has been seriously challenged by the departments and the larger towns for leadership in this area. Nor has it succeeded in projecting the notion of a strong regional and identity and culture, either internally within the region or externally to the outside world. A former regional prefect, Bernard Gérard, admitted as much when he spoke of Languedoc-Roussillon as having a *culture du paradoxe*: 'Occitan, Cevenese and Catalan, but also Cathar and Provençal, Languedoc-Roussillon is a region with many identities'. At least, the image of the region has changed from the notion of the *Midi rouge* to a more modern one of high-tech development and quality products but this has been more a result of the activities of policy entrepreneurs at the departmental and local levels than of the regional council.

Despite these difficulties in creating a common regional identity and culture, there is an appreciation on the part of different policy actors of the possibilities of linking economic development and cultural activities. According to Daniel Constantin (1998), regional prefect in 1998, it is the state which takes the lead in this with a budget of 195 million francs devoted to cultural activities in 1997 and 210 million francs in 1998. This covered a wide range of activities from heritage (*patrimoine*) to libraries (*la lecture publique*) with 280 persons directly employed by the Ministry of Culture and Communication and 8,252 employed in cultural activities in general. This made Languedoc-Roussillon fifth among French regions for the number of people employed in this sector (Préfecture de la Région

Languedoc-Roussillon, 1997). Culture is here understood in a very wide sense and few of these enumerated here are employed in cultural activities that are specifically regional.

Languedoc-Roussillon has developed a cultural policy more slowly and less coherently than Brittany, which, as we have seen, has itself been rather slow, despite being an area Jacques Blanc, an Occitan speaker, wished to develop. This is a result of two principal factors: the weakness of the regional institution and the fragmentation of the regional society but particularly of the cultural associations (Hammel, 1996). The antagonism between Catalan and Occitan associations is crucial here. Before the setting up of the region in 1982, two separate organisations were created in 1977. The *Centre d'Etudes, de Documentation et d'Animation de la Culture Catalane* (CEDACC) was founded in Perpignan following meetings between the mayor and a cultural activist called Paul Alduy. The *Centre International de Documentation Occitane* (CIDO) was established at Béziers by Paul Brousse and Yves Rouguette, both cultural activists. However, from the beginning the two organisations differed both in the personalities directing them and in their orientations.

In 1980, the *établissement public régional* set up un *Office Régional de la Culture* but the conflict continued. The transformation of the region in 1984 under the decentralisation laws failed to mitigate the conflict and it was only from 1985 onwards that it began to settle down. In 1986, the newly elected region began to develop a more coherent cultural policy with increasing resources devoted to regional culture. By 1987, the budget devoted to the *Mission de la Culture* was 5.5 million francs (Hammel, 1996). The most important initiative was the revamping of the CIDO by Jacques Blanc and the region, in collaboration with the municipality of Béziers, and its transformation into the *Centre Inter-Régional de Développement de l'Occitan* (CIRDOC). This placed relations between the region and the Occitan cultural movements on a new footing. The region has also contributed financially to the minority language schools. However, these initiatives have failed to create a common sense of identity among Catalan and Occitan cultural movements. Jacques Blanc has played the cultural card in the region but has been hampered by the reticence of his allies in the *Front National*, opposed in principle to minority cultures and by the suspicion of the cultural movements outside of the regional institutions. With regard to mobilisation around themes of identity, it is in fact, the departments and towns that are more important than the region. For example, the department of L'Hérault launched, with EU funding, a tourism project around the notion of the *Pays Cathare*. The region was practically absent from this project (Dedieu and Genieys, 1998). In 1999, the medium-sized towns of the region formed a new association called *Réseau Culturel des Villes Moyennes de Languedoc Roussillon* to co-ordinate their cultural activities (l'Indépendant, 2 March 2000). The state, too, through the *Direction des Affaires Culturelles* (DRAC) has taken a lead role in this domain (Groussard, 1996) although the Ministry of Culture warned them not to give too much support to minority languages, given France's difficulty over ratifying the Council of Europe's Charter on Minority Languages and Cultures (El Punt Perpinya, 15 January 2000).

Similar difficulties are evident in environmental policy issues. The region has its own *Direction de l'Environnement* but its main agency for environmental policy, set up in 1991, is the *Agence Méditerranéenne de l'Environnement* or AME (Région Languedoc-Roussillon, 1999). This association is largely financed by the region but also by contributions from the state, the EU and the local authorities. It seeks to promote a region-wide environmental approach along four axes: promoting sustainable development; maintaining and improving the quality and diversity of the environment; encouraging innovations; and stimulating a permanent debate on the environment. It strives to achieve these aims first by including an environmental dimension in those policy areas where the region was meant to take a lead under decentralisation: spatial planning; economic development, and the creation of *Parcs Naturels Régionaux* (PNRs). Secondly, it wishes to become involved in explicitly environmental policy areas: natural habitats; water; waste management; energy; and agriculture. Its favoured method is partnership with all those authorities and agencies involved in these areas. To its credit, it has been active in creating two PNRs (PNR du Haut-Languedoc, PNR de la Narbonnaise en Méditerranée) while a third is being created (Cerdagne, Capcir, Hautconflent). In 1996, it established the *Centre des Régions Euroméditerranéennes pour l'Environnement* (CREE). The method adopted by the AME is to initiate activities and then withdraw once they are under way rather than directly administer them subsequently. The most important frame of reference is the region, but the region understood as being situated in a broad Mediterranean context. The AME collaborates with a number of state field services especially the DIREN (*Direction Régionale de l'Environnement*), la DRIRE (*Direction Régionale de l'Industrie et Recherche*), l'ADEME (*Agence de l'Eau/Agence Bassin Saône Rhône Méditerranée*). It also works with the Ministries of Agriculture and Education. With regard to environmentalist associations, of which there are between 700 and 800 in Languedoc-Roussillon, they try to liaise with the larger, more representative ones, such as the *Société de Protection de la Nature – LR,* whose president is a member of the administrative board of the AME.

What is striking about these policy approaches by the region and the AME is the absence of any reference to a specific Languedoc-Roussillon regional identity. Rather, there is a manifest desire to be part of a wider Mediterranean cultural context and a recognition of *sub*-regional identities and cultures. To some extent, too, they reveal the importance of the external dimension for the region. More recently, the region has adopted a new initiative, the *pactes territoriaux de croissance,* signed with sub-regional local authorities, which, in 2001, numbered 19 (examples are *Terres romanes, Pyrénées, Plaine du Roussillon, Triangle d'Oc*). The idea here is to promote a balance between town and country, to stimulate the *forces vives* of an area around a project of regional development, and to encourage an opening out to the outside world, all within a context of sustainable development. On the other hand, the *pactes de croissance,* based on partnership with the other local authorities may signal a strategy to establish itself internally within the region.

CONCLUSIONS

This comparative survey of the historical, institutional and policy aspects of regional construction in Brittany and Languedoc-Roussillon illustrates the paradigm shift in the nature and functions of the state and the emergence of a new kind of territorial politics. Brittany and Languedoc-Roussillon have identical political and administrative institutions, but their histories and the nature of their identities are radically different. Brittany is a historic region with a high degree of coherence in its regional identity, which is based on the existence of a dominant minority language, Breton, and a number of historical customs. There are close links between its political, cultural and economic elites and it has developed a capacity for joint action even when there are internal disagreements.

We might conceive Brittany as consisting of three overlapping regions: a) the historic, cultural region; b) the economic region; c) the administrative region (*la Région*). The historic, cultural region has been strongly influenced by Catholicism even if this varies within the region. There is a certain *fond* of Catholic values especially the notions of the common good and solidarity, which have been modernised by entrepreneurial Catholic elites. Even if church attendance today has reached the same levels as other European societies, this value system has survived. Catholicism is also closely associated with the Breton language and, indeed, the Church helped to preserve the language and became a defender of Breton culture against the attacks of the Republican state. The second, economic, region is closely related to the historic, cultural region in the sense that the economic development of Brittany in the 1960s and recent attempts to convert this once again to a more environmentally friendly model both draw, with some success, on these older Catholic traditions. The language itself is in serious trouble but a wider Breton culture is flourishing today and the business community is investing heavily in this. Two of these regions are closely related and cover the five departments of the historic province. With regard to the third region, the region, the picture is rather less coherent and there is a certain *décalage* between it and the two others. However, even here there is a relatively high level of institutional capacity and the region has exploited the possibilities thrown up by decentralisation and regionalisation. Again, the Breton traditions of community and solidarity have played a role in this.

Languedoc-Roussillon, if examined under these three angles, presents a very different picture. Lacking a historic and cultural core, it is fragmented and pulled by larger areas on its borders – Catalonia and Occitania – although it can be considered as part of the larger Midi of France. Its two minority languages have not succeeded in co-operating despite the fact that they clearly share common interests. Economically, there has been a certain amount of success in recent years but this has been rather unbalanced with some strong sectors in the towns and along the littoral but with the departments of the interior among the poorest in France (for example Lozère). There is no regional business elite capable of working together with politicians and administrators in a common development project for the region. On the contrary, there is an intense conflict between modernisers, mostly found on the right of the political spectrum and traditionalists, mostly found on the left. The presence of the extreme-right *Front National* in the region has further exacerbated tensions, especially following its alliance with Jacques Blanc in the regional council. Even on the institutional level, the region is incapable of imposing itself on the other local authorities and has a low institutional capacity, abandoning whole policy areas to the departments and larger towns. It compensates for this weakness by engaging in international ventures either at the EU level or with other regions. But these ventures, too, have not known a great deal of success and may be simply alibis for the lack of internal action within the region. Perhaps, not to paint too black a picture of the region, it might be remarked that its environmental policy does seem to have developed in a satisfactory way.

Our two French case studies clearly illustrate the adoption by state, regional and local elites of the new paradigms outlined in the introduction. In each case, the region was confronted by socio-economic changes that were broader than their individual regions and even than the French state: economic transformation coupled with European Community agricultural policies. These wider forces of change threatened the internal social and economic conditions of the two regions and provoked processes of mobilisation from within of forces who sought to ally themselves with other, mainly state, actors. It is somewhat ironic that, because of the very different structures and composition of the two rural societies, the outcomes of these processes went in different directions: from mass-production to more customised quality production in Languedoc-Roussillon and from small family farms to an important agrifood industry in Brittany, although the Breton model is now being questioned and may go in the same direction as Languedoc-Roussillon. However, it must be concluded that only Brittany, building on its corporatist and consensual traditions and in possession of a strong and distinct culture, has succeeded in transforming itself from a weak, peripheral region to one that has experienced a certain amount of success. The cultural variable, using culture in its broader sense, has been crucial in the Breton case. The experience of Languedoc-Roussillon could not be more different. The region is almost entirely artificial despite its situation in the broader cultural sphere of the Midi de la France. The regional, departmental and municipal institutions are deeply divided against each other as are the political, economic and cultural elites of the region. Despite efforts by the region to exploit it, culture is, in fact, a divisive factor as is illustrated by the tension between the Catalan and Occitan activist movements.

6. The United Kingdom: Scotland and Wales

STATE AND NATION IN THE UNITED KINGDOM

The United Kingdom is an explicitly multinational state, as indicated in the very name of the state, created in successive unions of England and Wales in 1536 and then with Scotland in 1707 and Ireland in 1801. It was neither a unitary state on French lines, nor a federation like the United States of America. Its founding constitutional principle was that of parliamentary sovereignty, uniting political authority but not challenging the existence of its four distinct nations. At the same time, especially during the time of Empire, England was the dominant nation and London was the centre of political, economic and cultural power. Each of the other nations, related to this centre in distinct ways and each had its particular brand of society, politics and administration. While constitutional authority was unitary, there was a rather large degree of diversity across the various national civil societies and only sporadic efforts at forging a single national identity from the top, although there was a tendency, at least among English people, to conflate Britishness with Englishness, as can be remarked also in most European languages where *l'Angleterre* and *Inghilterra* are used to refer to what should be described as *le Royaume-Uni* or *il Regno Unito*.

This chapter focuses on Scotland and Wales as examples both of stateless nations and of European 'cultural regions'. In Scotland, national identity was carried by institutions that survived the Union of 1707, notably the education system, the established Church of Scotland and the law, reinforced by the tendency, especially from the late nineteenth century, to set up special Scottish institutions to handle new government tasks (Paterson, 1994; Harvie, 1994). Wales was less institutionally distinct but national identity was carried by the language, non-conformist Protestant religion and a political culture marked in the modern era by a particular brand of radicalism (Morgan, 1982). In the nineteenth century, there were attempts to penalise the speaking of Welsh, Irish and Scots Gaelic by the new national education systems in these countries, but the decline of these languages is also a result of other factors and not simply governmental policy. Following the Second World War the welfare state and interventionist economic policies were a force for centralisation and uniformity and during this period many native speakers of the minority languages switched to English, mainly for reasons of social advancement. Economic and political pressures from the peripheral nations were accommodated by diversionary regional policies, bringing new investment; by favourable treatment in public spending; and through administrative devolution. Since 1885 an increasing part of Scottish administration had been handled by the Secretary (of State) for Scotland and in 1965 a Secretary of State for Wales was appointed with a similar, if smaller brief. Both Secretaries had the dual role of carrying out central policy in the nations and representing the nations' needs at the centre.

Strains in this system grew from the 1970s and were exacerbated during the years from 1979 to 1997 when Scotland and Wales consistently voted in a large majority of Labour MPs but got a Conservative government, due to the preponderance of the English electorate. The Labour government proposed devolved assemblies in Scotland and Wales and put them to referendum in 1979, but the proposals foundered when the Welsh one was turned down by a massive majority and the Scottish one, although supported by a majority of those voting, failed to pass the threshold set by Parliament. During the 1990s, however, opinion in Scotland in favour of devolution solidified and the Labour Party, previously divided on the issue, became more firmly committed. The incoming Labour government of 1997 moved quickly to issue White Papers on devolution and hold referendums on its proposals. In Scotland these passed by a large margin, while in Wales they gained a small majority on a low electoral turnout. As of 1999, Scotland has a Parliament with legislative and executive powers over all matters not expressly reserved to Westminster. A National Assembly for Wales has administrative and secondary legislative powers over a specified list of functions. A Northern Ireland Assembly has a different format again, while in England there are only regional development agencies and indirectly elected regional assemblies. The system is thus highly asymmetrical, with each part of the United Kingdom having its own system of government in a different relationship to the centre.

Since the 1980s diversionary regional policy in the United Kingdom has been run down in favour of smaller scale initiatives in urban areas and a focus on reviving entrepreneurship and endogenous growth. This is line with European trends and implies a greater differentiation of policy and an integration of various development measures, including industrial development, training and research and development, at the regional level. This gives considerable scope for distinct development models to evolve. Yet there are limitations on the autonomy of the devolved institutions and some continuing centralising influences. Taxation is reserved to the centre, apart from a limited tax-varying power in Scotland, and the devolved bodies are financed by a block grant determined by a formula originally put in place in 1978 for the Scottish and Welsh Offices. While the devolved institutions can spend this block freely, they cannot offer their publics higher or lower levels of expenditure overall. The principal macro-economic instruments are likewise reserved to the centre, although Scotland and Wales have considerable discretion in the use of the instruments of development policy within their own areas, including regional development grants, control over their own development agencies, training and infrastructure. Aid to industry is governed by a concordat with the centre to prevent destructive competition for investment. The devolved territories are explicitly permitted by the legislation to act in European matters, and have their own offices in Brussels, although representation in European decision making takes place through the UK delegation, with Scottish and Welsh participation (Loughlin, 2001). This too is subject to concordats between central and devolved administrations. Since 1999, moreover, a degree of unity has been maintained by the fact that the central government is under Labour control while Scotland and (since 2000) Wales are governed by Labour-Liberal Democrat coalitions. This means that the scope for policy divergence has yet to be put seriously to the test, although in the early years there were some key initiatives in matters of student fees and care for the elderly.

SCOTLAND

Scotland in the United Kingdom

Scotland has about 8 per cent of the United Kingdom's population, a share that has been falling since the early twentieth century due to emigration and a low birth rate. Its period of economic greatness was in the late nineteenth century, based on heavy industry and imperial markets, although the Highlands mainly served the role of supplier of manpower to the industries of the central belt (Lee, 1995). After the First World War, Scotland suffered a steep economic decline relative to the southern regions of England and it was very badly hit in the Depression of the 1930s, its image changing from that of workshop of the Empire to a distressed area. Industrial decline weakened political self-confidence and hit the Labour movement hard, so that Scottish trade unions radicals, previously rather nationalistic, abandoned their support for Home Rule and sought protection within the British state (Keating and Bleiman, 1979). Business, previously strongly free trading and independent, turned to government for tariff protection or sold out to English and foreign capital (Harvie, 1981). Following the Second World War, Scotland was subjected to a wave of interventionist initiatives aimed at steering development its way and providing the infrastructure for expansion. The 1960s and 1970s saw active interventions by the central government to guide the motor industry to Scotland, linked to the decision to establish a new steel works at Ravenscraig (divided at the last minute with Llanwern in Wales, the steel companies' preferred location). There were even ambitious plans to industrialise and urbanise the Highlands. By 1974 the whole of Scotland was a development area eligible for government investment subsidies. These policies achieved some catch-up with England and from the early 1970s North Sea oil developments helped growth, especially in the north east (Lee, 1995). The recession of the early 1980s, however, devastated Scottish industry, wiping out all the plants brought to Scotland under the special initiatives of the 1960s. It also eliminated a large part of the remaining indigenous Scottish-owned industrial sector and did long-term damage to the Conservative Party.

There was a certain amount of catch-up in the early 1990s as Scotland, being less over-extended in credit and the property boom, suffered less in the second recession of the Thatcher years. Together with the structural shake-out in the old industries, this meant that Scotland's economic profile was now rather similar to that of Britain as a whole. The decline of state and state-aided industries, together with the reduction in regional policy support, meant that it was less dependent economically on central government policy than in the post-war era; but it had become much more dependent on foreign capital (Ashcroft and Love, 1993). Indigenous enterprise was still rather weak and there was a poor rate of new firm formation. There was dynamism in some sectors, notably in banking and financial services, for which Edinburgh is a significant centre, although these have become increasingly internationalised. Scotch whisky has also boomed, especially in export markets, although this too is largely controlled outwith Scotland. Scotland was also dependent on fiscal transfers from England. While the fiscal balance is a highly politicised topic and subject to endless controversy, it does appear that Scottish expenditure levels are appreciably higher than those in the English regions, and are not balanced by equivalent Scottish contributions to the Exchequer (Heald, 1994).

Culture and Identity

Scotland's position within the United Kingdom has long permitted Scots to maintain a dual identity, usually seeing no incompatibility between being Scottish and English but since the 1970s the Scottish element has come to predominate (McCrone, 2001). As class attachments have declined, Scots are also more likely to feel affinity with their co-nationals rather than with English people of the same social class (McCrone, 2001). Since there is no language issue to speak of, identity rests on a number of markers, no one of which is ever exclusive or even necessary – birth, ancestry, residence and commitment. This indeterminacy and the relative ease with which newcomers can assimilate, even in the first generation and certainly in the second, has allowed Scotland to project a civic form of nationalism bound by a set of common beliefs or myths (Keating, 2001a).

Yet when we probe the nature of these common beliefs and values we find that there are several Scottish stereotypes, not all of them entirely consistent. Among the most persistent is the idea of egalitarianism and equality of opportunity, linked to a belief in democratic process said to be inspired by the practice of the Church of Scotland with its lack of hierarchy. These beliefs, which have some basis in historic practice, can, however, lend themselves to a capitalist or a socialist conclusion (Reicher and Hopkins, 2001). The capitalistic version sees Scots as scorning non-achieved status and as entrepreneurial, linking into the common stereotype of the canny Scot concerned with the value of things and skilled in the handling of money. Margaret Thatcher as Prime Minister embellished this by rediscovering Adam Smith and the thinkers of the Scottish Enlightenment and pressing them into service as a kind of proto-Thatcherite school of thought. Left-wing versions build on egalitarianism and democracy with different conclusions. Early Scottish labour leaders were given to invoking Scottish traditions of radicalism to justify a popular form of radicalism rather far removed from the statist socialism of the mid-twentieth century Labour Party (Keating and Bleiman, 1979). From the 1920s the left-wing image was reinforced with the myth of 'red Clydeside', the radical workers' movement of the First World War era, mythologised by some as the lost Scottish revolution and dismissed by others as little more than a backlash by the skilled labour aristocracy against dilution and the threat of the new unskilled workers. The image of Scotland as a land of heavy industry dominated some representations even beyond the left, although this was arguably an unjustifiable projection of Clydeside onto the whole country. Another prominent image was provided by Glasgow as the site of urban stress and poverty immortalised in the inter-war novel 'No Mean City'; indeed the 'condition of Glasgow' question came to preoccupy a whole generation of government officials. Incidents like the work-in at Upper Clyde Shipbuilders in the early 1970s thus tapped the image of heavy industry as Scotland's lifeblood, romanticised memories of the Clydeside workers' movement, and Scottish traditions of self-help. There is even a recurrent theme in Scottish cultural commentary that sees a manichean dualism as a defining feature of the national ethos. Stevenson's 'Jeckyll and Hyde' famously depicts this within a single individual while Gregory Smith in the early twentieth century wrote of the Caledonian Antyzyzygy, a theme taken up by Hugh MacDiarmid with his desire to be 'whaur extremes meet'.

To these discordant images of Scottishness we must add the depoliticisation of culture during much of the nineteenth and twentieth centuries. It is a commonplace among Scots intellectuals to complain about the reduction of Scottish culture to tartanry and the kailyard, the latter being a school of escapist literature that depicted a small-town Scotland living largely in social harmony, beset only by petty jealousies and personality conflicts among stereotypical characters. Perhaps uniquely among industrial nations, Scotland failed to produce a great novel of social realism depicting the industrial strife of nineteenth century capitalism, although McCrone (2001) among others warns against too exclusive an attention on the kailyard, which threatens itself to become a stereotype. Beveridge and Turnbull (1989) put the depoliticisation of culture down to an inferiority complex typical of subordinated people but this would not explain why the Scots did not, like other stateless nations, experience a cultural awakening in the nineteenth century based on a revalorisation of the inferior culture. An alternative explanation is the relative ease with which Scots were able to enter the dominant culture and the outlets available to them within the British state and empire. Yet the weight of tartanry and kailyard lies heavy and is regularly boosted by episodes like the film *Braveheart*, to give Scottishness an archaic image inconsistent with economic and social modernisation. There is also a recurrent fear among Scots intellectuals of parochialism which often extends to Scottish culture in general and serves again to make culture a difficult instrument of modernisation and engagement with the world.

This has all been changing since the 1970s with the rise of Scottish nationalism, the modernisation of Scottish society within an indigenous frame and something of a cultural renaissance. New Scottish cultural expressions tend to be more politically engaged, to address contemporary issues and, rather than seeking an essentialised Scottishness, to see Scotland as a forum in which social issues are addressed, explored and occasionally resolved. Parochialism is less feared now that Scotland can be projected as a European culture, rather than a provincial branch of British culture, while even symbols like the kilt or the pipes, dismissed by progressives a generation ago as part of the old mythology, can be given their proper place as part of a distinctive but modern and evolving culture. The experience of the Conservative government between 1979 and 1997 which gained a dwindling minority of Scottish votes helped redefine Scotland as a political and social unit cleaving to values that had been abandoned in England.

Broadly shared opposition to Conservative government helped revive the movement for Scottish home rule, leading it to victory in 1998. At the same time, shared identity and the threat to the welfare state fed each other to construct a view of Scotland attached to the welfare settlement that had been abandoned down south. In fact, opinion data show the Scots to be only moderately more egalitarian and supportive of the welfare state than the English since the latter had not in fact swung radically to the right. The difference between the two is that Scotland had a vehicle for expressing opposition to neo-liberalism in the form of national identity, which seems to have become in some ways a substitute for social class as the basis for social solidarity (Brown et al., 1999). So the welfare state, previously an instrument of British nation-building, could become an element in Scottish nation-building instead. If there is a Scottish effect it is perhaps not that the Scots are natural social democrats but that they have retained a 'moral economy' in which there are common understandings of what is fair and the acceptable limits to socially divisive policies (Hearn, 2000). This may provide moral resources for resistance to measures like Thatcher's poll tax but whether it can provide the basis for mobilisation around an alternative model of development is another matter. Culture and identity in Scotland are only now being thought of as resources for development or the bases for a distinct development model as found in other European cultural regions.

Yet surveys have consistently shown that Scots are rather poor entrepreneurs (Ashcroft and Love, 1993). The rate of new firm formation is low and polls have indicated that Scots may indeed be rather risk-averse. A 2001 poll for the Global Entrepreneurship Monitor comparing Scotland with other 'small modern nations' found Scots to be more frightened of failure that people from Norway, Denmark, Israel and New Zealand, although marginally ahead of the Irish (GEM, 2002). Entrepreneurial levels were also lower than in the United Kingdom as a whole. The worst figures were from the old industrial areas of western Scotland, where traditional attitudes to employment seem to have persisted and hampered the transition to the new model of industrial development.

Political Leadership

There are competing visions about Scotland's future, exaggerated by political competition among the main parties. For most of the post-war period Scotland was managed as part of a single UK economy under regional development policies pursued by both Conservative and Labour governments. Nationalism was a minor force before the 1970s. Given the wide scope of the responsibilities of Scottish Office ministers and their absence for much of the time in London, policy leadership in many fields fell to the civil service. A modernising bureaucracy, especially in the Scottish Development Department and the specialised development agencies, was committed to change according to the current principles of planning and regional policy. Scotland in fact pioneered much of regional planning in the United Kingdom, with the Clyde Valley Plan of 1946, the Toothill Report of 1962 and the West Central Scotland Plan of 1973. In 1974-5 the entire structure of local government was overhauled with the establishment of large multipurpose regional councils on lines originally advocated by the Scottish Development Department. The Scottish Council (Development and Industry) bringing together private business, local government and other actors, was another important influence in the 1960s. Big measures were taken but these were largely depoliticised and consensual.

Among the parties, Labour was in the ascendancy in Scotland from the late 1950s and formed the UK government from 1964 until 1979 with the three and a half year hiatus of the Heath administration. Labour's aim was to develop Scotland by mobilising the resources of the UK state, which meant tying it into the central government and opposing anything, including political devolution that might put its privileged access to the centre in jeopardy. The meant a double game of stressing distinctive Scottish needs and mobilising the Scottish lobby, while damping down expectations of constitutional change. Labour sustained the old heavy industries of Scotland, part of its power base, while encouraging the arrival of new manufacturing plants. At the same time, its position in the cities was maintained through local political machines, which engaged in large-scale urban redevelopment while controlling the distribution of patronage in the form of prized council houses and jobs in council employment. After years of tension with the modernising bureaucracy in the Scottish Office, the local machines went into decline from the late 1960s and were dealt a major blow by the introduction of merit systems for allocating houses and jobs, and the reorganisation of local government in 1974–5. The system of managed dependency culminated in 1974 when the returning Labour government set up the Scottish Development Agency and declared the whole of Scotland to be a Development area eligible for regional assistance. Already the mid-1970s, however, the old system was in crisis under pressure from a resurgent nationalism and the Labour government was forced to introduce proposals for an elected Scottish Assembly. This would not, however, have had the lead role in economic development, since this was felt to clash with UK economic unity and Labour's desire to tap into UK resources. So the economic development machinery was to remain largely under the control of the Secretary of State for Scotland, who would continue as a UK minister.

Conservative governments between 1979 and 1997 broke with the consensus on regional development, insisting that Scotland was suffering from a 'dependency culture' born of excessive reliance on the public sector, public spending and state assistance to industry. In response, they applied the same strategy of privatisation, deregulation and attempting to cut back public spending as they did elsewhere in the United Kingdom, but accompanied by some distinctively Scottish rhetoric, invoking the Scottish myths of enterprise and financial acumen (Midwinter et al., 1991). There was some effort to rebuild a Scottish bourgeoisie, by stimulating small business and giving business people a larger role in public policy development and implementation. The Scottish Development Agency was renamed Scottish Enterprise, lost its social responsibilities and was largely decentralised to Local Enterprise Companies under business leadership. Yet privatisation was not used to rebuild a local business class by giving preference to Scottish owners and there was an absolute refusal to countenance political devolution, in contrast to the former leader Edward Heath, who seems to have seen devolution as part of a strategy to encourage Scottish self-reliance. Closure of the heavy industries cost Scotland dearly in jobs, but also undermined the old trade union and Labour alliance and opened the way to new forms of development.

New Labour, as the party was known on its return to power after 1997, had moved back to the party's historic support for Scottish home rule, had abandoned its former interventionism and support for manufacturing and heavy industries, and was committed to economic modernisation. Believing in the liberal market economy with only light intervention, it had less interest in keeping economic powers at the central level, and the Scottish Parliament and Executive inherited nearly all of the economic functions of the Scottish Office. This permitted the elaboration of a more distinct Scottish development strategy, albeit within the parameters of overall UK policy. Yet pressure from the nationalist quarter led Labour to be very cautious about striking out on its own or implying that Scotland could manage without the UK framework. Instead, it reverted to its old unionist rhetoric, emphasising Scotland's financial dependence on the central state.

After 1997 the main opposition force was the Scottish National Party (SNP). Previously a vaguely right of centre party whose official policy was based on Social Credit principles (Hanham, 1969), the SNP has evolved into a social democratic party committed to independence within the European Union. It used to take as its role model the Nordic democracies, most of which were outside the EU until 1995 and occasionally still evokes Norway, but since the late 1990s it has also held up the example of Ireland. In contrast with some of our other cases, however, the SNP does not engage much in the business of nation-building within Scotland, taking it as read that Scotland is already a mature nation ready for independence. Scotland is presented as a naturally rich nation, with oil, whisky, financial services and high technology industries, but held back by membership of the United Kingdom which forces it to accept macro-economic policies designed for the south of England. There was a brief flirtation with the Irish model of low corporate taxation and attraction of foreign capital but generally the SNP does not present a clear picture of an independent Scotland's position within global markets. Nor is there a clear internal development model, linking nation, culture and development such as we find in Catalonia or Flanders.

It is perhaps the very weakness of clearly articulated visions of Scotland as a trading nation that has facilitated a degree of consensus in practice following devolution. While Labour and the SNP differ radically on Scotland's constitutional future, both are prepared to adopt current wisdom about regional development policies. Both share a vaguely social democratic vision in which social inclusion is a necessary part of the development effort and neither evokes culture a great deal. The Scottish Parliament itself which provides a new focus for interest group activity and social compromise, also pulls policy visions back towards the centre and the emphasis on shared ideas and values.

Institutions

The centre of attention in Scotland has now shifted from the system of administrative devolution around the Scottish Office, to the elected Scottish Parliament. This has extensive powers over matters not reserved to the centre and has inherited a well-established territorial bureaucracy. Moreover, in contrast to other European cases, there are not in most fields central government departments operating in the same fields or setting the general rules meaning that Scottish discretion is rather large (Keating, 2001c). In economic matters, however, there is a close linkage into UK departments through the concordats and the requirement to work within overall state policies. Scottish departments are also weakened by their limited policy capacity due to their small size and the consequent need to learn from elsewhere. Devolution has not meant a radical change in Scottish administration, since most of the infrastructure was already there in the days of the Scottish Office. Much of the detailed work in development continues to be carried out by existing agencies, notably Scottish Enterprise and Highlands and Islands Enterprise originally founded in the 1960s and 1970s. Devolution has, on the other hand, politicised areas of policy previously treated as a matter of technical efficacy, brought a wider range of interests into the policy process, and broadened the development policy agenda.

A marked feature of Scotland is that before devolution in 1999 it had its own interest groups and policy communities (Kellas, 1989; Midwinter et al., 1991; Paterson, 1994; Brown et al., 1996). Some of these were purely Scottish; others were affiliated with UK groups; and others were regional branches of UK groups; and in a few cases there was no Scottish level at all, or groups were organised on a regional basis within Scotland. There was no consistent rationale for the distinction, since some groups operated on a Scottish basis for purely historical reasons; for example the Scottish Trades Union Congress which operated in parallel to its UK counterpart, had its origins in a decision of the TUC in the late nineteenth century to exclude trades councils. Teachers were organised separately because of the historic distinctiveness of Scottish education, which was one field in which the Scottish Office was able to make its own policy within overall UK guidelines. The main business groups were organised at a UK level while most Scottish trades unions were absorbed into their UK counterparts during the course of the twentieth century.

Scotland thus had its own civil society and some observers have detected in the post-war regeneration schemes and even in Conservative policy after 1979 a form of Scottish corporatism, forging a local consensus around shared interests within a protected corner of the British state (Moore and Booth, 1989; Paterson, 1994). In practice Scottish organs in both state and civil society lacked the autonomy that might have delivered this. Especially in relation to economic policy matters, this was less a self-regulating system than a territorial lobby, able to mobilise a territorial lobby on shared economic interests cutting across sectoral, class and party divisions while not in any way attenuating them (Keating, 2001d). Nor did this foster a shared vision of Scottish self-government. When devolution came back on the agenda in the 1970s, opinion was divided, with big business and some of the groups that enjoyed insider status under the old system of administrative devolution, especially those close to the Conservative Party, opposed (Lynch, 1998). Yet despite the fears of some groups about competing in a new Scottish arena, everyone since 1999 accepts the new rules of the game. On the other hand, notions of shared culture and identity, which might be expected to undergird a consensus on Scotland's development, have been challenged in new ways.

It was rather easy, before devolution, to invoke the Scottish cultural stereotypes in defence of various policy positions and agree on matters of shared interest, since these statements in general had few consequences. It was also easy to retail the routines of village life in a small society, such as are found in other European regions. Devolution has in some ways strengthened this Scottish frame of reference. There is a shared emotive commitment to the idea of Scotland and the promotion of Scottish interests and strong pressure on groups to be seen as good citizens in the new dispensation. The fate of the Conservative Party, which was seen during the 1980s and 1990s as increasingly 'anti-Scottish' weighs heavily on some groups and there is a concern to establish their legitimacy and defend themselves in a more exposed political environment. This is reflected in support for symbolic matters like the distinct Scottish bank notes, in instances of corporate philanthropy, and in a willingness to engage in the extensive process of consultation which the Scottish Executive and Parliament have launched. Groups cannot opt out of Scottish politics as easily in the past and must address each others' concerns. So business groups will accept the legitimacy of the Scottish Executive's social inclusion strategy, while unions and social interest groups will accept the need for economic competitiveness.

On the other hand, devolution has politicised the policy process, introduced new actors, and forced actors to face conflicts of interest and competition for resources. Operating within the same policy arena and must come up with their own policy ideas. Many of them found it something of a shock to be asked what their own ideas for policy were. As a result, the village story about consensualism will no longer serve its purpose and a new one has to be learnt. Moving from the politics of managed dependency to autonomy, Scotland has become a 'normal' political society in which groups confront each other directly instead of displacing conflict to the outside.

There has been a shift in the general orientation and priorities among the Scottish, UK and European levels of policy making. Historic factors play a role here, with groups that have traditionally worked at the Scottish level continuing to do so, while most have sought some sort of presence at all levels until they see how the new system settles down. Yet there are emerging patterns, which we can analyse by reference to three sets of institutional factors. First is the location of the group and its members, whether within Scotland, at the UK level or international. In the case of business firms and sectors, this would refer to the ownership of the firms and the location of their production. In the case of trades unions or social organisations, this would refer to the location of their members. Second is the field of operation of the group or, in the case of firms, the market. Third is the level at which the activity is regulated.

Big firms doing business in Scotland are mostly externally owned, are regulated mainly at UK and European levels and trade in UK and global markets. We find, accordingly, that the main focus of attention for their representative groups (the Confederation of British Industry (CBI) and the Institute of Directors) are UK government departments. They do, however, have to pay attention to the Scottish level more than in the past, because some matters affecting them, such as transport or planning policy, are devolved, and they do have to play in the Scottish arena to sustain legitimacy in the face of increased political exposure. Small businesses tend to be Scottish-owned and to operate in the Scottish market. Like large firms, they are generally regulated at the UK or European levels but, as elsewhere in Europe, are also dependent on locally produced public goods including grants, infrastructure and the services of Scotland's network of business support agencies. Small business tends to invoke Scottish themes more easily, has been rather more favourable to devolution than big business, and its federation had observer status at the Scottish Constitutional Convention of the 1990s. It has not enjoyed the insider status of the five big business federations and there was much resentment when the big five got together in 2000 to improve their status in Scotland and their lobbying activities. This has led small business groups to pay more attention to the Scottish level and to the Scottish Parliament in particular. Agriculture and fisheries are sectors where businesses are locally owned and operated, while regulated at Scottish and European levels. Ironically, the joint effects of devolution and Europeanisation are to strengthen the networks at UK level, which is the nexus of the other networks.

Specific sectors may be cross-pressured, caught between more than one territorial frame of reference. Scotland is a major centre for banking and finance and many of the firms are still Scottish-owned. Yet they operate in global markets and are regulated at UK and European levels. Scottish banking and financial interests are concerned to maintain the health of the sector locally and to retain headquarters functions in Scotland but recognise that survival requires that they play a global game and engage in cross-border mergers and take-overs. Since the 1980s there have been several take-over battles in which the Scottish lobby was mobilised to retain ownership or headquarters within Scotland and, while the banks insist that they operate purely on market principles, there has been a political input here. The take-over of the National Westminster by the Royal Bank of Scotland in 1999, representing a Scottish expansion into England, was widely seen as damaging the political protection of Scottish banks and the Bank of Scotland was duly taken over by the Yorkshire-based Halifax in 2001. Yet the insistence of the Bank together with political pressure within Scotland ensured that the headquarters of the merged institution would be in Edinburgh. By this time not even the Scottish National Party was claiming that Scottish banks should be immune from internationalisation and cross-border mergers, but there was a shared view that the Scottish banks still had a distinct identity and role. The whisky industry is similarly cross-pressured. It is by definition a local industry since the marque is culturally very specific and can only be awarded to whisky produced in Scotland, but it is largely externally owned. Indeed there were some spectacular take-over battles in the 1980s. The industry is regulated at the UK level and sells in global markets, with the vast bulk of production being exported so that it bridges the specifically Scottish and the global levels.

Trade unions are nearly all organised on a UK basis, although the Scottish Trades Union Congress is completely separate from the British TUC, with unions affiliating to both. Labour regulation is a largely reserved matter and there is a tendency now to leave this to the TUC and UK-level of the unions. Training policy and responsibility for local development and responses to industrial closures, however, is devolved, so the unions are drawn into the Scottish networks. Trade unions have often invoked specifically Scottish themes in their campaigning, tied as they are to a local membership, and have largely supported the move to Scottish devolution since the 1960s. They are also concerned with a range of social issues and with public sector employment. This gives them a stronger orientation to the Scottish networks than is the case with employers, but at the same time they support the unitary UK economy and labour market. Social lobby groups and service organisations tend to be less well resourced than the others and operate usually at the Scottish level. This means that they can enter into policy networks in matters like housing, which are almost entirely devolved. They tend to be strong supporters of devolution since it has increased the points of access into the political system and given them more sympathetic interlocutors in the Parliament and its committees.

Devolution has strengthened the territorial policy community in Scotland and no group or sector can simply opt out of the Scottish level or appeal above the head of the Scottish decision makers as happened in the past. There is a broadly shared territorial identity which might facilitate social co-operation and, together with the strengthening of Scottish institutions, has reinforced the salience of the territorial framework for policy making and regulation. This, however, is only one territorial level in a complex multi-level system and different groups are oriented differently. There is some evidence of more inter-sectoral and cross-class dialogue and consultation than in the past, although this may also reflect the arrival in 1997 of the Labour government less hostile to the trade unions than its predecessor. The shared Scottish perspective does broaden the development agenda and means that all groups have to pay attention, at least verbally, to issues of social inclusion as well as economic competition. We have not, however, found evidence of a distinct Scottish capitalism, more inclined to collectivism and associationalism such as has been identified in some of the new regionalist literature (Cooke and Morgan, 1998).

External Relations

Scotland's territorial lobby, previously focused on the United Kingdom, spread out from the 1970s under the influence of globalisation and Europeanisation. As in domestic politics, this involved a delicate balance between collaboration in pursuit of shared territorial interests, and political competition at home. During the 1980s there were clashes with UK departments over the independent Scottish inward investment effort and the promotion of tourism abroad, but over time a 'modus vivendi' was reached in which Scotland was promoted as a distinct location but within the limits of overall UK policy. A similar approach was adopted towards Scottish involvement in the European Community/Union. As part of a unitary government, Scottish Office ministers were sometimes able to attend meetings of the Council of Ministers and their officials participated in the working parties. In 1992 a Scottish office was opened in Brussels, Scotland Europa, but ministers made clear that this was a platform for Scottish interests in general, not a political representation of Scotland.

Following devolution, these arrangements were modified but not abandoned. Scottish ministers were permitted to participate in the Council of Ministers as part of the UK delegation, pursuing the common UK line. Relations between the Scottish Executive and the central government on European matters were to be governed by a concordat, a non-statutory agreement which provided for extensive consultation and Scottish input but made clear that in the event of disagreement the final word would rest with London. Scotland's presence in Brussels was expanded with the establishment of Scotland House, containing both the old Scotland Europa and a separate delegation representing the Scottish Executive. This too was tied into the UK system of representation, being part of the 'UKREP family' (UKREP is the UK permanent representation to the EU) and co-operating with it extensively. These arrangements are designed for a situation in which both central and Scottish governments are controlled by the same party and would have difficulty surviving divided political control. At the same time, Scotland has been drawn into European trans-regional networks and lobbies, including those pressing for stronger regional representation in EU institutions. It has participated in meetings of the Regions with Legislative Powers and of the Constitutional Regions but has been rather reticent to commit itself to anything that might bring it into conflict with the centre.

Among Scottish interest groups, European issues and networks appeared less salient than might have been expected, given all the political talk about Scotland's place in Europe. They have tended to leave European matters to their UK counterparts or to pan-European sectoral groups to which they are affiliated, although the services of Scotland Europa in Brussels are also used to pursue specifically Scottish issues. There is a general acceptance of European integration as something beneficial to Scotland, although opinions on the single currency are divided along similar lines to that in England and Wales. Some economic interests favoured the single currency because of the current over-valuation of the pound and its effect on Scotland's manufacturing industry, but in general this was seen as a broad political question to be resolved on other grounds. Despite the general tendency since the 1980s to link the questions of devolution and Europe, the leader in Scotland of Business for Sterling (opponents of the single currency) was the same businessman who had fronted the pro-devolution body FORward Scotland in the referendum of 1999.

Scotland has no problem of name-recognition in Europe and there is a lot of interest in its constitutional settlement. Yet it faces the problem of overcoming the dated and stereotypical image of tartan and romantic Highland landscapes. Hence the effort to promote modern Scottish culture, through exhibitions of modern art and a Scotland Week in Brussels which gives time to questions of technology and change. This requires a repackaging of culture and a broadening of its scope, much as has happened within Scotland. An example often cited is Ireland, which accompanied an economic breakthrough in the 1990s with a revalorisation of Irish culture, linked now to images of dynamism and modernity. Yet, while Scotland is making an impact in Europe, Europe has been slower to make an impact in Scotland. The slogan Scotland in Europe is now used but the combination of local and European flags, is rarer than elsewhere in Europe.

Policy

It is difficult to discern a distinctively Scottish development model, probably because the experience of devolution is so recent, and the transition from the old system of managed dependency is incomplete. Yet certain trends are visible.

Culture in Scotland, when not ignored politically, was sometimes a battlefield, as partisans fought over the relative priorities of Scottish, British and international culture and over high versus popular culture. These controversies are less resonant now, perhaps because there is more cultural patronage available. During the course of the 1990s, culture was gradually transferred to the Scottish Office and following devolution is the exclusive responsibility of the Scottish Parliament and Executive, operating mainly through the Scottish Arts Council. There is neither a culture minister nor an arts council for the United Kingdom or even Great Britain as a whole. Cultural issues play out rather differently in Scotland to some of our other cases, since language questions occupy a small role and there is no dominant culture to replace the old stereotypes. Yet the projection of Scotland as the scene of cultural representations has strengthened with initiatives like the Museum of Scotland, which presents a national, if not nationalist, vision of the country across the centuries.

The Scottish Executive, with its greater local democratic legitimacy, has felt able to take a more active role in culture than did the old Scottish Office, which tended to leave matters to the Scottish Arts Council and other institutions. A National Cultural Strategy was launched in 2000 as a guide to action (Scottish Executive, 2000). This was at pains to emphasise the cultural pluralism of Scotland, including the contribution of incomers, from the Norse invaders to the 'new generations of Scots, in particular those from the Indian subcontinent'. Apart from a general commitment to promotion of the arts, a strong emphasis was placed upon the contribution of culture to social inclusion and on internationalisation. This was a document from a non-nationalist administration and the role of culture in nation-building was not emphasised, nor was there a stress on culture as an instrument of collective consciousness. The role of the arts as part of the economy and in tourist promotion was covered and there was a recognition of the role of the arts in raising general skills, but again this was not focused on the promotion of the development of Scotland as a whole.

A similar reticence about the role of culture is evident in the Scottish Executive's (2000) *Framework for Economic Development*. As in other parts of Europe, policy has moved on from diversionary regional aid to endogenous development in the context of global competition. The Labour-led coalition, like its New Labour counterparts in London, puts a big stress on the market economy, with a limited role for public intervention only in the case of market failure. Declining sectors and firms should not, in this view, be supported but must give way to new activities. There is a strong emphasis of skills and technology and a concern that Scotland is lagging behind its competitors in these areas. This is consistent with the policy of their pre-devolution Conservative predecessors, except that Labour combines this with a new emphasis on the need for social inclusion and sustainable development. Inclusion is extended to all social groups and to the regions of Scotland, although it is emphasised that 'The Executive is committed to an economy-led social justice agenda', again reflecting the priorities of Labour at the UK level. Education and training are, as elsewhere, identified as factors that can contribute both to growth and to social inclusion. Environmental policy is also seen as a potential contribution to growth. The paper does, it is true, recognise that these objectives may or may not be compatible and that trade-offs and hard choices might be necessary, but there is little hint of a distinct Scottish formula for doing this. Scotland's insertion into the global and European economies is presented as a challenge and an opportunity, although Europe is framed as little more than a market and a source of aid through the Structural Funds; there is no mention of alliances with other European regions on shared interests and projects or of an active Scottish role within Europe, apart from its links to the UK state. The paper marks the definitive end of aspirations to maintain or increase Scottish control as an object of policy, noting that 'It is not possible – and probably undesirable – to resist the loss of Scottish corporate headquarters'.

Hints at cultural issues do, however, pervade the Framework, without ever being really resolved. It remarks that 'the potential for coherence and co-operation between economic agents in Scotland is high due to its small size and a relatively cohesive community', but does not expand on the meaning and implications of this. At another point it notes that a 'culture of risk aversion and cautious attitudes prevail', and when discussing the lack of entrepreneurial skills says that 'cultural attitudes and approaches to risk are relevant here', but in neither case does it elaborate or tie the issue of culture and collective action to Scottish institution-building and national mobilisation. Most revealing is the concluding section (chapter 8) where the following paragraph occurs:

> One particular example of where a more detailed understanding would be potentially valuable arose in the course of our consultation exercise: namely the question of Scottish culture and its impact on economic development. Is it 'culture' which accounts for the comparatively low business birth rate, the anecdotal evidence of weak levels of basis skills in the economy, or the weaker levels of literacy compared to some continental countries? And how quickly is that culture changing? This *Framework* harbours the suspicion that economic culture is an important determinant of economic progress over time, but it has not found sufficiently deep analysis of the role of culture across different segments of the Scottish economy.

This hesitancy looks like a legacy of Scotland's recent institutional past, in which politics, culture and economic development were, for political reasons, kept in separate compartments. Scotland is still presented as a place where things might happen rather than a dynamic society giving birth to distinctive forms of social relations and collective action. Labour is still reticent about invoking Scottishness as a mobilising theme, for fear of giving heart to the nationalists and jeopardising the union. The nationalists, for their part, cling to Scottish independence as the solution to the nation's problems, without attending too much to the need to build the nation as a system of collective action to meet the challenges of globalisation and European integration. MacInnes (2001: 111) commenting on the Deputy First Minister's 'state of the nation' address on St. Andrew's Day 2000, noted that he 'made no claims about how a sense of national identity might be mobilised to pursue social or political ends within the British state or face the challenges of globalisation beyond it'. Gradually, however, an understanding may be emerging, as the Scottish level is strengthened and politicised, about the relationships among culture, economics and politics, and the need for a distinctive Scottish synthesis.

Social inclusion is a dominant theme in the policy in the rhetoric of the Scottish Executive. This corresponds to a similar emphasis at the UK level (although it is called combating social exclusion in England). The emphasis, consistent with New Labour ideology, is on opportunities rather than social engineering or redistribution but it does mark a change from the Conservative years when governments regularly attacked the 'dependency culture' of Scotland. Scotland is thus pursuing a modernised social democratic strategy, strongly conditioned by territorial institutions and shared identity, but with only a cautious invoking of cultural or nation-building themes.

WALES

Wales in the United Kingdom

Welsh politics, culture and identity are, to a much greater extent than with Scotland, the result of Wales's long history of intertwined relations with its big neighbour, England. The Act of Union, unlike the Acts of Union between Scotland and England in 1707 or between Ireland and England in 1801, completely assimilated Wales into the English political, administrative and ecclesiastical system. Wales did, however, retain its language and most Welsh people gravitated to non-conformist Protestantism especially after the religious revivals of the eighteenth and nineteenth centuries. The Church of England nonetheless remained the established church of both England and Wales until disestablishment in 1920 when the Welsh Anglicans set up a separate province known as the Church *in* Wales. In the nineteenth and early twentieth centuries, Anglicanism was largely identified with the English interest in Wales and disestablishment became a *cause célèbre* and a powerful force for defining Welsh non-conformist identity. Today, the Church in Wales is strongly identified with the Welsh nation as is illustrated by the fact that a requirement for becoming one of the seven Welsh bishops is a knowledge of the Welsh language.

Wales, like Scotland, the North and Midlands of England, and the North-East of Ireland, did participate in the development of Britain as the greatest industrial and imperial power of the nineteenth century. At one time,

Cardiff was the coal capital of the world and the South Wales valleys were great centres of industrial activity. However, the harsh working conditions of the Welsh working-class gave rise to radical politics in the form of Chartism or militant trade unionism. This was closely linked to Welsh religious non-conformity and a strong sense of solidarity and egalitarianism in the rural and working-class communities. There was a strong identification of a majority of Welsh people with parties which represented the peripheries of British politics, rather than Conservative Unionism. At first, it was the Liberal Party and, then the Labour Party, which represented this tradition. Despite these common historical experiences and a sense of overarching common identity, Wales emerged into the modern world as a nation deeply divided by several cleavages, which have hampered its search for nation-hood and a common purpose. These cleavages are: economic-geographic (described in this section); linguistic-ethnic (described below in the section on culture and identity); and political (described in the section on political leadership).

Culture and Identity

Despite the assimilation of Wales into the English polity in the sixteenth century, and despite subsequent attempts to penalise the Welsh language, the Welsh nevertheless preserved and even strengthened a separate linguistic and religious culture from those of England. Indeed, these two aspects were closely linked. First, the Bible was translated into Welsh by Bishop William Morgan, an eminent scripture scholar of his day, as early as 1588 (the Irish Bible appeared only in 1690 and the Scots Gaelic only in 1801, and Scots in 1983!). The Welsh Bible played the same role for Welsh as Luther's Bible did for German, giving the language both a high literary expression as well as unifying its literary form by giving it a common vocabulary, syntax and grammar. Although Morgan was an Anglican the non-conformist Protestant traditions were strongly Bible-based, rather than ritualistic, and reading of the Bible in Welsh and English, both at home and in the community's chapel, was an integral part of the lives of the majority of Welsh people until well into the twentieth century.

The linguistic cleavage between Welsh- and English-speakers goes back to the nineteenth century. For most of that century, the language of the majority of Welsh people was Welsh, although many of these were bilingual. Monoglot English-speakers were mainly members of the upper classes but these were joined by the new industrial proletariat in working in the coal-mines and steel-works. Many of these came from rural Wales and boosted the presence of Welsh in the valleys but gradually these switched to English, along with the immigrants, mainly from Ireland but also from Italy,

Poland and some British and other colonies such as the Caribbean and Somalia. By the early part of the twentieth century, Welsh had become a minority language, although Welsh-speakers tended to see themselves as 'true Welsh' (*fior cymreig*) and there was a great deal of antagonism between them and the English-speaking Welsh. The 1931 census figures show that 36.8 per cent of the population (above the age of 3) were Welsh-speakers. This had declined to 18.7 per cent by 1991, although there has been a slight reversal of this trend in recent years. These bald figures, however, do not reveal the complexities with regard to Welsh-speaking and English-speaking communities in Wales.

First, there is the problem of defining what Welsh-speaking means. Second, there is the question of the status of the language in public and social life. Third, there is the relationship between language, identity and politics. The census figures need further refinement by more focused questions exploring these issues. In June 2000, the Welsh Language Board published a report on 'The State of the Welsh Language', which gives a more nuanced picture (Welsh Language Board, 2000). With regard to the meaning of Welsh-speaking, this report defined Welsh-speakers as those who speak the language fluently or very well. It emerged that 11 per cent were fluent, 5 per cent spoke it fairly well, 2 per cent spoke some Welsh, 27 per cent spoke just a few words, while 55 per cent spoke no Welsh at all. Thus, those speaking some Welsh, including those speaking only a few words is the figure given in the 1991 census for those who speak the language, although, clearly, the number of competent Welsh-speakers is much less than this figure suggests. However, this rather sombre picture is modified by the increase in Welsh-speaking among younger age groups, thanks to the introduction of compulsory Welsh and the provision of Welsh-medium schools.

With regard to the language's status, the position is more positive. The same survey revealed that 75 per cent of those interviewed, English- as well as Welsh-speakers, consider that the language will continue as a living entity for the foreseeable future. 89 per cent of all respondents of both languages thought the language was important for Welsh culture. A significant proportion thought knowledge of the language was useful in obtaining employment and the demand for bilingual skills would grow especially in certain sectors (60 per cent thought education such an area; 48 per cent the local authority sector; and 44 per cent the health service). Even more encouraging for the future of the language was the finding that almost everyone (with only 6 per cent disagreeing) thought there should be more bilingual education than is currently available and that more English medium schools should teach some subjects in Welsh. These developments are significant when we compare attitudes to Welsh during the 1979 referendum on devolution when there was a great fear in the English-speaking community that a devolved Assembly would be dominated by 'Welshies'. The position of the language has also been strengthened in public policy terms through the setting up of S4C (*Sianel Pedwar Cymru* – Channel Four Wales), the Welsh Language Act of 1993 and the subsequent setting up of the Welsh Language Board to protect and promote the language.

The final point concerns the relationship between language and identity, and the relationship between these two and politics. First, it should be noted that 74 per cent of respondents to the WLB survey were born in Wales and, of the remainder, 21 per cent were born in England. 76 per cent of all respondents considered themselves to be Welsh but 96 per cent of Welsh-speakers did so. Welsh-speakers considered themselves to be more Welsh (96 per cent) than British while among English-speakers only 73 per cent felt this (Welsh Language Board, 2000). On the political level, the Welsh-speaking communities have tended to support Plaid Cymru; the Welsh-born English communities, the Labour Party or the Liberal Democrats; and those of English origin, the Conservative Party or the Liberal Democrats. However, Plaid Cymru has in recent years have tried (with some success) to penetrate into English-speaking areas Wales, such as the Valleys. While old Labour dominated the Welsh-speaking areas in the 1950s and 1960s, their attitude to the language was ambivalent and sometimes even hostile. New Labour, at least, has made efforts to improve its relations with the Welsh-language community. The Conservatives have also attracted some high-profile Welsh-speakers and Welsh-born English-speakers.

The new respectability of the Welsh language and the employment opportunities which have followed the new governmental language policy have led to the emergence of a Welsh-speaking urban elite, whose sociological characteristics are quite different from the traditional Welsh-speaker from the 'heartlands'. In certain sectors of public employment, such as education, the media or public administration, and in parts of the private sector, it is now a distinct advantage in employment terms to be a Welsh-speaker. As we shall see below, this is leading to new cleavages on the language issue in the area of employment, which may be exacerbated by the bilingual nature of the National Assembly for Wales.

Another cleavage, related to but not identical with, the language issue, is what might be called the 'ethnic' cleavage. In Wales there are three main ethnolinguistic groups: the Welsh-speaking Welsh; the English-speaking Anglo-Welsh, born in Wales; and the English-speaking incomers, the majority of whom were born in England and that these groups are dominant in defined geographical areas (Balsom and Jones, 1984). There is also a small minority of other ethnic groups. Some of these, such as the Irish,

Italian, Poles, Somalis, and Yemenis migrated into Wales at the end of the nineteenth century, as mentioned above. These have been more or less assimilated into the large English-speaking Welsh group, although they have retained a sense of identity with their original culture. There has been a more recent immigration from the Indian sub-continent and, to a lesser extent, from the West Indies, who have a more uneasy relationship with the Welsh population and, from time to time, experience racist abuse and violence similar to what happens in other parts of the United Kingdom.

These reflections illustrate the complexity of Welsh culture and identity, which is, in some respects, even more complex than Northern Ireland and certainly more so than Scotland. Nevertheless, despite the complexity, there is an overarching sense of Welshness even if this is difficult to define and which expresses itself in games such as rugby. There is a positive Welsh stereotype which has traditionally been seen as somewhat similar to that portrayed in John Ford's 1941 film *How Green was my Valley,* in which closely knit family and villages, in which workers, lead a happy, contented life, singing hymns in Welsh on their home from the mines or fields. Although this stereotype bears little relation to the reality of life in the mines, and although it makes contemporary Welsh people squirm, the myth of a communitarian and egalitarian Wales is still strong, particularly but not exclusively, in the Welsh-language communities. Related to this myth is the tradition of radical politics, itself closely linked to the tradition of religious non-conformity, where chapel congregations elected their pastors in an egalitarian fashion and where a Biblical sense of social justice was very strong. In the Welsh-language communities, there is a tradition, derived from the Bible, of the Welsh nation as the elect of God, with a special destiny marking it off from the big neighbour England (the seat of godlessness).

There is, however, another Welsh stereotype, which is less positive and wholesome. This is the one held by the outside world especially by the English media (that is the media controlled by English people in England). The stereotype presented to the outside world is often far from flattering. The Welsh are seen as impractical talkers and singers but incapable of entrepreneurship, as John Redwood, one the last Conservative Secretaries of State for Wales, put it. In this negative stereotype, the Welsh language is regarded with distaste but even with regard to English-speaking Welsh people, it is interesting that speaking with a Welsh accent is regarded unfavourably by producers of television commercials, while having a Scottish or even an Irish accent is regarded as chic. This negative image is often shared by Welsh people themselves, as for example, the Welsh-made film *Twin Town* and recent television shows, which present a dreary, unattractive picture of Welsh life, racked by unemployment, drugs, casual sex and violence. This self-image is also an expression of what might be termed a psychological, but deeply resented, dependency on the big neighbour England. Policy makers are aware of these problems and of how difficult it is to mobilise Welsh identity and culture in the same way that the Irish (with a rather similar historical experience) have managed to convert an external stereotypical image of backwardness into one that is positive, dynamic and attractive. In order to market itself in the manner of Ireland or Catalonia, Wales needs to develop an image that is neither the romantic *How Green was my Valley* of John Ford's film, nor the dreary rain-sodden urban landscapes of *Twin Town*, but one which points to the existence of both an exciting minority language and culture and to the new political institutions established by devolution.

So far, Welsh policy makers have failed to promote an identity which can serve as a mobilising tool for a development project. There is still a certain amount of ambiguity about the Welsh language itself: is it a symbol of backward-looking, regressive and moribund rural communities and a small Cardiff middle-class elite, or can it, on the contrary, be harnessed as an element of modernisation in the new Wales. In fact, it is both these things. Undoubtedly, elements of the negative stereotype may found in the Welsh-language, but also the old English-language, communities. On the other hand, the language has been enjoying a modest but significant revival over the past several years and, at least in Wales itself, there is a greater interest in it among English-speakers than ever before. The example of small stateless nations such as Catalonia or Quebec is to hand to show that a community speaking a minority language can also be dynamic, outward-looking and 'progressive'. Still, harnessing the language into a modernising economic development project still remains an uphill struggle. With regard to Welsh culture and identity more generally, the notion of 'cool Cymru' (the Welsh word for Wales) has been promoted in relation to the emergence of a new rock scene based in the city of Newport. The National Assembly set for itself the task of promoting such a positive image and a working party was established by the First Minister to examine the question. It is the hope of Welsh policy-makers that the Assembly itself as a new kind of bilingual institution will become the new symbol of Wales.

Political Leadership

Political leadership in Wales has been largely in the hands of the Labour Party, which has exercised a hegemonic control since the 1920s, with only short interludes such as the Tory gains of the 1960s and then in the 1980s. Until the wilderness years of the 1980s, the party has been strongly centralist and anti-nationalist, although there have been some minority voices in favour of devolution. The Labour Party saw its primary task as capturing both the levers of the state at Westminster and the 'commanding heights of the economy' in order better to redistribute the benefits of national wealth to its working class constituents. Welsh Labour, marked by a long tradition of militancy in the Valleys and industrial South Wales, but also by the great levels of poverty and deprivation experienced by their supporters were strongly attached to this perspective. The link to the centre (London) was seen as a lifeline for many of these people. Welsh nationalism was regarded with particular alarm as it was perceived as putting this lifeline in danger. Furthermore, nationalism was strongly associated with the imposition of the Welsh language on a population which, although it possessed a sense of Welsh identity, was now English-speaking. Labour inherited the mantle of the old nineteenth century Liberal Party, with the latter being reduced to a small minority party within the country. Today, this tradition is represented by the Liberal Democrats, a party which was formed in the 1980s (at the UK level). Although the Liberal tradition is associated with decentralisation and even federalism, the Welsh Liberal Democrats, or at least their grass-roots supporters, were rather lukewarm towards the 1979 devolution programme. This may be because much of their membership is drawn from the English-born incomers who identify with neither Labour nor the Conservatives but nor do they identify with a Welsh civil society or nation. The main opposition to the Labour Party in Wales until the 1997 General Election has been the Conservative Party, which, in Wales, has been strongly unionist and ambivalent towards the Welsh language (Tories have been traditionally anti-Welsh language but, on the other hand, the language made big gains under the last Tory Prime Minister, John Major). Although the Conservatives made important gains in the 1960s and 1980s, they failed to elect any candidates at all in the General Elections of 1997 and 2001. Finally, the main representative of Welsh nationalism has been *Plaid Cymru*, meaning the Party of Wales, whose support base has been mainly in the Welsh-speaking communities of north and west Wales. Plaid Cymru was previously more of a pressure group, agitating mainly on the issue of the language and a rather conservative brand of 'community politics'. Its breakthrough as a political party came in the 1960s when it managed to have some members elected, mainly in rural Wales. The Welsh Labour Party has been somewhat paranoid about Plaid Cymru and, in the 1970s, the party (with the Scottish National Party) was perceived to be enough of a threat to provoke the then Labour government of James Callaghan to launch the ill-fated 1979 devolution proposals as a way of staving off this threat.

This political and economic landscape began to change in the 1980s during the long period of Tory rule from 1979 until 1997. We can highlight the drastic economic transformation which undermined the old Labour support bases. This benefited the Conservatives for a short period but, as the realities of Thatcherite policies began to bite into public services and with the significant levels of deprivation which resulted from economic restructuring, Welsh public opinion turned against the central government in London. However, unlike in Scotland, this did not lead to a mobilisation around a common political project equivalent to the Scottish Constitutional Convention. Instead, the Labour Party became deeply divided between those who clung to 'old Labour' approaches and those who identified with the New Labour attempts to modernise the party - although this did not imply support for Blairism but rather a support for the new policy agenda which had been initiated by Neil Kinnock and which included devolution. It was this ambivalence towards devolution as well as the traditional antipathy towards Welsh nationalism as represented by Plaid Cymru that hampered the Yes campaign in the 1997 referendum when there was no coalition of interests campaigning for the new Assembly. The other interesting and important development during this period has been the transformation of Plaid Cymru from a rather conservative, rurally-based party campaigning on the language question into a much more broadly-based 'politically correct' party, which has begun to make inroads into the English-language community. This change was symbolised by the addition of the English version of the name to the party's title: Plaid Cymru the Party of Wales. These changes have worked themselves out in the elections to the National Assembly where Labour is still the majority party, but is now in a coalition with the Liberal Democrats. Plaid Cymru is the second party in numbers of seats and is the unofficial opposition party. The Conservatives have the smallest number of seats but now accept devolution, at least in part because it allows them to have some representation in Welsh politics.

The new Assembly was meant to inaugurate a new kind of politics, different from both Westminster and traditional local government. In practice, although there are distinctively new features of the system, Welsh politics, as in Scotland, has fallen back into the Westminster mode, albeit through coalition governments with the nationalists being the official opposition.

Institutions

It was only with the setting up of the Welsh Office and the establishment of a Secretary of State for Wales in 1964 that Wales began to develop its own distinctive political institutions. Most power was concentrated in the hands of the Secretary of State who had a seat in the UK Cabinet, and who exercised this power with the help of a small number of junior ministers.

The 'territorialisation' of Welsh public administration was a slow and erratic process. First, several public utilities such as water and electricity were not geographically bounded by the Welsh border but overlapped across the border with parts of England. Second, although it is true to say that Wales developed a kind of government, this bore more resemblance to a kind of colonial rule from Westminster rather than something that was recognisably democratic. On the contrary, government in Wales, especially during the long period of Conservative governments, tended to take the form of rule by quangos. 'Quangoisation' became an element of the Tory governments' onslaught against British local authorities when the latter transferred many of their functions to these non-elected agencies. In Wales, despite the low level of support for the Conservative party, they were often headed by Tory place-men, who had sometimes been defeated in parliamentary elections. Third, the operating culture of the Welsh Office and the Civil Service in Wales, was quite different from that of their counterparts in the Scottish Office despite their both being part of the 'imperial' or 'home' civil service, with the Scots displaying somewhat greater independence than the Welsh. This culture of dependency in Wales was due to a number of factors: the more recent formation of the Welsh Office (1964) compared to the Scottish Office (set up in 1885 with a Secretary of State with a seat in the Cabinet since 1926); the scant resources at the disposal of Welsh civil servants; a reflection of the more general culture of dependency in Wales mentioned above. Despite these limitations, Wales did have a system of administrative devolution from 1964 but one that was characterised by a large democratic deficit. The deficiencies of the Welsh Office and what was dubbed 'The Quango State' were severely criticised by many within Wales.

One of the strongest arguments in favour of devolution in 1997, therefore, was that Wales could develop as a dynamic European region only if this democratic deficit were filled. Despite the low turnout and the slim majority, both of which have been detrimental to both the legitimacy and the credibility of the new institution, the Welsh National Assembly has been set up and this has fundamentally changed the nature of the Welsh system of government and administration. Most politicians and interest group leaders (including those who opposed its setting up such as Tory Assembly Members and others) agree that the Assembly is here to stay and that devolution is irreversible. Another way of expressing this is to say that the Assembly has replaced the Welsh Secretary of State and the Welsh Office as the nexus of policy making within Wales. The role of the Secretary of State has been reduced and there is a question mark over the future of the office of Secretary of State in a devolved UK. The Welsh Office civil service has now been largely transferred to the Welsh National Assembly.

For Welsh civil servants this has been a 'sea change'. Today, they must work closely with a democratically elected body which is also on a steep learning curve. Furthermore, both members of the Assembly (AMs) and civil servants have a wide array of tasks. The old Welsh Office culture of dependency on Whitehall is of little help in this rather stressful and turbulent situation and it is true that the new Assembly, despite its irreversibility, still has to find its feet in this new devolved world.

To some extent this is a consequence of the limited powers that were given to the Assembly compared to the Scottish Parliament. First, unlike the Parliament, it has neither primary legislative powers nor tax-raising powers. Second, while the Parliament has 129 members, the Assembly has only 60, which is an insufficient number to carry out all the tasks that are asked of it.

The Assembly Preparatory Group which was set up to design the details of the new institutions tried to make a virtue out of these limitations by arguing that it was an opportunity to design an institution which was based neither on Westminster-style government nor on the traditions of local government but would borrow from best practice around the world. Thus, it was claimed that the Assembly would be inclusive, transparent, close to the people and (for its members) family-friendly as opposed to the exclusive, secretive, elitist and family-destructive system which operated in Westminster. These promises have been met to some extent as there is very easy access to the Assembly and its individual Members, open meetings of committees on most issues, and a working day which takes into account the needs of AMs with family commitments. However, the attempt to develop a new inclusive type of politics in Wales based on consensus among the parties has proved more elusive. The first Labour executive was elected without an absolute majority of votes and attempted to be 'inclusive' through the committee system. In the end, this proved impossible with the defeat of the executive on a number of important issues and the resignation of the First Secretary, Alun Michael, who was replaced by his opponent in the leadership election, Rhodri Morgan. Thus, 'inclusive' government led to great instability. In the end, Morgan had to resort to forming a coalition with the Liberal Democrats in an attempt to create greater stability in the government of the Assembly.

Government in Wales is now a balancing act between the executive, led by a First Minister, and several powerful committees. The committee system was an attempt to move beyond the divisive politics that characterised Westminster to one more characterised by consensus. The idea was that while the Cabinet would be composed principally of members of the biggest party (inevitably the Labour Party), the committee chairs would be shared among the opposition as well as the leading party. To some extent this has worked out in practice with committee members working together quite well. The actual functioning of the committees, however, has been rather uneven with, for example, European Affairs still having to find its feet (Loughlin, 2001) and others, such as economic development or agriculture and rural development playing a very important role.

External Relations

One of the strongest arguments put forward by the Blair government in favour of the Welsh Assembly was that devolved government was necessary for Wales to become a strong, dynamic region in the new Europe. This contrasted with the justification for the Scottish Parliament, which was couched much more in terms of Scotland receiving back the trappings of nationhood. Somewhat ironically, however, it is the European Affairs Committee of the Parliament which has developed a stronger European and international profile than the European Committee of the Assembly, which has found it difficult to find its feet (Loughlin, 2001). To some extent, this is a consequence of the differences between the two institutions as the Parliament must translate European legislation directly into Scottish law without waiting for Westminster, while the Assembly, having only powers of secondary legislation, is dependent on Westminster to do this. Another irony is that the Assembly, like Welsh local government, is considerably reducing its European commitments (such as membership of the Assembly of European regions (AER) or the Conference of Peripheral and Maritime Regions) and is content, instead, to rely on its representation via Westminster. This irony is probably easily explained by reference to the new political context. During the years of rather hysterical anti-European Conservative governments, sub-national authorities in the UK (including Tory-led southern English councils) went 'straight to Europe', bypassing central government. Today, with a more Europe-friendly central government of the same party, there is felt to be less need to do this. Furthermore, ministers from the devolved institutions may be present in meetings of the EU Council of Ministers, although they represent the UK as a whole rather than their own nations. Finally, there seems to be a good working relationship between the devolved assemblies and the UK representation in Brussels, which is an important intermediary body between the Commission and the Council, and is the locus where key decisions are taken. If the 'territorial' interests can be taken into account at this level, this is more important than investing resources in bodies such as the AER. This, at least, is the argument put forward.

A strong European orientation is seen to be necessary both because of Welsh economic backwardness and because of its successes. It backwardness has made it necessary to seek Objective 1 funds from the EU and the Assembly (although not its European but its Economic Affairs Committee) is now responsible for overseeing these funds. This means that it is necessary to have an input into the EU decision-making system, although funds are negotiated by Whitehall and Wales even required a special dispensation from the UK Treasury to get spending cover to use the funds. On the plus side, the restructuring of the Welsh economy outlined above has produced a more balanced economy in Wales where dependency on a few sectors has been reduced. There are, nevertheless, features that distinguish the Welsh economy from the UK economy as a whole. Manufacturing still plays a more prominent role in the Welsh economy than it does in the UK economy as a whole: it accounts for 27.8 per cent of Welsh GDP compared with 20.8 per cent of UK GDP (ONS, 1998). In terms of its exports, the Welsh economy is even more strongly integrated into the EU economy than the UK's, in 1991, with 72.1 per cent of exports from Wales going to the EU – compared with 60.8 per cent for the UK economy. Consequently, it may be said that there is a stronger case to be argued in Wales in favour of joining the European single currency. Having been integrated into the macro-economic framework of the UK and strongly integrated into the EU economy, several interviewees commented that, in conceptual terms, Wales had 'less of a problem' about integrating into the larger economy of the EU. This will be another key indicator to analyse in any future referendum on UK entry to the Euro.

Policy

Public policy in Wales has been dominated over the last twenty-five years by the level of restructuring that has taken place in the economy. With the decline of heavy industry, there are few remnants of the traditional industrial sectors that once dominated Welsh economic output. This restructuring led to the establishment of the Welsh Development Agency (WDA) in 1976, which was given the task of regenerating the economy of Wales. One of its key objectives was to attract foreign direct investment to compensate for the loss of jobs in traditional sectors and it has succeeded in attracting many large companies from overseas, notably from the USA, Europe and Japan. Whilst news of job creation was almost invariably greeted favourably, increasing concerns have been raised in the last few years over the sustainability of such a strategy. Many of the manufacturing jobs that were attracted to Wales on the basis of favourable commercial conditions – including relatively low wages – have now been lost to areas that have even lower labour costs (especially Eastern Europe). As a consequence, the debate more recently has shifted in favour of devoting more resources to indigenous business. This is reflected in a number of strategic initiatives that seek to promote economic prosperity in Wales.

Within these strategic initiatives, much attention has been focused on creating sustainable, high-value jobs. The WDA has sought to be at the forefront of some leading edge European practices, especially in the field of innovation (Rhisiart and Thomas, 2000). Another important area where Wales has traditionally lagged behind, as noted above, is entrepreneurship. Recognition of the problem led the National Assembly to issue a strategic document, *Entrepreneurship Action Plan for Wales*. The vision outlined within the document is of 'a bold and confident nation where entrepreneurship is valued celebrated and exercised throughout society and in the widest range of economic circumstances' (NAW, 2000). It will be a formidable task to transform that vision into the increased business birth rates that are required to help increase Welsh GDP per capita, which stands at only 82 per cent of the UK average (only Northern Ireland and the North East of England have lower percentages).

One of the strongest arguments put forward during the devolution debate was that Wales needed an Assembly to tackle these issues and to turn Wales into a powerful economic region in a new European context. Despite its limitations, it is clear that the Assembly, with its executive and committees, is developing a crucial role in shaping public policy in Wales. There is a fixed budget decided by the UK Cabinet but it is the Assembly which decides how to prioritise within this budget and may decide to emphasise for example health, rather than post-16 education. This, in effect, is the Assembly's most important role as the representative government of the people of Wales. But it has run into two difficulties. First, the sheer size of the task has stretched the capacity of both the Assembly members and the committees for many of whom this is their first experience of government and, indeed, political activity. This problem is largely related to the newness of the institution and the Assembly needs a period of time to 'find its feet'. The second problem is related to the distance of the Assembly in the eyes of public opinion mentioned above. Basically, the issue of which priorities to choose for the governance of Wales has failed to generate a healthy public debate with the possible exception of the agricultural crisis and the arrival of Objective 1 funds.

Another problem relates to the difficulties of groups and individuals who might be considered as members or potential members of policy communities in 'penetrating' the Assembly. Ironically, this is not because the Assembly is not 'transparent' enough but because it is *too* transparent. Many organisations simply did not know where the contact should be made and which were the appropriate parts of the institution that they should penetrate.

The key question from the point of view the theme of this book is whether the new institutions and the new policy-making system will be capable of generating a new kind of dynamic, innovative culture in Welsh society and how identity may be used or reformulated in this context. The evidence so far is mixed. It is probably true to say that the new Assembly is restructuring the policy-making system in Wales and there are signs of the beginnings of a new kind of approach that is more open and inclusive. Sectors such as local government, the trade unions and the voluntary sector which had been frozen out of the decision-making process by the Conservatives are now welcomed with open arms by the Assembly (most of whose members come from these sectors). The business sector, on the other hand, feels somewhat left out. Furthermore, as Welsh is, with English, one of the two working languages of the Assembly, the new institution is a concrete expression of the aspiration towards a bilingual society in Wales. On the other hand, there have been fears raised that the preference given to those who speak Welsh may lead to discrimination against non-Welsh-speakers. Nevertheless, the sting seems to have been taken out the language conflict and most Welsh people have accepted the language as part of their culture. Welsh-speakers on the other hand are more accepting of English-speakers as 'truly' Welsh. These new attitudes find expression in the bilingual Assembly. What is less certain, given the low public profile and the operating difficulties of the Assembly as presently constructed, whether it will be able to forge a more 'modern' and dynamic culture and identity capable of counteracting the negative stereotypes mentioned above. This was considered so important that in 2001 the First Minister set up a working party on identity to examine the issue.

In December 2001, the Assembly Government published its programme of economic development for the next ten years in a document optimistically entitled *A Winning Wales* (National Assembly for Wales, 2001). The general thrust of this strategy is that the government of the new Assembly will 'transform the economy of Wales, while promoting sustainable development' so that Wales will 'within a generation' achieve the same standard of living of the UK as a whole. Clearly influenced by the new regional development model based on innovation and learning (Cooke and Morgan, 1998), the strategy seeks to 'increase the knowledge, research and development, and innovation capacity in all parts of the Welsh economy'. There is an emphasis on spreading economic development to all parts of Wales and not just to the area around Cardiff. There is also an emphasis on partnership approaches involving communities and businesses with the National Assembly. The document sees the promotion of Welsh culture as a key element of the new strategy: 'We want Wales to be a country that has a distinctive and creative culture with bilingualism a growing reality. This culture will thrive where the relationship between people, their schools and colleges, their workplace and their environment is strong'. As if aware of the negative image that Wales sometimes has, alluded to above, it goes on: 'We want to promote a positive and confident image of Wales, both externally and internally, and capitalise on our natural advantages'. To round off this vision, both social inclusion and environmental concerns are included under the key theme of sustainable development as part of the new strategy. Finally, it is recognised that Wales is a part both of the UK and wider European economic systems. It remains to be seen whether the Assembly, or at least the Assembly Government, will be able to transform this vision, the creation of a new Welsh myth or stereotype, into concrete realities. 15 billion pounds are allocated, either directly or in related policy programmes, to do so and there is a detailed action programme. But we will know the answer to this question only in ten years time or longer.

CONCLUSIONS

The United Kingdom is a multinational state in which complexity and cultural pluralism have always received at least some symbolic recognition. Despite the hostility exhibited periodically to the Welsh language, there was no Jacobin strategy of cultural assimilation as in France. Yet central government monopolised political authority and active economic intervention including regional policy was always centralised. Now devolution has decentralised political authority to the smaller nations at the same time as decentralised economic strategies and endogenous development have come into fashion. The question of the relationship among national identity, culture, political institutions and development strategies is thus posed.

Both Scotland and Wales have entered devolution under the leadership of the Labour Party, so it is not surprising that their strategies follow the social democratic model as modified by New Labour, with an emphasis on combining competitiveness with social inclusion. Both administrations, facing nationalists as their principal opposition, have been wary of explicit nation-building measures or rhetoric that might give ammunition to the nationalists. Wales has made some use of new regionalist themes, which have been championed by prominent Welsh academics (Cooke and Morgan, 1998) to forge an image of itself as a performing region, drawing on its own traditions of solidarity and community. The Scottish Executive has been less interested in this, partly because it sees Scotland as a mature and plural nation rather than a solidary community. Scotland also has a long experience of regional development strategy based on the agency model, and this has not radically changed with devolution.

In both cases devolution has forced a rethinking of easy assumptions made during the opposition years of the 1980s and 1990s about social consensus and progressive values. This has in some cases proved difficult, especially given the often naïve hopes that devolution would usher in a new era of consensual and conflict-free politics. Yet there is also strong evidence of policy communities adjusting to devolution, strengthening their territorial organisation, and engaging in a new debate on development at the Scottish and Welsh levels (Keating and Loughlin, 2002). We have also found evidence that, by bringing in more actors and reducing the opportunities for powerful groups to by-pass the territorial level and go directly to the centre, devolution has broadened the development agenda and promoted more dialogue within Scotland and Wales. Groups must couch their demands in general interest terms to appeal to other participants in the policy process and the trade-offs that are the stuff of politics have to be made locally. Consequently, development agendas include issues of sustainable development, social inclusion and culture as well as economic competition. The impact of this on policy outcomes, however, can only be assessed in the longer term.

7.   Conclusion

CULTURE, COLLECTIVE ACTION AND DEVELOPMENT

Our aim in this book has not been to demonstrate exactly what causes some regions to develop faster than others. We certainly do not dispute that traditional factor endowments play a large role, as do the economies of scope and scale that arise from geographical proximity. Yet there is a broad consensus in the literature that there is something else at work, less tangible and related to the social construction of regions and our aim has been to explore this dimension. The literature also agrees on the critical importance of collective action and social mobilisation across disparate social and economic groups who might normally be antagonistic but can be brought into a common endeavour in the name of the region as a shared community. This has led us to examine the construction of regions as 'imagined communities' around the theme of development. Some regions, it is clear, do this better than others and are more successful in sustaining a common vision.

It is easy to attribute this to primordial or perennial features of each territorial society, taken as a whole. At the limit this becomes a mere rehearsal of regional stereotypes and a rather circular explanation of success and failure; as we have seen, regional actors themselves often invoke these stereotypes as a form of rationalisation. At the other extreme, we might present the capacity for a common vision and for social co-operation as something that can simply be wished into existence, telling regions that they can succeed merely by learning from the leaders or by adopting the right institutions and procedures. Our approach has two features. We do not attribute cultural features to regional society as a reified whole, but to actors working within a given institutional framework. Culture and norms therefore mediate between individuals and institutions and cannot be reduced to the one or the other. Secondly, we see culture neither as primordial, nor as something that can be created 'ex novo' merely by an act of will. It is the result, rather, or actors working with existing materials, reshaping them in the process.

The common identity forged by regional culture also permits actors to reconcile some rather discordant themes which might otherwise be sources of fragmentation and internal conflict. The first is the opposition of tradition and modernity so familiar to generations of sociologists, who see modernity as involving an increase in functional differentiation and a diminution of social attachments and solidarities based on territory or culture. The second is the tension between inward-looking and outward-looking conceptions of regional identity, since both seem to be necessary in a modern regional productive system. Third is the clash between economic development and social cohesion, traditionally managed at the level of the nation-state but increasingly mediated at the regional level. Here the common framework of identity and action can either allow a negotiated trade-off between growth and distribution, or permit the region to change to a more virtuous development path in which collective action can both enhance productive efficiency and sustain social solidarity. Fourth is the tension between the market and regional culture itself. While in the modernist paradigm, these are seen as in conflict, new models of development suggest that they may be compatible and even mutually sustaining.

While primordial explanations are ultimately non-explanations, our eight case studies suggest that raw materials do matter and that there is a degree of historic path-dependency. Yet the past, as historians know, tends to be seen through present-day lenses and the gap between tradition and modernity is amenable to intellectual reinterpretation. Catalonia and Flanders have a 'usable' past as historic trading regions in which the economic dimension plays an important role in the imagination of the territory – even if there have been some historic discontinuities. Brittany can also count on traditions of collective action, and a legacy of Christian-democratic efforts to modernise tradition as the condition of survival. Languedoc-Roussillon and Galicia have a self-image of failure which is self-perpetuating and social relations have indeed been highly fragmented for a long time. Languedoc-Roussillon lacks even a memory as a definable space or any tradition of autonomy. In Wales, traditions of communitarianism rooted in an older society have been invoked as a form of modern social capital. Yet this faces a contrary legacy from the industrial era. As in the west of Scotland and in Wallonia, a history of domination by heavy industry, big firms and Fordist production patterns has left a class polarisation, a lack of social co-operation and a poor record of entrepreneurship. These distinct patterns have become somewhat self-perpetuating to produce vicious or virtuous circles and positive and negative stereotypes which involve certain features of territorial societies being applied to the society as a whole to create a whole story of success or failure. Such patterns, in the case of Galicia or Languedoc-Roussillon, are hard to shift.

Yet regions are not completely trapped in their past and change can sometimes come quite rapidly, in response to external shocks or internal dynamics. Such change may help to strengthen social co-operation and consensus on development, or destroy them, fragment the territory and incorporate it into the global market on terms dictated from outside. The transition of Scotland and Wales from old industrial societies under the Conservative governments of the 1980s and 1990s involved massive disruption and a 'scorched earth' policy in which the social and cultural underpinnings of the old production model were rather deliberately destroyed. Scotland and Wales were excoriated for being trapped in a 'dependency culture' and 'collectivism'. There was consequently no effort to rescue those elements of the old industrial culture, or even the traditional skills, that might have value in the new conditions. There was a certain effort to rebuild a business class in Scotland, but this flew in the face of the overall effort to insert the economy into global markets, and a strong hostility to political devolution. There was, however, a reaction to this, which emphasised precisely the common territorial and cultural identity and the resulting political and social mobilisation may have helped move Scotland and Wales from the politics of opposition to more constructive institution-building after 1997. Brittany, on the other hand, had a less brutal and more successful transition from the 1950s onwards, with a role for the new local elites or *forces vives* who shifted the image of the region from one of backwardness to modernity. Like Scotland and Wales, Wallonia was hit by a massive industrial crisis in the 1980s which dealt a severe blow to regional self-confidence and self-perception, but recently local management of change has helped to forge a more positive self-image, rescuing elements of the industrial culture rather than consigning it all to the waste bin. Catalonia's economic restructuring in the 1980s was less radical but substantial and managed partly by local leadership committed, for political reasons, to sustaining a common vision. Languedoc-Roussillon's economic restructuring in the 1970s and 1980s was dominated in the early stage by the central state with no commitment to sustaining a regional vision and served further to fragment local identities and collective capacities. Regionalists failed to produce a counterbalance in the form of modernised tradition and were rendered largely irrelevant. Even when decentralisation came in the 1980s, it was the city leaders who were the beneficiaries. So a regional theme is now hardly available for development efforts.

Inward and outward conceptions of identity and action have been reconciled in most of our cases by the theme of the Europe of the regions as part of an evolving transnational order. Europe has facilitated the building of imagined regional communities by providing a new discursive space marked by themes of modernity and development. Europe gives a new legitimacy to regionalism by dissociating it from parochialism and tying it to the future. It also allows the regions to project themselves beyond the state and, by posing as actors in the transnational sphere, to reinforce identity back home. For regional nationalist parties, it also helps to blur the difference between independence and devolution within the state. This has proved immensely important in Catalonia and Flanders, which have pressed for more autonomy in time with steps to European integration, and have been very active in the Europe of the regions movement. The very indefinition of the goals of the European project helps actors with rather different aspirations co-operate in the pursuit of regional influence and European resources. Scotland and Wales were later-comers to the European game than Catalonia and Flanders, but since the late 1980s Europe has transformed their self-understanding to the point that their nationalist parties are the most pro-European in the United Kingdom (with the possible exception of Northern Ireland's SDLP). Neither Galicia nor Languedoc-Roussillon, on the other hand, has developed a shared vision of Europe.

Shared culture and identity does not, in our cases, banish class conflict in favour of solidarity and social cohesion. Class politics are still played out, but in a new framework in which the region plays a role, albeit not an exclusive one, in social mediation. So culture, identity and a shared vision, where they are consistent with development and change, can provide and a basis for social concertation, although to speak of regional corporatism would be an exaggeration. Development, rather, seems to flourish on the basis of 'weak ties' which do not monopolise social relations or lock actors into outdated patterns. Common regional identity is not, as sometimes imaged, a substitute for class identities or even necessarily a competitor. Yet shared territorial frame of reference does help regional concertation and exchange. Both labour and capital are torn between local and broader identities and solidarities, but we have detected a tendency in the more successful regions for both sides to strengthen their territorial presence. There is a strong regional bourgeoisie in Flanders, closely identified with the regional project and a weaker one in Catalonia. Scotland has a class of industrialists and financiers who identify with the territory, although they declined steadily during the twentieth century. Wales, Galicia, and Languedoc-Roussillon have very weak business classes, while the Walloon bourgeoisie was strongly Belgian in orientation and tied to the old heavy industries.

Labour has generally been more willing to play the regional card, although often in a defensive manner in declining industrial regions. At the same time, it defends state-wide social solidarity and redistribution especially, unsurprisingly, in economically dependent regions like Wallonia or Wales. Trade unions have continued to organise on a state-wide basis even in Belgium, the only exception among our cases being in Galicia. Yet with their popular basis, they have to be responsive to demotic regional and nationalist sentiment, while closures and other threats to employment often take on a local or regional form. Some trade unions, like those in Scotland, have addressed this by taking a very definite position in favour of devolution with a measure of local economic management, but within a strong state framework. Elsewhere, as in Galicia or Languedoc-Roussillon, the tension is unresolved. So we see in some of our cases that regionally-oriented social partners are able to use a common understanding of territorial community to engage in limited forms of social concertation at the regional level, while not effacing the class cleavage of industrial society. In other cases, this has not happened.

Several of our less successful cases (Languedoc-Roussillon, Wales, Galicia) are marked by strong patterns of clientelism. Clientelism is a complicated concept and sometimes difficult to distinguish from other forms of interest representation but one aspect is of key importance to our cases. This is the ability of clientelist systems to exploit territorial identities and encourage the territorial expression of grievances but then to satisfy these by the provision of divisible goods which discourage broad political mobilisation. Since the patrons are the intermediaries between the state and the regions and localities, they would be threatened both by a complete integration of the territory into the state and the consequent decline of territorial identity; and by regional autonomy, which would allow the region to allocate resources on its own and manage its own relations with the state. Clientelism is both a structural and a cultural phenomenon. In Galicia, in Wales (at least in the past) and in Languedoc-Roussillon, political structures have been shaped so as to require the presence of intermediaries in order to get things done, giving opportunities for patrons and, later, political parties, to fill the gap. At the same time, traditions of personalistic social and political relations have accustomed people to gaining favours through the intervention of patrons. So clientelistic systems are rather resilient and often appear self-perpetuating. Yet territorial community building can encourage a broader conception of the regional public domain and of a shared territorial interest. In these circumstances, identities and culture can provide the basis for a more constructive form of politics and social concertation. The immediate reciprocity of the clientelistic exchange is replaced by the more diffused reciprocity characteristic of high trust societies. Such has, to varying degrees, happened in Catalonia and Scotland.

Language use and policy best serve to illustrate the tensions and complementarities between culture and the economy. In Flanders and Catalonia, local languages are used as instruments of community-building, but combined with an emphasis on foreign language learning. Generally, the strategy has been successful, although local languages have thrived better in the public sector, the arts and education that in the economy, where governments have had to tread carefully. Galicia has its own language but this still carries the image of rurality and backwardness, which is only slowly being overcome. There is still a sharp disjuncture between a regional world of tradition and a Spanish world of progress and modernity. Wales and Brittany have their own languages, but these are spoken only by a minority of the population. After years of conflict, there is a growing consensus on the desirability of nurturing the languages as symbols of identity, even though not everyone will speak them. They are increasingly dissociated from the backward imagery by a new middle class, which has invested them with greater prestige, while government policy has ensured that speaking Welsh has now become a useful piece of human capital. The impact in the private economy, however, is still very limited.

CONDITIONS FOR SUCCESS

There is a risk of indeterminacy in all this and it might be tempting just to say that regions are different because they are different. This is a problem in any analysis of territorial politics and society, since multiple variables are at work in any case and it is their interaction in space, not their individual impact, that best explains variation. Yet we can draw some general lessons. We are not concerned here with all the conditions for economic success, merely with the construction and transmission of a vision of regional culture and identity and its role in collective action, concertation and mobilisation.

While the initial, *prima facie*, classification of the eight regions into successes and failures has been modified as we explored the details of each case, it does still hold to a considerable degree. Although economic performance is not, as we have emphasised, everything, it does provide a measurable test that largely confirms the hierarchy. Flanders and Catalonia are at or above the European average, Scotland just below it. Brittany, however, is a poorer performer, joining the other four regions at the bottom end of the table (see Appendix).

Our other, less quantifiable, judgements on institution-building and institutional performance largely confirm the initial categorisation, although showing more change than purely primordialist accounts might suggest.

One condition for success in the broad sense seems to be a shared territorial identity that is at the same time open and flexible. This is a difficult balance and there is always the danger of unleashing a populist nationalism on the one hand, or of destroying territorial identity on the other. It means that the region or nation is never complete but always being built, the future never closed but always open to divergent paths. The strategy and tactics of Catalan and Flemish leaders, often seen from outside as opportunistic or as hiding a secret agenda, is better explained by this constant process of building and rebuilding. A related condition is the existence of weak ties, which facilitate social co-operation, but do not lock actors into dysfunctional patterns of behaviour. It is this that underpins the rather light forms of development policy in Flanders or Catalonia, allowing government to intervene to help development, but to pull out of projects if they fail. It also allows new coalitions to be forged according to the needs of the time, as has happened in Brittany. Clientelistic links in Languedoc-Roussillon and Galicia, on the other hand, have hampered flexibility and new social and economic relationships. Scotland, with its continuing civil society based on institutions and memories rather than strong ethnic solidarities, has a stronger network of actors than Wales, where internal divisions are greater.

Successful regions do have a shared vision of development based upon a self-representation as dynamic and flexible societies. Myths play a role in this, understood as stories told in the society which may be true or false but whose effect is independent of their truth or falsehood. Such myths, which may be positive or negative, typically rest upon an account of history which is consistent with the situation of the present. It would be intellectually dishonest and ethically dubious to recommend to failing regions that they invent historical myths of greatness to match those of their more successful competitors. Yet revisiting history in a more respectable way does have a role to play. History has become a battleground in many regions, as revisionists challenge the old myths of both the positive and negative sort, seeking to understand the past in its own terms, not as a teleological prelude to the present. In this they have helped to understand key moments and phases in history, such as the weakness of heavy industry in the British periphery as early as the late nineteenth century; the failure of economic take off in eighteenth-century Galicia compared with Catalonia; or the dependent mode of development in nineteenth-century Languedoc. Such work can overcome the easy stereotypes that hamper social co-operation in failing regions, as well as reminding the successful regions that they do not owe all to their inherent virtue. It can also stimulate debates on the nature and meaning of the territorial identity, which can itself be a creative exercise.

Good history also helps us understand the concept of modernised tradition, in which there is more than one route to modernity and the past is incorporated in the present. Tradition may be seen as an obstacle to change, the enemy of modernity and particularly of economic development, where the latter is based on a functional division of labour and status is allocated by a culturally neutral market. Yet in successful regions, traditional culture has become newly fashionable, sustaining a vision of the region while projecting a dynamic image. The battles over the projection of Scottish culture illustrate this, with some people deploring ventures like Tartan Day in the United States as depicting an outmoded, conservative and stereotypical Scottish culture and insisting on a more modern, but still Scottish, image. The more successful regions seem to overcome this opposition, creating new cultural syntheses is successive generations. Catalonia, a leading centre of modernism in the early twentieth century, has been notably successful here. Brittany, too, modernised tradition, with ventures in music, literature and fashion. Galician culture, on the other hand, has not succeeded in this synthesis and is not used as a motif for mobilisation for change, development and external promotion.

Institutions are also important and, while elected regional governments in themselves cannot change a regional culture and social relations, they do play a role. It is common in the literature on regionalism to talk of 'governance' as a new mode of regulation replacing government in the traditional sense. The idea is that power has shifted from formal political institutions into networks spanning the various levels of the state and transnational regimes, and the public and private sectors. Yet our studies suggest that regional government, where it exists, does matter and that mere governance will not always fulfil the tasks of mobilisation and collective action. Elected government gives a symbolic legitimacy to the region as a political space and endows it with the one form of legitimation that, in a democratic society, trumps all others. It also creates an institutional boundary within which the actors must operate, making it difficult for any of them to defect as they could in a system of loose concertation or 'governance'. Business in Scotland was generally hostile to devolution, but now accepts the need to play within the new rules of the game; the same thing happened in Catalonia in the 1980s. This in turn affects representations of culture and identity by creating a common discursive space in which the social partners must recognise the relevance of being Scottish or Catalan. Even in Galicia, where other conditions look unfavourable, there has been a strengthening of regional identities and frames of action as a result of the progressive strengthening of the elected regional government. Wallonia seems to be following a similar trajectory. The French cases, on the other hand, have weak elected regional governments which neither provide a symbolic reference point for identity, nor possess the resources and powers which might constrain actors to play within the regional framework.

A shared constitutional vision is also important in shaping a shared culture and identity. Governments in Flanders in recent years have had somewhat differing views on the constitution but these have been variations on a theme of seeking more autonomy within an evolving Europe. Separatists and centralists have both been marginalised. Walloon elites seem to be accommodating to an autonomy which they did not originally seek. Catalan politics are dominated by a nationalist party that is non-separatist and a socialist party that is rather regionalist, creating differences of emphasis and pace rather than radically opposed visions. Parties in Wales seem closer together now that Plaid Cymru has explicitly renounced independence and the other three parties are committed to devolution. Such a convergence has not yet occurred in Scotland, and politics are polarised around the competing visions of devolution and independence in Europe, but even here the collapse of the old anti-devolution position provides for a measure of agreement on developing and strengthening the Scottish Parliament as the main expression of Scottish nationality and the focus for the development effort. Galician constitutional debates, on the other hand, are highly fragmented, among the various wings of the ruling *Partido Popular* and an ideologically heterogeneous nationalist party. Visions of Languedoc-Roussillon are similarly fragmented, a situation complicated further by the rise of the extreme right. Brittany, too, lacks a clear constitutional vision or even a consensus on what the boundaries of the region are.

Finally, this is an area in which political leadership plays a strong role. We are talking here of a complex process of synthesising divergent elements, including symbolic representation, social concertation and policy, into a project for a region. Parties and leaders have a degree of freedom here to construct the imagined regional community and to do it in various ways. Some maintain hegemony through clientelistic manipulation, some seek to tie the region into state politics, and some seek regional autonomy. Catalan nationalists have a primary interest in building the nation and advancing its autonomy and their development strategy is a reflection of this. Manuel Fraga in Galicia has opted for a regionalism that is consciously placed in the context of unitary Spanish state and is keenly aware of the opportunities and limitations that his provides. Scottish nationalists seem to take the nation for granted and have engaged in little of the conscious nation-building that we have seen in Catalonia or Flanders. Brittany in the 1950s and 1960s saw a new generation of leaders around the CELIB, committed to a new vision of regional development. Wallonia and Languedoc-Roussillon have not produced strong leaders, either individual or collective, to shape their project.

The task of region building around development is easier for some regions than others because their economic problems are less severe. Flemish regionalism rode a rising tide of prosperity from the 1960s and there was a complementarity between the economic and cultural aspirations.

Wallonia and Wales, on the other hand, have suffered severe economic crises and have been economically dependent on the state. This has not surprisingly inhibited the development of an ideology of self-help and autonomy until rather recently. Some regions also have more by way of cultural and institutional endowments than others. Scotland and Catalonia have a strong sense of identity, now complemented by autonomous institutions and this facilitates the task of leadership. When comparing the success or otherwise of regions over any period of time, we must therefore take account of their starting point and the scale of the task to be accomplished. From this perspective, we can appreciate the consolidation of Galicia as a community and institutional set over the last twenty years, even if its performance in most respects lags behind that of Catalonia. Languedoc-Roussillon has a formidable set of obstacles to overcome. The hierarchy of regions does change over time, as we have seen in the reversal of the positions of Flanders and Wallonia.

REGIONAL STRATEGIES

Looking at our eight cases in the round, we can detect common themes and important variations. In all cases there is a recognition of the importance of the regional dimension in development, and new regionalist ideas about competitiveness and internal co-operation find a strong echo. All are of course constrained by European and global market conditions and the state remains a key level for economic adaptation. Yet, within these constraints, there is scope for institution-building and mobilisation around development, leading to significant variations in policy and approach. Some have developed more clearly articulated development projects than others and the character of these do differ in sometimes subtle but important ways. The territorial framework has forced leaders to consider policy across a range of functional fields, rather than reducing development to a single key. Social cohesion does feature as an element in this, often tied to the theme of competitiveness. None of the regions is now committed to the 'low road' of inserting the region into the global economy on whatever terms are available but all have sought with different degrees of success to shape their response. Environmental policy has perhaps surprisingly emerged less strongly as a common territorial interest or motif.

Within these common patterns, we have discerned some patters. Flanders and Catalonia are led by centre-right administrations committed to a market-driven approach with the public sector supporting rather than leading. They may be seen as examples of bourgeois regionalism (Chapter 1) in tune with much current thinking on regional development. At the same time, they are engaged in a process of nation-building, although this has been somewhat downgraded in Flanders since the days of Van den Brande. Culture is a fundamental element in both, with a strong emphasis on language and presenting a modern and progressive image to the world. Social cohesion, especially in Catalonia, is tied to a discourse about nation-building and solidarity.

Wallonia, Wales and Scotland are more social democratic in orientation, stressing social inclusion, environmental sustainability and a continuing role for organised labour. On the other hand, they neither can nor aim to engage in state-led interventionist policies and large-scale planning that have characterised social democratic approaches in the past. After a period of Conservative rule sustained by majorities from England, in which the emphasis was on the low-cost road to development, Scotland and Wales are seeking new avenues. They have been led by non-nationalist parties who emphasise the need for continuing support from the central state, but have gradually been adapting to the new regionalism of decentralised development. The link between culture and economic development is not stressed as much as in Flanders or Catalonia, although the human resources and traditions receive some mention and, in Wales, there is some reference to the culture of community and co-operation. There are nation-building processes at work, which were strengthened by shared opposition to Conservative governments in the 1980s and 1990s, but, with the administrations in Scotland and Wales facing nationalist oppositions, they have been wary of giving sustenance to these by too overtly pushing for a stronger role. Community building at the territorial level is also modified by support from the dominant Labour Party for a continuing strong welfare state. Wallonia, too, has moved away from a traditional social democracy based on central state planning, to a regional social democracy incorporating new regionalist themes – but with continuing support for a Belgian welfare state as the principal redistributor. So while in these social democratic regions, social solidarity is expressed increasingly on a regional basis, this does not preclude support for the state-wide welfare state.

Galicia and Languedoc-Roussillon have yet to convert fully to the ideas of the new regionalism and remain clientelistic in their organisation and operation. Their political fragmentation, while serving to maintain existing elites in their position, has militated against organisation for economic development or the forging of a shared vision for development. Nor do such development efforts as they have made fit easily into our categories. Instead, fragmentation and clientelism allow a multiplicity of competing development themes but prevent the adoption of priorities. Brittany, one of the leaders of regionalist thinking in the 1960s, has received less prominence since the 1980s, as its indigenous leaders were incorporated into the French party system on both left and right, but it has retained elements of social cohesion that have allowed it to organise its efforts better than Languedoc-Roussillon.

Culture does therefore matter to development. It provides a framework for collective action and a rationale for social co-operation. It explains how institutions that might be rather similar in formal structure can operate differently, as we have seen particularly from the Spanish and French cases. Culture may sustain a positive or negative self-image and may facilitate or hinder change. Operating at the level of ideas and relationships, it is itself open to change and we have seen how purposive action can achieve that. So culture can be both the independent variable, the factor that explains performance, or the dependent variable, subject to change on the part of political and social leaders. Thus we have a virtuous cycle in which good performance leads to positive self-evaluation, or a negative cycle of self-deprecation and failure of social co-operation. It is possible for a region to progress from one trajectory to another, but only if the problem is recognised in the first place.

Bibliography

Agnew, J. (1987), *Place and Politics. The Geographical Mediation of State and Society*, London: Allen and Unwin.

Aitchison, J. and H. Carter (2000), *Language, economy and society: The changing fortunes of the Welsh language in the twentieth century*, Cardiff: University of Wales Press.

Álvarez Corbacho, X. (1995), *La agonía del municipalismo gallego*, Santiago de Compostela: Fundación Caixa Galicia.

Amin, A. (1999), 'An Institutionalist Perspective on Regional Economic Development', *International Journal of Urban and Regional Research*, 23, 2, pp. 365–78.

Amin, A. and J. Tomaney (1995), 'The Challenge of Cohesion', in A. Amin and J. Tomaney, (eds), *Behind the Myth of European Union. Prospects for Cohesion*, London: Routledge.

Amin, A. and N. Thrift (1994), 'Living in the Global', in A. Amin and N. Thrifts (eds), *Globalization, Institutions, and Regional Development in Europe*, Oxford: Oxford University Press.

Anciaux, B. (2000), *Beleidsnota Cultuur 1999-2004*, available at http://www. vlaanderen.be/ned/sites/regering/beleidsnota, accessed on 11/5/00.

Anciaux, B. (2000) *Beleidsnota De Vlaamse Rand 1999-2004*, available at http://www.vlaanderen.be/ned/sites/regering/beleidsnota, accessed on 11/05/00.

Anderson, B. (1991) *Imagined Communities. Reflections on the origin and spread of nationalism*, revised edition 1983, London: Verso.

Andrés Orizo, F. and A. Sánchez Fernández (1991), *El systema de valors dels Catalans. Calatunya dins l'enquesta europea de valors dels anys 1990*, Barcelona: Institut Català d'Estudis Mediterranis.

Ashcroft, B. and J.H. Love (1993), *Takeovers, Mergers and the Regional Economy*, Edinburgh: Edinburgh University Press.

Artobolevskiy, S.S. (1997), *Regional policy in Europe*, London: Jessica Kingsley.

Aunger, E. A. (1993) 'Regional, national and official languages in Belgium', *The International Journal of the Sociology of Language*, 104, pp. 31-48.

Bachtler, J. (1993), 'Regional Policy in the 1990s. The European Perspective', in R.T. Harrison and M. Hart (eds), *Spatial Policy in a Divided Nation*, London: Jessica Kingsley.

Bachtler, J. (1997), 'New Dimensions in Regional Policy in Western Europe', in M. Keating and J. Loughlin (eds), *The Political Economy of Regionalism*, London: Frank Cass.

Badie, B. (1995), *La fin des territoires. Essai sur le désordre international et sur l'utilité sociale du respect,* Paris: Fayard.

Bagnasco, A. and C. Trigilia (1993), *La construction sociale du marché. Le défi de la troisième Italie,* Cachan: Editions de l'Ecole Normale Supérieur de Cachan.

Balsom, D. and B. Jones (1984), 'The Faces of Wales', in I. McAllister and R. Rose, *The Nationwide Competition for Votes. The 1983 British General Election,* London: Pinter.

Balzac, H. de (1829), *Les Chouans,* Paris: Gallimard. (1972 edition).

Begg, I., M. Lansbury and D. G. Mayes (1995), 'The case for decentralized industrial policy', in P. Cheshire and I. Gordon (eds), *Territorial Competition in an Integrating Europe,* Aldershot: Avebury.

Beiras, X.M. (1995), *O atraso económico de Galicia,* 3rd edition, Santiago de Compostela: Laiovento.

Bergman, E., G. Maier and F. Tödtling (1991), 'Reconsidering Regions', in E. Bergman, G. Maier and F. Tödtling (eds), *Regions Reconsidered. Economic Networks, Innovation and Local Development in Industrialized Countries,* London: Mansell.

Berthet, T. and J. Palard (1997), 'Culture politique réfractaire et décollage économique. L'exemple de la Vendée du Nord-Est', *Revue française de science politique,* 47.1, pp. 29–48.

Beveridge, C. and R. Turnbull (1989), *The Eclipse of Scottish Culture,* Edinburgh: Polygon.

BNG (Bloque Nacionalista Galego) (1998), *VIII Asemblea Nacional, Galiza sairá gañada. Con intelixéncia e illusion. Ponéncias asemblearias,* (June), Ourense: BNG.

Boerzel, T.A. (1999), *The domestic impact of Europe: institutional adaptation in Germany and Spain,* doctoral thesis, Florence: European University Institute.

Bouveroux, J. (1998), 'Nationalism in Present-Day Flanders', in K. Deprez and L. Vos, (eds), *Nationalism in Belgium. Shifting Identities, 1780-1995,* Houndmills: Macmillan.

Borrás, S. (1993), 'The "Four Motors for Europe" and its Promotion of R&D Linkages. Beyond Geographic Contiguity in Interregional Agreements', *Regional Politics and Policy,* 3, 3, pp. 163-76.

Boyer, Robert and Daniel Drache (eds) (1996), *States against markets. The limits of globalization*, London: Routledge.

Bretagne Eau Pure (n.d), *Bretagne Eau Pure: une formidable mobilisation*, Rennes: Bretagne Eau Pure.

British Regional Studies Association (1983), *An Inquiry into Regional Problems in the United Kingdom*, London: British Regional Studies Association.

Brown, A., D. McCrone and L. Paterson (1996), *Politics and Society in Scotland*, London: Macmillan.

Brown, A., D. McCrone, L. Paterson and P. Surridge (1999), *The Scottish Electorate. The 1997 General Election and Beyond*, London: Macmillan.

Bru de Sala, X. (1997), 'Universalidad y Capitalidad', in X. de Bru, A. Grau, R. Lobo, M. Oranich, M. Parrellada, G. Garcia, A. Pons and J.-M. Puigjaner (eds), *El Modelo Catalan*, Barcelona: Flor del Viento.

Cabana, F. (1998), 'Els principals grups econòmics a Catalunya', in S. Giner (ed.), *La societat catalana*, Barcelona: Generalitat de Catalunya.

Cabrera, J. (1992), *La nación como discurso. El caso galego*, Colección Monográfico, 126, Madrid: Centro de Investigaciones Sociológicas.

Cambré, B., Billiet, J. and M. Swyngedouw (1997), *De kennis van de Vlamingen en hun houding tegenover de Vlaamse Overheid. Resultaten van de effectpeiling*, Leuven: Katholieke Universiteit.

Cappellin, R. (1995a), 'Una politica regionale nazionale "orientata al mercato" tra i nuovi modelli organizzativi e federalismo', in G. Gorla and O.V. Colonna (eds), *Regioni e Sviluppo: Modelli, politiche e riforme*, Milan: Franco Angeli.

Cappellin, R. (1995b), 'Regional Development, Federalism and Interregional Cooperation', in H. Eskelinen and F. Snickers, (eds), *Competitive European Peripheries*, Berlin: Springer.

Casademunt, A. and J. Molins (1998), 'Les organitzacions empresarials a Catalunya', in S. Giner (ed.), *La societat catalana*, Barcelona: Generalitat de Catalunya.

Castells, M. (1997), *The Information Age: Economy, Society and Culture, volume II, The Power of Identity*, Oxford: Blackwell.

Castells, A. and M. Parellada (1998), 'L'economia catalana en el context espanyol i europeu', in S. Giner (ed.), *La societat catalana*, Barcelona: Generalitat de Catalunya.

Clavera, J. (1990), 'El debat sobre el lluire canvi: el cas de Catalunya davant la integració en la Comunitat Europea', in M. Parés i Maicas and G. Tremblay (eds), *Catalunya, Quebec: Autonomía i Mundialització*, Barcelona: Generalitat de Catalunya.

Coleman, J. (1988), 'Social Capital in the Creation of Human Capital', *American Journal of Sociology*, 94 Supplement, pp. 95-120.

Constantin, D. (1998), 'La Culture pour valoriser et mailler le territoire', in

L'État en Région, Montpellier: Préfecture de la Région Languedoc-Roussillon.

Cooke, P. and K. Morgan (1998), *The Associational Economy. Firms, Regions, and Innovation*, Oxford: Oxford University Press.

Cooke, P., P. Boekholt and F. Tödtling (1999), *The governance of innovation in Europe: regional perspectives on global competitiveness*, London: Pinter.

Costa Clavell, X. (1976), *Perfil conflictivo de Galicia*, Barcelona: Galba.

Courchene, T. (1995), 'Celebrating Flexibility: An Interpretative Essay on the Evolution of Canadian Federalism', C.D. Howe Institute, Benefactors Lecture, 1994, Montreal.

Courchene, T. (1999), 'Ontario as a North American Regional State', *Regional and Federal Studies*, 9, 3, pp. 3-37.

Courchene, T. (2001), *A State of Minds. Toward a Human Capital Future for Canadians*, Montreal: Institute for Research in Public Policy.

Crouch, C., P. Le Galès, C. Trigilia and H. Voelzkow (2001), *Local Production Systems in Europe. Rise or Demise?* Oxford: Oxford University Press.

Crozier M, F. Dupuy and J.-C. Thoenig (1983), *Sociologie de l'administration française*, Paris: Armand Colin.

Cuadrado Roura, J. (1981), 'La política regional en los planes de desarollo', in R. Acosta España (ed.), *La España de las Autonomías*, Tomo 1, Madrid: Espasa-Calpe.

Davies, J. (1994), *A History of Wales*, London: Penguin.

De Jouvenal, H. and M.-A. Roque (1991), *Catalunya a l'horitzó 2010. Prospetiva mediterránea*, Barcelona: Enciclopedia Catalana.

De Schryver, R. (1988), 'Vlaams bewustzijn en interpretatie van het Belgische verleden. Vragen rond wederzijdse beïnvloeding', *Handelingen der Zuidnederlandse Maatschappij voor Taal- en Letterkunde en Geschiedenis*, XLII, pp. 73-92.

De Winter, L. (1998), 'Etnoterritoriale identiteiten in Vlaanderen: Verkenningen in een politiek en methodologisch mijnenveld', in Swyngedouw, M., J. Billiet, A. Carton and R. Beerten (eds), *De (on)redelijke kiezer. Onderzoek naar de politieke opvattingen van Vlamingen. Verkiezingen van 21 mei 1995*, Leuven: Acco.

De Winter, L. and A.-P., Frognier (1999), 'Les identités ethno-territoriales: Exploration dans un champs de mines politique et méthodologique', in A.-P. Frognier and A.-M. Aish (eds), *Des élections en trompe-l'œil. Enquête sur le comportement électoral des Wallons et des Francophones*, Bruxelles: De Boeck Université.

Décision Environnement (1995), *Spécial Bretagne*, 36, mai 1995.

Dedieu, O. and W. Genieys (1998), Du local à l'Europe: La transformation des réseaux d'action locale. L'invention du *Pays Cathare*', in E. Négrier (ed.), *L'Europe en Région: une évaluation de la mise en oeuvre de la politique régionale européenne en Languedoc-Roussillon (1989-1997)*, Montpellier: Université de Montpellier.

De Rynck, S. (2002), *Changing Public Policy : the Role of the Regions*, Brussels:PIE-Peter Lang

Deschouwer, K. (2000), 'Belgium's quasi-regional elections of June 1999', *Regional and Federal Studies*, 10, 1, pp. 125-132.

Deschouwer, K. (2001), 'Symmetrie, Kongruenz und Finanzausgleich: die regionale Ebene in Belgien seit den Wahlen von 1999', *Jahrbuch des Föderalismus 2001*, Nomos Verlaggesellschaft, Baden-Baden, pp. 203-216.

Deschouwer, K. (2002), 'Falling apart together. The changing nature of Belgian consociationalism, 1961-2001', *Acta Politica*, 37, pp. 68-85

Deschouwer, K. and T. Jans (2001), 'L'avenir des institutions, vu de Flandre', in A. Leton (ed), *La Belgique. Un état fédéral en évolution*, Bruxelles: Bruylant

Destatte, P. (1998), 'Present-Day Wallonia. The Search for an Identity without Nationalist Mania', in K. Deprez and L. Vos (eds), *Nationalism in Belgium. Shifting Identities, 1780-1995*, Houndmills: Macmillan.

Deutsch, K. W. (1972), *Nationalism and social communication: an inquiry into the foundations of nationality*, Cambridge (Mass.): MIT Press.

Dewael, P., J. Sauwens, and B. Anciaux (2000), *Policy Memorandum 2000 - 2004 Foreign Policy of Flanders*, available http://www.flanders.be/public/authority/ government/policy/index.asp, accessed at 11/5/00.

Drevet, J.-F. (1991), *La France et l'Europe des Régions*, Paris: Syros.

Dunford, M. (1988), *Capital, the State, and Regional Development*, London: Pion.

Dunford, M. (1994), 'Winners and Losers: the new map of economic inequality in the European Union', *European Urban and Regional Studies*, 1, 2, pp. 95-114.

Escobar, M. and M. van der Meer (1995), *Trade union membership in Spain*, Madrid: Fundación Juan March.

Euroregió (1991), *Euroregió, Eurorégion*, Perpignan: Eurorégion, Languedoc-Roussillon, Midi Pyrénées, Catalunya.

Fach, W. (2001), 'Symbolische Regionalpolitik. Eine Problemskizze', *Comparativ*, 11, pp. 7-12.

Favereau, F. (1993), *Bretagne Contemporaine: Langue, Culture, Identité*, Morlaix-Montroulles: Editions Skol Vreizh.

Flaubert, G. (1885), *Voyages en Bretagne – par les champs et par les grèves*, 1989 edition, Brussels: Editions Complexe.

Folch-Serra, M. and J. Nogue i Font (2001), 'Civil Society, Media and

Globalization in Catalonia', in M. Keating and J. McGarry (eds), *Minority Nationalism in the Changing International Order,* Oxford: Oxford University Press.

Fontaine, J. (1998), 'Four Definitions of Culture in Francophone Belgium', in K. Deprez and L. Vos (eds), *Nationalism in Belgium. Shifting Identities, 1780-1995,* Houndmills: Macmillan.

Fonteyn, G. (1998), *De nieuwe Walen. Met een inleiding over het Belgisch model,* Tielt: Lannoo.

Ford, C. (1993), *Creating the Nation in Provincial France: religion and political identity in Brittany,* Princeton, N.J : Princeton University Press.

Fraga Iribarne, M. (1991), *De Galicia a Europa. España y su urgente regionalización frente a los retos del nuevo milenio,* Barcelona: Planeta.

Frankenber, P. and J. Schuhbauer (1994), 'Raumbezogene Identität in der Geographie', in G. Bossong, M. Erbe, P. Frankenberg, C. Grivel and W. Lilli (eds), *Westeuropäische Regionen und ihre Identiät. Beitrage aus interdiszipliärer Sicht,* Mannheim: J&J.

Friedmann, J. (1991), 'The Industrial Transition: A Comprehensive Approach to Regional Development', in E. Bergman, G. Maier and F. Tödtling (eds), *Regions Reconsidered. Economic Networks, Innovation and Local Development in Industrialized Countries,* London: Mansell.

Fukuyama, F. (1992), *The End of History and the Last Man,* New York: Free Press.

Fukuyama, F. (1995), *Trust: The Social Virtues and the Creation of Prosperity,* London: Hamish Hamilton.

Fundación Encuentro (1997), *Informe España, 5,* Madrid: Fundación Encuentro.

Gagnon, A.-G. (2001), 'Le Québec, une nation inscrite au sein d'une démocratie étritique', in J. Maclure and A.-G. Gagnon (eds), *Repères en Mutation. Identité et citoyenneté dans le Québec contemporain,* Montreal: Québec Amérique.

Galasso, G. (1978), *Passato e presente del meridionalismo,* Naples: Guida.

García Barbancho, A. (1979), *Disparidades Regionales y Ordenación del Territorio,* Barcelona: Ariel.

García Ferrando, M., E. López-Aranguren, and M. Beltrán (1994), *La conciencia nacional y regional en la España de las autonomias,* Madrid: Centro de Investigaciones Sociológicas.

García Pérez, B. and A. López Mira (1996), *O Nacionalismo Galego e O Futuro do Nacionalismo,* Pontevedra: O Gato da Moureira.

Garfoli, G. (1991), 'Local Networks, Innovation and Policy in Italian Industrial Districts, in E. Bergman, G. Maier and F. Tödtling (eds), *Regions Reconsidered. Economic Networks, Innovation and Local Development in Industrialized Countries,* London: Mansell.

Gavignaau-Fontaine, G. (1998), 'L'extinction de la "viticulture pour tous" en Languedoc (1945-1984)', in *Pôle Sud*, 9, pp. 57-70.

Gellner, E. (1983), *Nations and Nationalism*, Oxford: Blackwell.

GEM (2002), *Global Entrepreneurship Monitor, Scotland 2001*, Glasgow: Hunter Centre for Entrepreneurship, University of Strathclyde.

Generalitat de Catalunya (1992), *Departament d'Industria i Energia, Quadernos de Competivitat. La internalització*, Barcelona: Generalitat.

Generalitat de Catalunya (1997), *El coneixement del català. Anàlisi de les cens lingüístic de 1991*, Barcelona: Generalitat.

Genieys, W. (1998), 'Le retournement du Midi viticole', *Pôle Sud*, no. 9, novembre, pp. 7-25.

Genieys, W. and E. Négrier (1998), 'Un Tableau Général du Languedoc-Roussillon' in E. Négrier (ed.), *L'Europe en Région: une évaluation de la mise en oeuvre de la politique régionale européenne en Languedoc-Roussillon (1989-1997)*, Montpellier: Université de Montpellier.

Giddens, A. (1998), *The third way. The renewal of social democracy*, Cambridge: Polity Press.

Gifreu, J. (1993), 'Cultura, Llengua i Comunicació Deprés del Tractat de Maastricht', *Revista de Catalunya*, 75: 10-20.

Gilbert, Y. (1989), *Le Languedoc et ses images*, Paris: L'Harmattan.

Giner, S., L. Flaquer, J. Busquet and N. Bultà (1996), *La cultura catalana: el sagrat i el profà*, Barcelona: Edicions 62.

Goossens, J. (1975) "Talal", in *Grote Winkler Prins, Compendia Vlaanderen*, Brussel: Elsevier Sequoia, pp. 374-379.

Goossens, J. (2000) 'De toekomst van het Nederlands in Vlaanderen', *Ons Erfdeel*, 43, pp. 3-13.

Gouvernement Wallon (1999) *Déclaration de Politique Régionale du Gouvernement Wallon. Wallonie Horizon 2004: Rénover et mobiliser*, available at http://gov.wallonie.be/gov/dpr/dprtop.html, accessed at 11/5/00.

Gouvernement Wallon (2000) *Contrat d'Avenir pour la Wallonie*, available at http://gov.wallonie.be/gov/caw/cawtop.html, accessed at 11/5/00.

Granovetter, M. (1973), 'The Strength of Weak Ties', *American Journal of Sociology*, 78, pp. 1360-80.

Gras, C. and G. Livet (eds) (1977), *Régions et régionalisme en France: du XVIIème siècle à nos jours*, Paris: Presses Universitaires de France.

Gravier, J.-F. (1947), *Paris et le désert français*, Paris: Le Portulan.

Groussard, J.-C. (1996), 'La Culture en Languedoc-Roussillon', *L'État en Région*, No. 35, Autumn/Winter, pp. 6-7.

Grutman, R. (1993) 'What is in the name "Walloon"?', *International Journal of the Sociology of Language*, 104, pp. 117-118.

Hadjmichalis, C. and N. Papamios (1991), '"Local" Development in southern Europe: Myths and Realities', in E. Bergman, G. Maier and F. Tödtling (eds), *Regions Reconsidered. Economic Networks, Innovation and Local Development in Industrialized Countries*, London: Mansell.

Hall, P. A. and R.C.R. Taylor (1996), 'Political Science and the Three New Institutionalisms', *Political Studies*, 44 5, pp. 936-57.

Hammel, E. and P. Gardy (1991), *L'Occitan en Languedoc-Roussillon*, Perpinyà: Trabucaïre.

Hammel, E. (1996), *Aide-Mémoire: Langues et Cultures Régionales et Région Languedoc-Roussillon (1985-1986)*, Perpignan: Llibres del Trabucaire.

Hanham, H.J. (1969), *Scottish Nationalism*, London: Faber.

Hansen, N., B. Higgins and D. J. Savoie (1990), *Regional Policy in a Changing World*, New York and London: Plenum Press.

Harding, A. (1999), 'Review Article: North American Urban Political Economy, Urban Theory and British Research', *British Journal of Political Science*, 29, pp. 673-98.

Harvie, C. (1981), *No Gods and Precious Few Heroes. Scotland, 1914-1980*, London: Edward Arnold.

Harvie, C. (1994), *The Rise of Regional Europe*, London: Routledge.

Harvie, C. (1995), *Scotland and Nationalism. Scottish Society and Politics, 1707-1994*, 2nd edition, London: Routledge.

Hasquin, H. (1996), *Historiographie et politique en Belgique*, Bruxelles/ Charleroi: Editions de l'Université de Bruxelles/Institut Jules Destrée.

Hayward, J.E.S. (1969), 'From functional regionalism to functional representation in France', *Political Studies*, vol XVII, March, pp. 48- 75.

Hayward, J.E.S. (1983), *Governing France: the one and indivisible republic*, London: Weidenfeld and Nicolson. (2nd edition).

Heald, D. (1994), 'Territorial Public Expenditure in the United Kingdom', *Public Administration*, 72, pp. 147-75.

Hearn, J. (2000), *Claiming Scotland. National Identity and Liberal Culture*, Edinburgh: Polygon.

Henry, A. (1974), *Histoire des mots Wallon et Wallonie*, 3rd revised and expanded edition, Mont-sur-Machienne: Institut Jules Destrée.

Hirst, P. and G. Thompson (1999), *Globalization in Question*, London: Polity.

Hobsbawm, E. and T. Ranger (eds) (1983), *The Invention of Tradition*, Cambridge: Cambridge University Press.

Hoffmann-Martinot, V. (1999), 'Les grandes villes françaises: une démocratie en souffrance', in O. Gabriel and V. Hoffmann-Martinot (eds), *Démocraties urbaines: l'état de la démocratie dans les grandes villes de 12 démocraties urbaines*, Paris: L'Harmattan.

Hooghe, L. (ed.) (1996), *Cohesion Policy and European Integration.*

Building Multi-Level Governance, Oxford: Clarendon.

Hooghe, L. and M. Keating (1994), 'The Politics of EU Regional Policy', *Journal of European Public Policy,* 1, 3: pp. 368–93.

Houthaeve, R. (1996), 'Spatial Planning in Flanders. Looking for Strengths and Weaknesses Through its Regional Approach', in J. Alden and P. Boland (eds), *Regional Development Strategies. A European Perspective,* London: Jessica Langley.

Hudson, R. (1999), '"The Learning Economy, the Learning Firm and the Learning Region": A Sympathetic Critique of the Limits to Learning', *European Urban and Regional Studies,* 6, 1, pp. 59–72.

Hugo, V. (1874), *Quatre-vingt-treize,* Paris: Gallimard. (1979 edition).

Institut Culturel de Bretagne (1988), *Bretagne: Clés en Mains,* Rennes: Institut Culturel de Bretagne/Skol-Uhel ar Vro. (Collective work).

Jackman, R.W. and R.A. Miller (1996), 'A Renaissance of Political Culture?', *American Journal of Political Science,* 40, 3, pp. 632-59.

Jones, B. and D. Balsom (eds) (2000), *The Road to the National Assembly for Wales,* Cardiff: University of Wales Press.

Jordana, J. and K.-J. Nagel (1998), 'Trade Unionism in Catalonia: Have Unions Joined Nationalism?', in P. Pasture and J. Verberckmoes (eds), *Working-Class Internationalism and the Appeal of National Identity,* Oxford: Berg.

Kantor, P. (1995), *The Dependent City Revisited. The Political Economy of Urban Development and Social Policy,* Boulder: Westview.

Keating, M. (1983), 'Decentralisation in Mitterrand's France', *Public Administration,* 61, 3, pp. 237-52.

Keating, M. (1985), 'The Rise and Decline of Micro-nationalism in Mainland France', *Political Studies,* XXXIII, 2, pp. 1-18.

Keating, M. (1986), 'Revendication et Lamentation. The Failure of Regional Nationalism in Languedoc', *Journal of Area Studies,* 14.

Keating, M. (1988), *State and Regional Nationalism. Territorial Politics and the European State,* London: Harvester-Wheatsheaf.

Keating, M. (1993), *Comparative Urban Politics. Power and the City in the United States, Canada, Britain and France,* Cheltenham: Edward Elgar.

Keating, M. (1998a), *The New Regionalism in Western Europe. Territorial Restructuring and Political Change,* Aldershot: Edward Elgar.

Keating, M. (1998b), 'Nationalism, Nation-Building and Language Policy in Quebec and Catalonia', in H-G. Haupt, M.G. Müller and S. Woolf (eds), *Regional and National Identities in Europe in the XIXth and XXth centuries,* Amsterdam: Kluwer.

Keating, M. (2001a), *Nations against the State. The New Politics of Nationalism in Quebec, Catalonia and Scotland,* 2nd edition, London: Palgrave.

Keating, M. (2001b), *Plurinational Democracy. Stateless Nations in a Post-Sovereignty Era*, Oxford: Oxford University Press.

Keating, M. (2001c), *Devolution and Public Policy in the United Kingdom*, London: Institute for Research in Public Policy.

Keating, M. (2001d), 'Scottish Autonomy, Then and Now', *Scottish Affairs*, special issue, pp. 91-103.

Keating, M. and D. Bleiman (1979), *Labour and Scottish Nationalism*, London: Macmillan.

Keating, M. and J. Loughlin (2002), 'Territorial Policy Communities and Devolution in the United Kingdom', *EUI Working Papers*, 2002/1, Florence: European University Institute.

Kellas, J. (1989), *The Scottish Political System*, 4th edition, Cambridge: Cambridge University Press.

Kerremans, B. (1997), 'The Flemish Identity: Nascent or Existent?', *Res Publica*, 39, 2, pp. 303-314.

Kerremans, B. and J. Beyers (1996), 'The Belgian Sub-National Entities in the European Union: Second or Third Level Players?', *Regional and Federal Studies*, 6, 2, pp. 41-55.

Kesteloot, C. (1998), 'The Growth of the Walloon Movement', in K. Deprez and L. Vos (eds), *Nationalism in Belgium. Shifting Identities, 1780-1995*, Houndmills: Macmillan, pp. 139-152.

Klinkenberg, J.-M. (1999), 'Het Frans in/van België', in K. Deprez and L. Vos (eds), *Nationalisme in België. Identiteiten in Beweging, 1780-2000*, Antwerpen: Houtekiet.

Kohler-Koch, B. (1998), *Interaktive Politik in Europa. Regionen im Netzwork der Integration*, Opladen: Leske and Budrich.

Labrie, N. (1993), *La construction linguistique de la Communauté européenne*, Paris: Honoré Champion.

Lafont, R. (1967), *La révolution régionaliste*, Paris: Gallimard.

Le Bihan, J. (1993), 'Culture Bretonne et Développement', Conférence prononcée à Perros-Guirrec, journée d'été de l'OBE (Organisation des Breton de l'Extérieur).

Le Bourdonnec, Y. (1996), *Le Miracle Breton*, Paris: Calmann-Lévy.

Le Coadic, R. (1998), *L'Identité bretonne*, Rennes: Presses Universitaires de Rennes.

Le Faou P. and J.-L. Latour (2000), *La dynamique culturelle bretonne*, Rennes: Conseil Economique et Social, Région de Bretagne.

Le Nail, B. (1996), 'L'identité bretonne', *Pouvoirs Locaux*, 31, IV, pp. 85-92.

Leca, J. (2000), 'Sur la gouvernance démocratique: entre théorie et méthode de recherche empirique', *Politique européenne*, 1, pp. 108-129.

Lee, C.H. (1995), *Scotland and the United Kingdom. The economy and the union in the twentieth century*, Manchester: Manchester University Press.

Lem, W. (1995), 'Identity and History: Class and Regional Consciousness in Rural Languedoc', *Journal of Historical Sociology*, Vol. 8, no. 2, pp. 198-220.

Lindley, P. (1982), 'The framework of regional planning, 1964-1980', in B. Hogwood and M. Keating (eds), *Regional Government in England*, Oxford: Clarendon.

Lobo, R. (1997), 'La cultura y la lengua, origen y substrato del catalanismo político', in X. de Bru, A. Grau, R. Lobo, M. Oranich, M. Parrellada, G. Garcia, A. Pons and J.M. Puigjaner, *El Modelo Catalan*, Barcelona: Flor del Viento.

López Mira, Á. (1996), *Territorio e Democracia. Un modelo de participación democrática para Galicia, nacionalidad histórica*, La Coruña: Edicios do Castro.

Loughlin, J. (1989), *Regionalism and Ethnic Nationalism in France: a Case Study of Corsica*, Florence: European University Institute.

Loughlin, J. (1999), 'Wales: a dynamic region or a 'fractured' nations?', Paper presented at the inaugural conference of the Institute of Irish-British Studies, University College, Dublin.

Loughlin, J. (2000), 'Regional Autonomy and State Paradigm Shift in Western Europe', *Regional and Federal Studies*, 10. 2, pp. 10-34,

Loughlin, J. (2001), 'La Dimension Européenne de la Dévolution en Grande-Bretagne', *Pouvoirs locaux*, Vol. 49, no. 11, juin 2001, pp. 115-120.

Loughlin, J. and S. Mazey (eds) (1995), *The End of the French Unitary State: Ten Years of Regionalization in France, 1982-1992*, London: Frank Cass.

Loughlin, J. and C. Olivesi (eds) (1999), *Autonomies insulaires: vers une politique de différence pour la Corse*, Ajaccio: Albiana.

Loughlin, J. and F. Letamendia (2000), 'Lessons for Northern Ireland: the Peace Processes in the Basque Country and Corsica', *Irish Studies in International Affairs*, Volume 11, November, pp. 147-162.

Lovering, J. (1999), 'Theory Led by Policy: The Inadequacies of the "New regionalism"', *International Journal of Urban and Regional Research*, 23, 2, pp. 379-95.

Lynch, P. (1998), 'The Scottish Business Community and Devolution', in H. Elcock and M. Keating (eds), *Remaking the Union. Devolution and British Politics in the 1990s*, London: Frank Cass.

Machin, H. (1977), *The Prefect in French Public Administration*, London: Croom Helm.

MacInnes, J. (2001), 'Dual National Identity in Scotland and Catalonia', *Scottish Affairs*, Special Issue, pp. 104-121.

Maddens, B., R Beerten and J.Billiet (1994), *O dierbaar België? Het natie-bewustzijn van Vlamingen en Walen*, Leuven: K.U.Leuven / ISPO.

Maddens, B., R. Beerten and J. Billiet (1998), 'The National Consciousness of the Flemings and the Walloons. An Empirical Investigation', in K. Deprez and L. Vos, (eds), *Nationalism in Belgium. Shifting Identities, 1780-1995*, Houndmills: Macmillan.

Maíz, R. (1996), '*Nación de Breogán*: Oportunidades políticas y estrategías enmarcadores en el movimiento nacionalista gallego (1886-1996)', *Revista de Estudios Políticos*, 92, pp. 33-75.

Maíz, R. (1997), *A Idea de Nación*, Vigo: Xerais.

Maíz, R. and A. Losada (2000), 'Institutions, Policies and Nation Building: the Galician Case', *Regional and Federal Studies*, 10, 1, pp. 62-91.

March, J.G. and J.-P. Olsen (1984), 'The New Institutionalism: Organizational Factors in Political Life', *American Political Science Review*, 78, pp. 734–748.

Mathias, J. (2000), *Regional Interests and Regional Actor Behaviour in the Context of EU Regional Policy*, Cardiff: Unpublished PhD Thesis, Cardiff University.

McCrone, D. (2001), *Understanding Scotland. The Sociology of a Nation*, 2nd edition, London: Routledge.

McCrone, D., A. Morris and R. Kelly (1995), *Scotland - the Brand. The Making of Scottish Heritage*, Edinburgh: Edinburgh University Press.

McEwen, N. (2001), 'The Nation-Building Role of the Welfare State in the United Kingdom and Canada', in T. Salmon and M. Keating (eds), *The Dynamics of Decentralization. Canadian Federalism and British Devolution*, Montreal: McGill-Queen's University Press.

McRoberts, K. (2001), *Catalonia. Nation Building Without a State*, Toronto: Oxford University Press.

Mella, C. (1992), *A Galicia Posible*, Vigo: Xerais.

Midwinter, A., M. Keating and J. Mitchell (1991), *Politics and Public Policy in Scotland*, London: Macmillan.

Monnier, J.-J. (1998), *Le comportement politique des Bretons*, Rennes: Presses Universitaires de Rennes.

Moore, C. and S. Booth (1989), *Managing Competition. Meso-Corporatism, Pluralism and the Negotiated Order in Scotland*, Oxford: Oxford University Press.

Moral, F. (1998), 'Identidad regional y nacionalismo en el Estado de las Autonomías', *Opiniones y actitudes*, 18, Madrid: Centro de Investigaciones Sociológicas.

Morgan, K. (1982), *Rebirth of a Nation. Wales, 1880-1980*, Oxford: Oxford University Press.

Morgan, K. (1997), 'The Learning Region. Institutions, Innovation and

Regional Renewal', *Regional Studies*, 31, pp. 491–503.

Morvan, Y. (1991), 'Les Acteurs du système économique breton', in G. Prémel and A. Huet (eds), *Bretagne: contribution au débat sur l'Europe des Région*, Rennes: Ubacs.

Morvan, Y. (1997), *Demain, La Bretagne ou La métamorphose du modèle Breton*, Rennes: Editions Apogée.

Muller, P. (1989), *Airbus. L'Ambition européenne: Logique d'Etat, logique de marché*, Paris: L'Harmattan.

Murphy, A. B. (1988), *The regional dynamics of language differentiation in Belgium, a study in cultural-political geography*, Chicago IL: University of Chicago.

Mutti, A. (1996), 'Politiche di sviluppo per le regione meridionali', *Il Mulino*, XLIV.357, pp. 83-97.

National Assembly for Wales (2000), *National Assembly for Wales – making it happen*, Cardiff: National Assembly for Wales.

National Assembly for Wales (2001), *A Winning Wales: the National Economic Strategy of the Welsh Assembly Government*, Cardiff: National Assembly for Wales.

Négrier, E. (1998), "Échanges politiques territorialisés et Action publique européenne", in E. Négrier and B. Jouve (eds), *Que gouvernent les régions d'Europe? Échanges politiques et mobilisations*, Paris: L'Harmattan.

Négrier, E. (ed.) (1998a), *Le Patrimoine en Région: le cas du Languedoc-Roussillon*, Montpellier: Université de Montpellier.

Négrier, E. (ed.) (1998b), *L'Europe en Région: une évaluation de la mise en oeuvre de la politique régionale européenne en Languedoc-Roussillon (1989-1997)*, Montpellier: Université de Montpellier.

Nicolas M. (1982), *Histoire du mouvement breton (Emsav)*, Paris: Syros.

Office for National Studies (1998) *1991 census: key statistics for urban and rural areas. The South West and Wales*, London: The Stationery Office.

Ohmae, K. (1995), *The End of the Nation State: The Rise of Regional Economies*, New York: The Free Press.

Ohmae, K. (2001), 'How to Invite Prosperity from the Global Economy Into a Region', in A. J. Scott (ed.), *Global City-Regions. Trends, Theory, Policy*, Oxford: Oxford University Press.

Olson, M. (1982), *The rise and decline of nations: economic growth, stagflation, and social rigidities*, New Haven: Yale University Press.

Orizo, F. and A. Sánchez Fernández (1991), *El sistema de valors dels catalans. Catalunya dins l'enquesta europea de valors dels anys 90*, Barcelona: Institut d'Estudis Mediterranis.

Osiander, A. (1994), *The States System of Europe, 1640–1990. Peacemaking and the Conditions of International Stability*, Oxford:

Clarendon.

Parellada, M. and G. Garcia (1997), 'La doble convergencia de la economía catalana con España y Europa', in X. de Bru, A. Grau, R. Lobo, M. Oranich, M. Parrellada, G. Garcia, A. Pons and J. Mª Puigjaner (eds), *El Modelo Catalán*, Barcelona: Flor del Viento.

Paterson, L. (1994), *The Autonomy of Modern Scotland*, Edinburgh: Edinburgh University Press.

Pérez, F., J.-F. Goerlich and M. Mas (1996), *Capitalización y crecimiento en España y sus regiones 1955-1995*, Bilbao: Fundación BBV.

Peters, B.G. (1999), *Institutional Theory in Political Science. The New Institutionalism*, London: Pinter.

Peterson, P. (1981), *City Limits*, Chicago: University of Chicago Press.

Petschen, S. (1992), *La Europa de las regiones*, Barcelona: Generalitat de Catalunya.

Phlipponneau, M. (1981), *Décentralisation et Régionalisation. La grande affaire*, Paris: Calman-Levy.

Piattoni, S. (1997), 'Local Political Classes and Economic Development. The Cases of Abruzzo and Puglia in the 1970s and 1980s', in M. Keating and J. Loughlin (eds), *The Political Economy of Regionalism*, London: Frank Cass.

Plumb, J.H. (1967), *The Growth of Political Stability in England, 1675-1725*, London: Macmillan, pp. xvi-xvii. Quoted in J. Steinberg, *Why Switzerland?* 2nd edition, Cambridge: Cambridge University Press, 1996.

Pôle Sud (1998), numéro spécial, 'La "Grande Transformation" du Midi Rouge', no. 9, novembre.

Portes, A. (2001), 'Social Capital: Its Origins and Applications in Modern Sociology', *Annual Review of Sociology*, 24, pp. 1-24.

Porter, M. (2001), 'Regions and the New Economics of Competition,' in Allen J. Scott (ed.), *Global City-Regions. Trends, Theory, Policy*, Oxford: Oxford University Press.

Poussier, J.-L. (1997), *Bretagne*, Paris: LEC/Edition.

Préfecture de la Région Languedoc-Roussillon (1997), *Emplois culturels en Languedoc-Roussillon*, Montpellier: Secretariat Général pour les Affaires Régionales, Préfecture de la Région.

Putnam, R. (1993), *Making Democracy Work. Civic Traditions in Modern Italy*, Princeton: Princeton University Press.

Putnam, R. (2000), *Bowling Alone. The collapse and revival of American community*, New York: Simon and Schuster.

Putnam, R. (2001), 'Social Capital: Measurement and Consequences', *Isuma. Canadian Journal of Policy Research*, 2.1, pp. 41-52.

Quairiaux, Y. and J. Pirotte (1978), 'L'image du Flamand dans la tradition populaire wallon depuis un siècle', *Res Publica*, XX, 391-406.

Quévit, M. (1978), *Les causes du déclin wallon*, Bruxelles: Vie Ouvrière.

Rapport Mauroy (2000), *Refonder l'action publique locale: rapport au Premier ministre / Commission pour l'avenir de la décentralisation présidée par M. Pierre Mauroy*, Paris: La Documentation française.

Real Academia Galega (1990), *Estudio sociolingüístico da comarca ferrolá*, A Coruña: Real Academia Galega.

Real Academia Galega (1995), *Usos lingüísticos en Galicia*, A Coruña: Real Academia Galega.

Real Academia Galega (1996), *Actitudes lingüísticas en Galicia*, A Coruña: Real Academia Galega.

Région Bretagne (1997), *Forces et faiblesses de l'économie bretonne: Eléments statistiques et d'analyse*, Rennes: Région de Bretagne.

Région Bretagne (1998), *1998: Guide des Actions du Conseil Régional*, Rennes: Région de Bretagne.

Région Bretagne (1999), *La conférence régionale de l'environnement de Bretagne*, Rennes: Région de Bretagne.

Région Bretagne (n.d.), *Le Conseil régional s'engage: préservation, gestion et valorisation du patrimoine naturel en Bretagne, Contrats Nature*, Rennes: Région de Bretagne.

Région Languedoc-Roussillon (1998a), *Pratiques et représentations du Catalan*, Montpellier: Hôtel de Région.

Région Languedoc-Roussillon (1998b), *Pratiques et représentations de l'Occitan*, Montpellier: Hôtel de Région.

Région Languedoc-Roussillon (1999), *Agence Méditerranéenne de l'Environnement*, Montpellier: Hôtel de Région.

Reicher, S. and N. Hopkins (2001), *Self and Nation*, London: Sage.

Rhisiart, M and M. Thomas (2000), 'Innovative Wales' in *Wales in the 21st Century. An Economic Future*, London: Macmillan.

Riera, I. (1998), *Los catalanes de Franco*, Barcelona: Plaza & Janés.

Ritaine, E. (1989), 'La modernité localisée. Leçons italiennes sur le développement régional', *Revue française de science politique*, 44, 3, pp. 154–77.

Robertson, R. (1992), *Globalization: social theory and global culture*, London: Sage.

Rondin, J. (1985), *Le Sacre des Notables. La France et la décentralisation*, Paris: Fayard.

Roudat, D. (1999), *De la Géopolitique: Celtitude, Celticité, Panceltisme*, DEA Mémoire, Université Paris VIII.

Sabel, C. F. (1993), 'Studied Trust: Building New Forms of Cooperation in a Volatile Economy', in R. Swedberg (ed.), *Explorations in Economic Geography*, New York: Russel Sage Foundation.

Saey, P., Ch. Kesteloot, and Ch. Vandermotten (1998), 'Unequal Economic

Development and the Origin of the Federalization Process', in K. Deprez and L. Vos (eds), *Nationalism in Belgium. Shifting Identities, 1780-1995*, Houndmills: Macmillan.

Sánchez, J.E. (1998), 'L'estructura empresarial i productive de Catalunya', in S. Giner (ed.), *La Societat Catalana*, Barcelona: Generalitat de Catalunya.

Sangrador García, J.-L. (1981), *Estereotipos de las nacionalidades y regiones de España*, Madrid: Centro de Investigaciones Sociológicas.

Sangrador García, J.-L. (1996), *Identidades, actitudes y estereotipos en la España de las Autonomías, Opiniones y Actitudes*, No 10, Madrid: Centro de Investigaciones Sociológicas.

Sarasa, S. (1998), 'Associacionisme, moviments socials i participació cívica', in S. Giner (ed.), *La societat catalana*, Barcelona: Generalitat de Catalunya.

Sassen, S. (2001), 'Global Cities and Global City-Regions: A Comparison' in A.J. Scott (ed.), *Global City-Regions. Trends, Theory, Policy*, Oxford: Oxford University Press.

Schramme, A. (1999), *Vlaanderen en zijn grote buitenland. De opbouw van het internationaal cultuurbeleid van Vlaanderen 1965-1988*, Tielt: Lannoo.

Schuller, T., S. Baron and J. Field (2000), 'Social Capital: A Review and Critique', in S. Baron, J. Field and T. Schuller (eds), *Social Capital. Critical Perspectives*, Oxford: Oxford University Press.

Scott, A.J. (1996), 'Regional Motors of the Global Economy', *Futures*, 28, 5, pp. 391–411.

Scott, A.J. (1998), *Regions and the World Economy. The Coming Shape of Global Production, Competition, and Political Order*, Oxford: Oxford University Press.

Scott, A.J. (2001), 'Global City-Regions', in A. J. Scott (ed.), *Global City-Regions. Trends, Theory, Policy*, Oxford: Oxford University Press.

Scott, A.J. and M. Storper (1992), 'Industrialization and Regional Development', in A.J. Scott and M. Storper (eds), *Pathways to Industrialization and Regional Development*, London and New York: Routledge.

Scott, A.J., J.A., E.W. Soja and M. Storper (2001), 'Global City-Regions', in A.J. Scott (ed.), *Global City-Regions. Trends, Theory, Policy*, Oxford: Oxford University Press.

Scottish Executive (2000), *The Way Forward: Framework for Economic Development in Scotland*, Edinburgh: Scottish Executive.

Siguan, M. (1996), *L'Europe des Langues*, Liège: Mardaga.

Smith, A., (1998), 'L'Europe, le Midi et le vin', in *Pôle Sud*, no. 9, novembre, pp. 125-135.

Steen, I. (1999), 'Van Nederlandse naar Vlaamse Cultuur', in K. Deprez and L. Vos (eds), *Nationalisme in België. Identiteiten in Beweging, 1780-2000*, Antwerpen: Houtekiet.

Steinberg, J. (1996), *Why Switzerland?* 2nd edition, Cambridge: Cambridge University Press.

Steinmo, S., K. Thelen and F. Longstreth (eds) (1992), *Structuring Politics. Historical Institutionalism in Comparative Perspective*, Cambridge: Cambridge University Press.

Stöhr, W. B. (1989), 'Regional Policy at the Crossroads', in L. Albrechts, F. Moulaert, P. Roberts and E. Swyngedouw (eds), *Regional Policy at the crossroads: European perspectives*, London: Kingsley.

Stone, C. (1989), *Regime Politics. Governing Atlanta, 1946-1988*, Lawrence: University of Kansas Press.

Storper, M. (1995), 'The Resurgence of Regional Economies, 10 Years Later', *European Urban and Regional Studies*, 2, 3, pp. 191–221.

Storper, M. (1997), *The Regional World. Territorial Development in a Global Economy*, New York and London: Guildford.

Swedberg, R. (1993), 'Introduction', in R. Swedberg (ed.), *Explorations in Economic Geography*, New York: Russel Sage Foundation.

Taeldeman, J. (1999), 'Welk Nederlands voor Vlamingen?', *Nederlands van Nu*, XL, pp. 33-52.

Tarrow, S. (1978), 'Regional Policy, Ideology and Peripheral Defense: The Case of Fos-sur-Mer', in S. Tarrow, P. J. Katzenstein and L. Graziani (eds), *Territorial Politics in Industrial Nations*, New York and London: Praeger.

Taylor B. and K. Thomson (eds) (1999), *Scotland and Wales: nations again?* Cardiff: University of Wales Press.

Temple-Boyer, S. (1993), *Rapport de stage*, Institut d'Etudes Politiques de Paris, La Région Languedoc-Roussillon, Direction de l'Enseignement, des Sports et de la Culture. Mission Culture.

Thomas, M.D. (1972), 'Growth Pole Theory: An Examination of Some of its Basic Concepts', in N.M. Hansen (ed.), *Growth Centers in Regional Economic Development*, New York: Free Press.

Tilly, C. (1990), *Coercion, Capital and European States, AD 990–1990*, Oxford: Blackwell.

Tollebeek, J. (1994) *De ijkmeesters. Opstellen over de geschiedschrijving in Nederland en België*, Amsterdam: Bert Bakker.

Touraine, A., F. Dubet and M. Wieviorka (eds) (1981), *Le Pays contre l'Etat*, Paris: Seuil.

Touzard, J.-M. and J.-P. Laporte (1998), 'Deux décennies de transition viticole en Languedoc-Roussillon: de la production de masse à une viticulture plurielle', *Pôle Sud*, no. spécial, 'La Grande Transformation du Midi rouge', pp. 26-47.

Trigilia, C. (1996), 'Una nuova occasione storica per il Mezzogiorno?', *Le Regioni*, XXIV.1, pp. 93–101.

Vagman, V. (1994), *Le mouvement wallon et la question bruxelloise*, Bruxelles: CRISP. (Courrier Hebdomadaire no. 1434-1435).

Van Dam, D. (1997), *Flandre, Wallonie, le rêve brisé, quelles identités culturelles et politiques en Flandre et en Wallonie?* Ottignies: Quorum.

Van den Brande, L. (1995), *Policy Priorities 1995-1999. "Flanders International"*, Brussels: Ministry of Flanders.

Van Mechelen, D. (2000), *Beleidsnota Economie 1999-2004*, available at http://www.vlaanderen.be/ned/sites/regering/beleidsnota/, accessed at 28 April 2000.

Vandeputte, O., P. Vincent, and T. Hermans (1986), *Dutch. The language of twenty million Dutch and Flemish people*, Rekkem: Stichting Ons Erfdeel vzw.

Verpeaux, M. (1999), 'La Décentralization depuis les lois en 1982', in *Les Collectivités Locales en Mutation*, Paris: La Documentation Française.

Versmessen, E. (1995), 'In the kingdom of paradoxes: the Belgian regional and national elections of May 1995', *Regional and Federal Studies*, 5, 2, pp. 239-246.

VEV (Vlaams Economisch Verbond) (1999), *Open regio, blik op de toekomst. De kracht van instituties in Europese regio's*, Antwerp: VEV

Virós, M. R., R. M. Canals, and F. Pallarés (1991), 'Influència en l'opció electoral d'alguns factors sòcio-demogràfics i polítics. Perfil dels electorats', in Equip de Sociología Electoral (Universitat Autónoma de Barcelona), *Estudis Electorals*, 10, Barcelona: Fundació Jaume Bofill.

Wannop, U. (1995), *The Regional Imperative. Regional Planning and Governance in Britain, Europe and the United States*, London: Jessica Kingsley.

Weale, A., G. Pridham, M. Cini, D. Konstadalopoulos, M. Porter and B. Flynn (2000), *Environmental Governance in Europe,* Cambridge: Cambridge University Press.

Welsh Language Board (2000), *The State of the Welsh Language,* Cardiff: Welsh Language Board.

Wils, L. (1993), *Van Clovis tot Happart. De lange weg van de naties,* Leuven: Garant.

Witte, E., Craeybeckx, J. and A. Meyen (1990), *Politieke Geschiedenis van Belgie van 1830 tot heden*, Antwerpen: Standaard Uitgeverij.

Woolcock, M. (2001), 'The Place of Social Capital in Understanding Social and Economic Outcomes', *Isuma. Canadian Journal of Policy Research*, 2.1, pp. 11–17.

Yuill, D., K. Allen, J. Bachtler, K. Clement and F. Wishlade (1993),

European Regional Incentives, 1993-4, 13th edition, London: Bourker-Saur.

Zolberg A. R. (1974), 'The making of Flemings and Walloons. Belgium, 1830-1914', *The Journal of Interdisciplinary History,* 5, 2, pp. 180-235.

Other sources:

De Standaard
El País
El Punt Perpinyá
La Croix
L'Indépendent
Le Monde
Le Soir
Le Télégramme
La Tribune
Newsletter

Appendix

Table 1: Economic Statistics, EU, four states and regions (Eurostat)

	GDP per capita, 1997	Unemployment, 1999 %	Activity rate 1999 %	Population change 1987–1997
Brussels	169.1	14.0	51.2	- 0.2
Flanders	114.3	5.6	52.8	0.4
Belgium	114.0	8.8	51.9	0.3
UK	101.9	6.1	61.9	0.4
Catalonia	100.0	10.8	51.9	0.1
EU15	100.0	9.4		
France	99.1	11.4	55.8	0.5
Scotland	97.2	7.6	60.4	0.3
Wallonia	88.0	13.1	50.4	0.4
Wales	83.7	6.9	56.3	0.0
Britttany	82.1	9.3	54.3	0.4
Spain	79.8	16.1	47.6	0.2
Languedoc Roussillon	74.2	17.8	49.5	1.0
Galicia	63.6	16.8	47.6	- 0.3

Index